CW00832684

POCKET MEC

Mercedes _____
A-Class and Vaneo
A160 CDI, A170 CDI, A170 L CDI
1.7 Litre CDI Engine
1998 to 2004

BY PETER RUSSEK

ORDER NO.: 471

Published by
Peter Russek Publications Ltd.
3rd Floor, Block C
Commercial Square
High Wycombe, Bucks, HP11 2RH
Tel.: High Wycombe (01494) 440829
(01494) 526882
Fax: (01494) 473980
E-mail: russek@globalnet.co.uk
www.russek-manuals.co.uk

ISB. NO. 1-898780-47-1

**WITH FAULT FINDING SECTION
AT END OF MANUAL**

The publisher would like to thank Daimler Chrysler U.K. Ltd. for their invaluable support in producing this manual.

Drawings produced by S. Semmens. Copyright Peter Russek Publications Ltd.

No liability can be accepted for any inaccuracies or Omissions in this workshop manual, although every possible care has been taken to make it as complete and accurate as possible Every care has also been taken to prevent personal injury or damage to equipment when working on the vehicle We have tried to cover all models produced to the day of publication, but are unable to refer to all modifications and changes for certain markets or up-dating of models.

PREFACE

Small though this Workshop Manual is in size, it lacks no detail in covering most of the servicing and repair of the Mercedes-Benz A-Class diesel models from 1998 to 2004. Covered are the standard models "A160 CDI", (short version) introduced during 1998, the "A170 CDI" and the "A170 L CDI" (long version) from March 2001. Also covered are the "Vaneo" Minivan 1.7 CDI models, introduced for model year 2002. Vaneo All engines have a 1.7 litre direct injection diesel engine.

Depending on the version the engine fitted to the A160 CDI has a performance of 60 BHP (44 kW) or 75 BHP (55 kW) from 2002. The A170 CDI has been marketed with an engine performance of 90 BHP (66 kW) to the end of 2001 and 75 BHP (55 kW) after 2001. The A170 L CDI model from 2002 has, however, a performance of 95 BHP (70 kW) since its introduction during 2002.

Vaneo models are available in two engine versions, a 75 BHP and a 91 BHP version.

Brief, easy-to-follow instructions are given, free from all necessary complications and repetitions, yet containing all the required technical detail and information, and many diagrams and illustrations.

Compiled and illustrated by experts, this manual provides a concise source of helpful information, all of which has been cross-checked for accuracy to the manufacturer's official service and repair procedures, but many instructions have derived from actual practice to facilitate your work. Where special tools are required, these are identified in the text if absolutely necessary and we do not hesitate to advise you if we feel that the operation cannot be properly undertaken without the use of such tools.

The readers own judgement must ultimately decide just what work he will feel able to undertake, but there is no doubt, that with this manual to assist him, there will be many more occasions where the delay, inconvenience and the cost of having the van off the road can be avoided or minimised.

The manual is called "Pocket Mechanic" and is produced in a handy glove pocket size with the aim that it should be kept in the vehicle whilst you are travelling. Many garage mechanics themselves use these publications in their work and if you have the manual with you in the vehicle you will have an invaluable source of reference which will quickly repay its modest initial cost.

A general faultfinding (troubleshooting) section is included at the end of the manual and all items listed are taken from actual experience, together with the necessary remedies to correct faults and malfunctioning of certain parts.

0. INTRODUCTION

Our "Pocket Mechanics" are based on easy-to-follow step-by-step instructions and advice, which enables you to carry out many, jobs yourself. Moreover, now you have the means to avoid these frustrating delays and inconveniences which so often result from not knowing the right approach to carry out repairs which are often of a comparatively simple nature.

Whilst special tools are required to carry out certain operations, we show you in this manual the essential design and construction of such equipment, whenever possible, to enable you in many cases to improvise or use alternative tools. Experience shows that it is advantageous to use only genuine parts since these give you the assurance of a first class job. You will find that many parts are identical in the range covered in this manual, but our advice is to find out before purchasing new parts - **Always buy your spare parts from an officially appointed dealer.**

0.0. General Information

The manual covers the listed Mercedes-Benz passenger vehicles (and the Minivan) with the following engines:

A160 CDI (short version) – 1.7 litre engine with direct diesel fuel injection (CDI) injection. Model identification 168.007, engine 668.941. Available models, depending on country are: Classic, Elègance, Avantgarde, From 2003 Classic Style. Engine performance 60 B.H.P. (44 kW). From 2002 a engine with 75 B.H.P. (55 kW) has been fitted.

A170 CDI (short version) – 1.7 litre engine with direct diesel injection (CDI). Model identification 168.008 engines (engine 668,940) 168.009 (engine 668.942). Engine performance 90 B.H.P. (66 kW). From model year 2001 75 B.H.P. (55 kW).

A170 L CDI (long version) – 1.7 litre engine with direct diesel injection (CDI). Model identification 168.109, engine 668.942. From 2002. Available models, depending on country are: Classic, Elègance, Avantgarde, From 2003 Classic Style. Engine performance 95 B.H.P. (70 kW)..

Vaneo – Already available since summer 2001, i.e. model year 2002 are the Vaneo Minivans, based on the A-Class passenger cars (model identification 414) which are fitted with a 1.7 litre engine. Two engine versions. Engine performance 75 B.H.P. (55 kW) or 91 B.H.P. (67 kW).

- The engine operates with a direct diesel engine (CD) with four valves in a light-alloy cylinder head. The valve seat inserts are made of hardened steel and are pressed into the cylinder head. The overhead valves operate in brass valve guides.
- Two overhead camshaft ensures the opening and closing of the valves.
- An intercooler is fitted to A170 CDI models.

Many different body versions and model numbers are used in the range of vehicles marketed. The above list indicates the various model identification numbers which are important if parts are required. These numbers are sometimes referred to, mainly in the technical data sections and you should familiarise yourself with the model number of your vehicle. We should like to stress that not all vehicles are sold in any particular country.

All vehicles covered in the manual are fitted with a five-speed manual transmission of the type "716", but again the transmission has a different type designation in accordance with the fitted engine. A 5-speed automatic transmission can also be fitted (type 722).

The front suspension consists of spring struts and suspension arms, the rear suspension is fitted with coil springs and trailing arms. A stabiliser bar is fitted to the front and rear suspension.

Disc brakes at the front and drum brakes at the rear or disc brakes at the front and rear (all Vaneo models) make up the brake system, assisted by a brake servo unit. The vacuum for the servo unit is supplied by a vacuum (exhauster) pump. ABS can be fitted as standard or is available as optional extra. Models can also have a so-called "ASR" system (anti-slip system) or are build with the drive dynamic "ESP". system.

The rack and pinion steering is servo-assisted.

0.1. Identification

When your purchases the vehicle you will have received various data cards which have all important vehicle details, as for example chassis number and component numbers as well as identification of optional equipment, etc. You Owner's Manual will give you further instructions on the use of these cards.

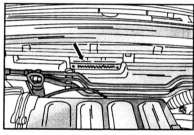

Fig. 0.1 – The location of the type identification plate on the bulkhead of the engine compartment.

You will know the location of the type identification plate at the position shown in Fig. 0.1, giving you the chassis number, the vehicle series number (168 or 414), etc. You will find more information at the lower end of the passenger door, shown in Fig. 0.2, i.e. max. permissible weight, max. permissible weight on front and rear axles

and other important data.

Fig. 0.2 – The location of the type identification plate in the door opening.

The engine number is stamped into the cylinder block but not at the position normally expected. The number is stamped from below into the cylinder block near the oil sump. The protective panel under the engine compartment must be removed to check the engine number. The number consists of the engine type

"166...." And the engine serial number. Transmission, rear axle and steering also have a serial number.

Always quote the complete chassis number and/or engine number and the model year, when ordering parts. Important is also the actual model number, which will indicate the construction of the vehicle, i.e. a short or long version.

0.2   Filling Capacities

Fuel tank: ....54 litres
Engine:
- Complete re-fill: ....5.0 litres

- Oil change with filter:...5.0 litres
- Min. oil fill capacity: ....5.0 litres

Cooling System:
- With manual transmission:..6.5 litres
- With automatic transmission:..6.5 litres
- Frost protection to –37° C:..................................... 3.25 litres of anti-freeze
- Frost protection to –45° C:...................................... 3.6 litres of anti-freeze

Transmission: ....2.0 litres
Automatic transmission (total capacity):...5.5 litres
Power assisted steering: ....0.8 litres

0.3.   General Servicing Notes

The servicing and overhaul instructions in this Workshop Manual are laid out in an easy-to-follow step-by-step fashion and no difficulty should be encountered, If the text and diagrams are followed carefully and methodically. The "Technical Data" sections form an important part of the repair procedures and should always be referred to during work on the vehicle.

In order that we can include as much data as possible, you will find that we do not generally repeat in the text the values already given under the technical data headings. Again, to make the best use of the space available, we do not repeat at each operation the more obvious steps necessary - we feel it to be far more helpful to concentrate on the difficult or awkward procedures in greater detail. However, we summarise below a few of the more important procedures and draw your attention to various points of general interest that apply to all operations.

Always use the torque settings given in the various main sections of the manual. These are grouped together in separate sub-sections for convenient reference.

Bolts and nuts should be assembled in a clean and very lightly oiled condition and faces and threads should always be inspected to make sure that they are free from damage burrs or scoring. DO NOT degrease bolts or nuts.

All joint washers, gaskets, tabs and lock washers, split pins and "O" rings must be replaced on assembly. Seals will, in the majority of cases, also need to be replaced, if the shaft and seal have been separated. Always lubricate the lip of the seal before assembly and take care that the seal lip is facing the correct direction.

References to the left-hand and right-hand sides are always to be taken es if the observer is at the rear of the vehicle, facing forwards, unless otherwise stated.

Always make sure that the vehicle is adequately supported, and on firm ground, before commencing any work on the underside of the car. A small jack or a make shift prop can be highly dangerous and proper axle stands are an essential requirement for your own safety.

Dirt, grease and mineral oil will rapidly destroy the seals of the hydraulic system and even the smallest amounts must be prevented from entering the system or coming into contact with the components. Use clean brake fluid or one of the proprietary cleaners to wash the hydraulic system parts. An acceptable alternative cleaner is methylated spirit, but it this is used, it should not be allowed to remain in contact with the rubber parts for longer than necessary. It is also important that all traces of the fluid should be removed from the system before final assembly.

Always use genuine manufacturer's spares and replacements for the best results.

Since the manufacturer uses metric units when building the cars it is recommended that, these are used for all precise units. Inch conversions are given in most cases but these are not necessarily precise conversions, being rounded off for the unimportant values.

Removal and installation instructions, in this Workshop Manual, cover the steps to take away or put back the unit or part in question. Other instructions, usually headed "Servicing", will cover the dismantling and repair of the unit once it has been stripped from the vehicle it is pointed out that the major instructions cover a complete overhaul of all parts but, obviously, this will not always be either necessary and should not be carried out needlessly.

There are a number of variations in unit parts on the range of vehicles covered in this Workshop Manual. We strongly recommend that you take care to identify the precise model, and the year of manufacture, before obtaining any spares or replacement parts.

Std.: To indicate sizes and limits of components as supplied by the manufacturer. Also to indicate the production tolerances of new unused parts.

O/S Paris supplied as Oversize or Undersize or recommended limits for such parts, to enable them to be used with worn or re-machined mating parts.

U/S O/S indicates a part that is larger than Std. size U/S may indicate a bore of a bushing or female part that is smaller than Std.

Max.: Where given against a clearance or dimension indicates the maximum allowable If in excess of the value given it is recommended that the appropriate part is fitted.

TIR: Indicates the Total Indicator Reading as shown by a dial indicator (dial gauge).

TDC: Top Dead Centre (No. 1 piston on firing stroke).

MP: Multi-Purpose grease.

0.4.   Recommended Tools

To carry out some of the operations described in the manual we will need some of the tools listed below:

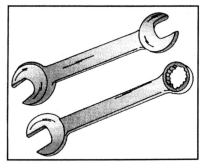

Fig. 0.3 – A double open-ended spanner in the upper view and an open-ended/ring spanner in the lower view. Always make sure that the spanner size is suitable for the nut or bolt to be removed and tightened.

As basic equipment in your tool box you will need a set of open-ended spanners (wrenches) to reach most of the nuts and bolts. A set of ring spanners is also of advantage. To keep the costs as low as possible we recommend a set of combined spanners, open-ended on one side and a ring spanner on the other side. Fig. 0.3 shows a view of the spanners in question. Sockets are also a useful addition to your tool set.

A set of cross-head screwdrivers, pliers and hammers or mallets may also be essential. You will find that many bolts now have a "Torx" head. In case you have never seen a "Torx" head bolt, refer to Fig. 0.4. A socket set with special t "Torx" head inserts is used to slacken and tighten these screws. The size of the bolts are specified by the letter "T" before the across-flat size.

Fig. 0.4 – A graduated disc is used to "angle-tighten" nuts and bolts. "Torx" head bolts are shown on the R.H. side.

Circlip pliers may also be needed for certain operations. Two types of circlip pliers are available, one type for external circlips, one type for internal circlips. The ends of the pliers can either be straight or angled. Fig. 0.5 shows a view of the circlip pliers. Apart from the circlip pliers you may also need the pliers shown in Fig. 0.6, i.e. side cutters, combination pliers and water pump pliers.

Fig. 0.5 – Circlip pliers are shown in the upper view. The type shown in suitable for outside circlips. The lower view shows a pair of pointed pliers.

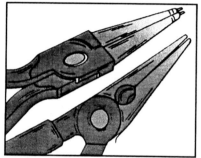

Every part of the vehicle is tightened to a certain torque value and you will therefore need a torque wrench which can be adjusted to a certain torque setting. In this connection we will also mention a graduated disc, shown in Fig. 0.4, as many parts of the vehicle must be angle-tightened after having been tightened to a specific torque. As some of the angles are not straight-forward (for example 30 or 60 degrees), you will either have to estimate the angle or use the disc.

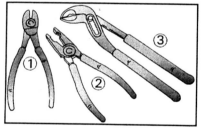

Fig. 0.6 – Assortment of pliers suitable for many operations.
1 Side cutter
2 Combination pliers
3 Water pump pliers

Finally you may consider the tool equipment shown in Fig. 0.7 which will be necessary from time to time, mainly if you intend to carry out most maintenance and repair jobs yourself.
shows

0.5. Before you start

Before you carry out any operations on your vehicle it may be of advantage to read the following notes to prevent injuries and damage to the vehicle:

- Never carry out operations underneath the vehicle when the front or rear is only supported on the jack. Always place chassis stands in position (refer to next section). If no chassis stands are available and if the wheels are removed place on wheel on top of the other one and place them under the side of the vehicle where you work. If the jack fails the vehicle will drop onto the two wheels, preventing injury.

8

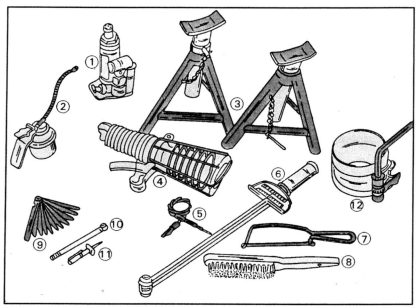

Fig. 0.7 – Recommended tools to service and repair your vehicle.

1 Hydraulic jack
2 Oil can
3 Chassis stands
4 Electric hand lamp
5 Test lamp (12 volts)
6 Torque wrench

7 Small hand saw
8 Wire brush
9 Feeler gauges
10 Tyre pressure gauge
11 Tyre profile depth checker
12 Piston ring clamp band

- Never slacken or tighten the axle shaft nuts or wheel bolts when the vehicle in resting on chassis stands.
- Never open the cooling system when the engine is hot. Sometimes it may, however, be necessary. In this case place a thick rag around the cap and open it very slowly until all steam has been released.
- Never drain the engine oil when the engine is hot. Drained engine oil must be disposed of in accordance with local regulation.
- Never allow brake fluid or anti-freeze to come in contact with painted areas.
- Never inhale brake shoe or brake pad dust. If compressed air is available, blow off the dust whilst turning the head away. A mask should be worn for reasons of safety.
- Remove oil or grease patches from the floor before you or other people slip on it.
- Do not work on the vehicle wearing a shirt with long sleeves. Rings and watches should be removed before carrying out any work.
- If possible never work by yourself. If unavoidable ask a friend or a member of the family to have a quick look to check that's everything is OK.
- Never hurry up your work. Many wheel bolts have been left untightened to get the vehicle quickly back on the road.
- Never smoke near the vehicle or allow persons with a cigarette near you. A fire extinguisher should be handy, just in case.

- Never place a hand lamp directly onto the engine to obtain a better view. Even though that the metal cage will avoid direct heat it is far better if you attach such a lamp to the open engine bonnet.

0.6.   Jacking up of the Vehicle

Always make sure that the jack used to lift the vehicle is adequate for the vehicle weight. Additional weight must always be removed from the luggage compartment and the inside of the vehicle.

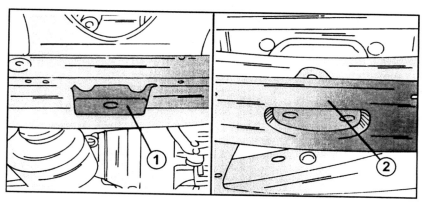

Fig. 0.8 – Jacking up the front of the vehicle in the L.H. view. Place the jack head underneath the rubber block (1). The R.H. view shows where the jack is placed under the axle (2).

To jack up the vehicle completely, first jack up the front end. Chock the rear wheels to prevent the vehicle from rolling off the jack or apply the handbrake. Place a mobile jack underneath the centre of the front axle carrier, as shown on the L.H. side of Fig. 0.8. A hard rubber block indicates the jacking point.

The rear of the vehicle is lifted with a mobile jack as shown on the R.H. side underneath the centre of the rear axle.

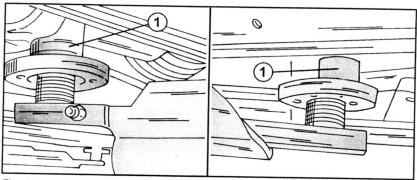

Fig. 0.9 – Chassis stands (1) are placed underneath the vehicle as shown, on the left underneath the front axle, on the right underneath the rear axle. The locations are the same where the car is supported in a workshop when a lift is used.

10

To lift one side of the vehicle use the jacking points on the side of the body, as described in your Owners Manual.

After the vehicle is lifted place three-legged chassis stands on the left and right underneath the axle as shown in Fig. 0.9. The L.H. view shows where the stands are placed underneath the front of the vehicle, the R.H. view shows where the stands are placed underneath the rear end.

Before the vehicle is jacked up always check the condition of the ground where the jack or chassis stands are located. Soft ground will allow jack or chassis stands to sink in, making the whole assembly unstable.

Take care that the vehicle cannot tip-over when the first side is lifted. Ask a helper to support the vehicle from the other side. Never work underneath the vehicle without adequate support.

---

1   ENGINES

1.0   Technical Data

Fitted Engines:
- A160 CDI, model 168.007:   Engine 668.941
- A170 CDI, short version, model 168.008:   Engine 668.940
- A170 CDI, short version, 168.009:   Engine 668.942
- A170 L CDI, long version, model 168.109:   Engine 668.942
- Vaneo – model 414, 414.700:   On of the above

Number of Cylinders:	Four
Firing order:	$1 - 3 - 4 - 2$
Arrangement of cylinders:	In-line
Camshaft:	Overhead camshaft
Arrangement of valves	Overhead
Number of valves:	Four per cylinder
Number of camshafts:	Two
Capacity – all engines:	1689 c.c.
Cylinder bore:	84.00 mm
Piston stroke:	80.00 mm

Compression Ratio:
- A 160 CDI in model 168.006:   19.5 : 1
- A 160 CDI in model 168.007:   19.0 : 1
- A 170 CDI in model 168.008:   19.5 : 1
- A 170 CDI in model 168.009 and 168.109:   19.0 : 1

Max. B.H.P. (DIN):
- A160 CDI, model 168.006:   44 kW (60 BHP) at 3600 rpm
- A160 CDI, model 168.007, Vaneo: 55 kW (75 BHP) at 3600 rpm
- A170 CDI, model 168.008, Vaneo: 66 kW (90 BHP) at 4200 rpm
- A170 CDI, models 168.009 and 168.109   70 kW (95 BHP) at 4200 rpm

Max. Torque:
- A160 CDI, model 168.006:   160 Nm at 1500 rpm
- A160 CDI, model 168.007:   160 Nm at 1500 rpm
- A170 CDI, model 168.008:   180 Nm at 1600 rpm
- A170 CDI, models 168.009 and 168.109:   180 Nm at 1600 rpm

Crankshaft bearings   5 friction bearings

Cooling system   Thermo system with water pump, thermostat, cooling fan, tube-type radiator. With or without separate expansion tank.

Lubrication   Pressure-feed lubrication with gear-type oil pump, driven with chain from crankshaft. With full-flow and by-pass oil filter

Air cleaner   Dry paper element air cleaner

1.1.   Engine – Removal and Installation

The removal of the engine is carried out together with the front axle carrier. The workshop uses a special table to lower the axle carrier. We therefore recommend to read the following instructions and then decide if you want to attempt to remove the engine. A suitable hoist or crane is required to lower the front axle carrier after it has been removed from its attachment. Remember that the weight of the assembly is around 200 kg, i.e. the lifting tackle and/or jack must be suitable to carry the weight/ The following instructions are given in general for all models.

- Place the front end of the vehicle on chassis stands when work is carried out underneath the vehicle.

- If an automatic transmission is fitted drain the oil. To do this, unscrew the drain plug from the oil sump and allow the oil to drain into a suitable container. Always replace the plug sealing ring. The plug is tightened to 2.2 kgm (16 ft.lb.).

- Drain the coolant from radiator and cylinder block as described in section "Cooling System".

- If a heated windscreen washer system is fitted remove the washer fluid reservoir.

- Disconnect the battery earth cable. Refer to section "Electrical System" for details.

- Remove the front bumper as described below. Also remove the intercooler (charge air cooler) if an engine of type 668.940 or 668.942 is fitted. The operations are also described below. In the case of engine type 668,941 a cross pipe is fitted in place of the intercooler.

- The next operations are carried out by referring to Fig. 1.1. First remove the intake scoop (1) and the air intake duct (2).

- Disconnect the vacuum line (3) from the turbo charger and the vacuum line (9) from the EGR valve (exhaust gas return valve). A further vacuum line (4) must be disconnected from the boost pressure sensor and the vacuum line (5) for the brake servo unit from the vacuum pump. This is a quick-release fitting. Press together the two catches shown by the arrows, at the same time withdrawing the connection.

- Disconnect the induction hose (12) from the turbo charger.

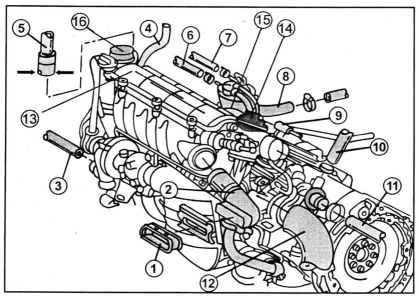

Fig. 1.1 – Details for the removal of the engine together with the front axle carrier. The details also refer to the removal of the intake module.

1 Air intake scoop
2 Air intake duct
3 Vacuum hose
4 Vacuum hose
5 Vacuum line, brake servo
6 Fuel pipe

7 Fuel pipe
8 Coolant hose
9 Vacuum hose
10 Coolant hose
11 Coolant hose
12 Charge air hose

13 Intake module
14 Mixing chamber
15 Oil filter
16 Oil filler neck

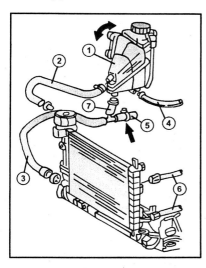

Fig. 1.2 – Connection of coolant hoses (2 to 5) to the expansion reservoir. The connections of the two pipes (6) on models with automatic transmission are tightened to 2.5 kgm (18 ft.lb.).

Disconnect the fuel pipes (6) and (7) from the fuel filter. **Attention:** No fire, sparks, open flames or smoking during this operation. Try to avoid inhaling fuel vapour. Fuel can be collected in a suitable container. Seal the fuel lines with a suitable plug.

•   Disconnect the coolant hoses (10) and (11) after slackening of the hose clamps from the thermostat housing and the return line (8) to the heater. New hose clamps should be used during installation.

•   The remaining coolant hoses are removed next. Fig. 1.2 shows the connection.. Disconnect the hoses (2), (4) and (7) from the expansion tank (1). Unlock the striker at the expansion tank and remove the tank (1). Use new hose clamps during

13

installation. The coolant hose (3) at the bottom of the radiator must also be disconnected and unclipped along the longitudinal member where it is marked with the arrow. Again a new hose clamp must be used during installation.

- If an automatic transmission is fitted, disconnect the fluid lines (6) from the oil cooler. Seal the open ends of the pipes. The oil cooler in incorporated into the water cooler. The connections of the pipes are tightened to 2.5 kgm (18 ft.lb.) during installation.

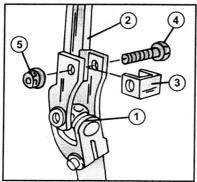

Fig. 1.3 – Separating and steering universal joint. The numbers are referred to in the text.

- Detach the steering joint in Fig. 1.3. Unscrew the joint (1) from the steering shaft (2) and take off the thrust piece (3). During installation tighten a new self-locking nut (5) to and the bolt (4) 2.0 kgm (14.5 ft.lb.). Certain models are here fitted with a so-called nut bracket which in this case must be replaced.

- Remove the positive wire (1) and the control wire (2) for the power-assisted steering from the L.H. frame side member shown in the L.H. view of Fig. 1.4

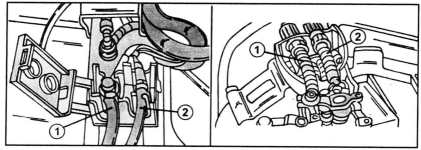

Fig. 1.4 – The L.H. view shows where the positive wire (1) and the control wire (2) for the power-assisted steering are disconnected from the L.H. frame sidemember. The R.H. view shows the two gear shift cables (1) and (2).

- Disconnect the two gear-shift cables (1) and (2) in the R.H. view of Fig. 1.4 by turning the locknuts counter-clockwise, releasing them from the bracket and then pushing the cable ends off the ball heads. During installation ensure that the shift cables are securely attached to the ball heads.

- Disconnect the electrical connectors at the turning angle sensors, expose the electrical cable and place it to one side (only models with automatic clutch operating system).

The remaining operations are carried out by referring to Fig. 1.5:

- Detach the suspension strut (5) from the strut dome. During installation guide the pins on the suspension struts into their guides, shown by the arrows. Tighten the bolt (4) to 4.0 kgm (29 ft.lb.).

- Remove the brake calipers (8) from the steering knuckle and remove together with the fitted brake pads and the connected brake hose. Tie the calipers to the body, using a piece of wire. The self-locking bolts (9) must be replaced.

14

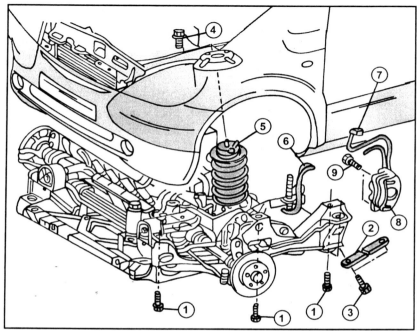

Fig. 1.5 – Details for the removal and installation of the front axle carrier together with the engine. The numbers are referred to below.

- Separate the plug connector from the brake pad wear indicator sensor (7) and the wheel speed sensor (6) in the top of the wheel housing. The plug for the brake pad wear indicator sensor can only be fitted from the front.
- Remove the complete exhaust system.
- Follow the fluid hose for the clutch operation, remove the visible clip towards the top out of the transmission and withdraw the hose from the transmission. Some fluid will run out. Close the hose end in suitable manner. Replace the sealing ring during installation of the hose.

Fig. 1.6 – A special lifting plate (1) is used in the workshop underneath the front axle carrier to lower the subframe with the engine during removal.

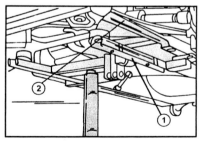

- Release the Poly drive belt as described under a separate heading and lift it off the compressor if an air conditioning system is fitted. Also on these vehicles remove the compressor and attach it to the underfloor with the refrigerant lines and electrical cables connected
- The subframe must now be supported from below. The workshop uses a special removal tool as shown in Fig. 1.6. With a jack and a suitable plate and the help of the illustration you may be able to arrange a make-shift support.

- Remove the struts (2) in Fig. 1.5 from the front axle carrier at the underfloor. Tighten the bolts to 6.0 kgm (43.5 ft.lb.) during installation.
- Take off the wheel housing liners on the left and right from the underfloor and fold them downwards to reach the bolts (1) in Fig. 1.5. Unscrew the eight bolts. During installation first screw in all bolts and then tighten them evenly to a torque of 12.0 kgm (86.5 ft.lb.).
- Carefully lower the engine with the front subframe until you have access to the starter motor and alternator. Proceed with caution to avoid damage to the coolant hoses, A/C hoses (if air conditioning is fitted) and the electrical cables. During installation lift the front axle carrier with the guide pin into the bore in the longitudinal member..

Fig. 1.7 – Attachment of the gear change cable if a manual transmission is fitted. The numbers are referred to below.

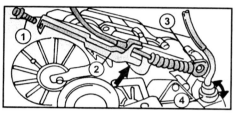

- If a manual transmission is fitted, unhook the gear change cable (3) from the shift linkage (2) in Fig. 1.7, remove the bolt (1) and remove the bracket from then transmission and free it from the support (arrow). Unlock the plug (4) on the transmission (R.H. arrow) and pull it out.
- Disconnect the earth cable together with the fixture at the oil sump.
- Disconnect the cable harness from the starter motor. Note the tightening torques during installation. Terminal "50" 0.6 kgm, terminal £30" 0.9 kgm. Also disconnect the cables from the alternator. Again note the tightening torques, Terminal "D+" 0.6 kgm, terminal "B" 1.8 kgm.
- Carefully lower the engine with the front axle carrier fully until it can be removed. Proceed with care to avoid damage to hoses, cables, leads, etc. A helper is required to observe the carrier and engine during removal.

The installation is a reversal of the removal procedure. Note the special points already given during the removal instructions. If an automatic transmission is fitted check the fluid level or have it checked at the earliest opportunity, as the fluid lines have been disconnected from the radiator. The clutch system must be bled of air as described in the relevant section. Fill the engine with coolant and engine oil. After starting the engine check for leaks.

Removal and Installation of front Bumper

As already mentioned the bumper must be removed in order to gain access to various parts. Remove the bumper as described below, but note that there are some differences, depending when the vehicle was built. Fig. 1.8 shows the attachment to the end of February 2001:

- Open the bonnet.
- Remove the bolts (1), (2) and (3). From March 2001 an alteration has been carried out, i.e. the bumper is attached with the bolts (1) to the light units. The bolts are tightened to 0.3 kgm during installation.
- Remove the clips (4). Use new clips if the old ones are no longer in good condition.
- Open the engine bonnet.

16

Fig. 1.8 – Details for the removal and installation of the front bumper. The numbers are referred to in the text.

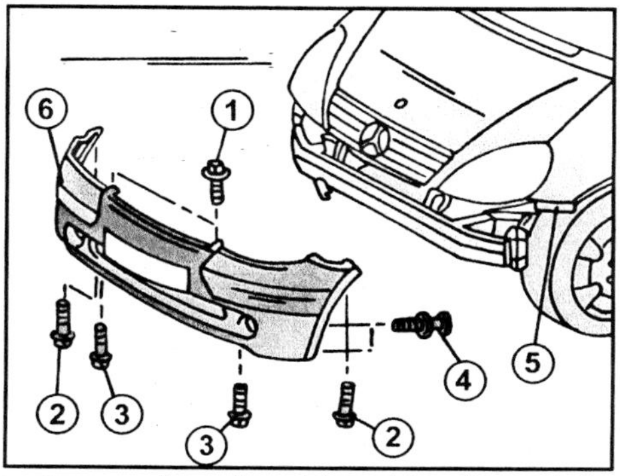

- Remove the bolts (1), (2) and (3) in the illustration. From March 2001 the bumper is secured with the bolts (1) to the light units. The bolts are only tightened to 0.3 kgm during installation.
- Remove the clips (4). Fit new clips if necessary during installation.
- The bumper can now be withdrawn, but two persons will be required. First unclip the bumper from the side guides (5) and then withdraw it towards the front. Specially observe the bumper at the points shown by the arrows to prevent damage to the paint work. During installation the bumper (6) is guided into the side guides and then pushed fully in position.
- Certain models are fitted with a "Parctonic" system (PTS). In this case withdraw a plug connector from the L.H. and R.H. fog lamp and separate an electrical connection.

The installation is a reversal of the removal procedure. Check the adjustment of the fog lamps or have it checked professionally.

Removal and installation of the charge air cooler (intercooler)

The charge air cooler is only fitted to engine types 668.950, 669.942 or 668.914. Fig. 1.9 shows where the cooler is located. Remove as follows:

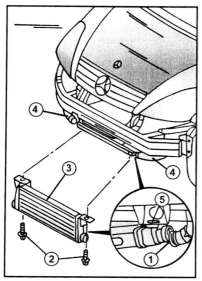

Fig. 1.9 – Details for the removal and installation of the charge air cooler.
1 Seal
2 Self-tapping screws
3 Charge air cooler
4 Charge air pipes
5 Rubber mounting

- Remove the front bumper as described above.
- Turn the quick-locks at the at the charge air pipes (4) sufficiently until they release at the charge air cooler (3) and then push back the quick-locks. During installation push on the quick-locks at the charge air cooler (circle insert) until they lock into place. The seals (1) must always be replaced.
- Unscrew the R.H. charge air pipe (4) from the front axle carrier.
- Separate the L.H. and R.H. charge air pipes (4) from the charge air cooler (3).
- Unscrew the bolts (2) and remove the cooler from the front axle carrier.

During installation insert the mounting studs

of the charge air cooler into the rubber bushes (5) in the front axle carrier. Replace the rubber bushes if no longer in perfect condition.

Separating the Engine from the Front Axle Carrier

The removal of the engine from the front axle carrier after the assembly has been removed from the vehicle is described under a separate heading further on in this section. This also includes the attachment of the engine to the carrier. The installation of the assembly can then be carried out as described above.

1.3.   Engine - Dismantling

All engines are sensitive to dirt or other contamination. It is therefore essential to make sure that no foreign matter can enter the pipes, connections, etc. during the dismantling operations.

Dismantling of the engine will be made much easier, if a swivelling engine stand is available. Otherwise place the engine/transmission on a work bench, supporting is adequately to prevent if from falling over.

Before commencing dismantling, block up the inlet and exhaust openings and give the exterior of the engine a thorough cleaning to remove all loose dirt and oil. Pay particular attention to all joint surfaces, brushing these to remove loose debris which might otherwise find its way into the interior of the engine.

Many of the parts are made of aluminium alloy and must be treated accordingly. Only use plastic or rubber mallets to separate parts, if necessary.

As a complete strip-down of the engine is in most cases not necessary, and many of the operations can be carried out with the engine fitted or lowered together with the front axle carrier, you will find in the following text a description of individual operations which can be carried out with the engine fitted and removed. Combining these, will give you the complete dismantling of the engine.

1.3.   Engine - Overhaul
1.3.0.   Cylinder Head and Valves – Technical Data

Cylinder Head:
Max. Distortion of Cylinder Head Faces:
- Longitudinal direction: 0.08 mm
- Across the face: 0.00 mm
Max. deviation of faces between upper and
  lower sealing faces (parallel to each other)   0.10 mm

Valves
Valve seat angle   45° + 15'
Valve Stem Diameter:
- Inlet valves   5.960 – 5.990 mm
- Exhaust valves   6.955 – 7.045 mm
Valve seat width: 1.7 – 1.9 mm

Valve Seats
Valve seat width: 1,7 – 1,9 mm

18

Valve seat angle:	45° +15'
Upper correction angle:	15°
Lower correction angle:	60°

Valve Guides
Inlet valve Guides:

- Outer diameter – Std.	12.540 – 12.551 mm
- Outer diameter – Repair size	12.564 – 12.571 mm
- Inner diameter:	6.000 – 6.015 mm
	or 7.000 – 7.015 mm

Basic bore in cylinder head:

- Std.	12.500 – 12.510 mm
- Repair size	12.530 or 12.700 mm

Interference fit of valve guides – All guides:

- Std.	0.009 – 0.021 mm
- Repair size	0.011 – 0.024 mm

1.3.0.1. Cylinder Head

The following information should be noted when work is carried out on a cylinder head: The items to be removed before the actual removal of the cylinder head are described under different headings.

- The cylinder head is made of light-alloy. Engine coolant, engine oil, the air required to ignite the fuel and the exhaust gases are directed through the cylinder head. Valves, valve springs and valve tappets are fitted to the cylinder head. Also in the cylinder heads you will find the camshafts.

- The exhaust manifold and the inlet manifold are bolted to the outside of the head. The fuel enters the head on one side and exits on the other side, i.e. the head is of the well-known "crossflow" type.

- The cylinder head is fitted with various sender units, sensors and switching valves, responsible for certain functions of the temperature control.

- As the cylinder head is made of light alloy, it is prone to distortion if, for example, the order of slackening or tightening of the cylinder head bolts is not observed. For the same reason never remove the cylinder head from a hot engine.

- A cylinder head cannot be checked in fitted position. Sometimes the cylinder head gasket will "blow", allowing air into the cooling system. A quick check is possible after opening the coolant reservoir or radiator cap (engine fairly cold). Allow the engine to warm-up and observe the coolant. Visible air bubbles point in most cases to a "blown" gasket. Further evidence is white exhaust smoke, oil in the coolant or coolant in the engine oil. The latter can be checked at the oil dipstick. A white, grey emulsion on the dipstick is more or less a confirmation of a damaged cylinder gasket.

The following description refers to some operations which may be necessary on the cylinder head.

Cylinder Head Cover – Removal and Installation

Figs. 1.10 and 1.11 show details for the removal and installation of the cylinder head cover. The removal and installation is carried out as follows. Again you will find points to be observed during installation mentioned for each operation. Certain operations are described as necessary.

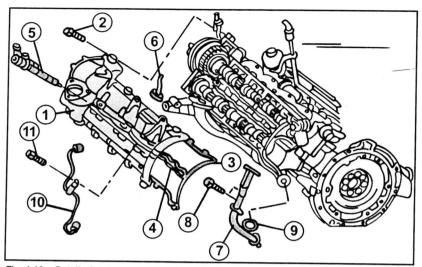

Fig. 1.10 – Details for the removal and installation of the cylinder head cover. See also Fig. 1.11 for continuation.

1 Cylinder head cover	5 Injector	9 Clip
2 Torx-head bolt	6 Plug, camshaft pos. Sensor	10 Pressure pipe
3 Outer shaped rubber gasket	7 EGR pipe	11 Torx-head bolt
4 Inner shaped rubber gasket	8 Torx-head bolt	

Fig. 1.11 – Removal and installation of the cylinder head cover (cont. from Fig. 1.10).

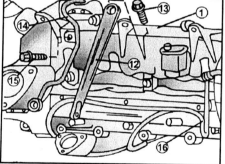

12   Turbo charger support
13   Torx-head bolt
14   Oil feed line (turbo charger)
15   Torx-head bolt
16   Glow plug cable harness

- Remove the injectors as described in the chapter in question (diesel injection).
- Remove the oil filler neck as described below. Note that a modified version has been fitted from September 2000. The operation is rather complicated if the older version is fitted, as the intake module must be removed. The operations are also described further on in this section.
- Remove the electric shut-off valve (see below).
- Detach the fuel rail from the cylinder head cover and place it to one side, with the fuel lines connected. Tighten the bolts to 0.9 kgm during installation.
- Separate the plug connector (6) from the camshaft position sensor. The plug is located between cylinders 3 and 4 (cylinder 1 on the side of the timing gear).
- Disconnect the oil supply line (14) to the turbo charger.
- Disconnect the cable harness for the glow plugs (16) from the cylinder head cover (1).

20

- Remove the support for the turbo charger (12) and the exhaust recirculation pipe (7).
- Disconnect the high pressure pipe (10) and remove it. The union nuts on high pressure pump and fuel rail are tightened to 2.3 kgm (16.5 ft.lb.). The hexagon of the connectors must be prevented from rotating by applying an open-ended spanner.
- Unscrew the cylinder head cover (1) from the cylinder head and remove it together with the two pre-formed rubber gaskets (3) and (4). The gaskets, one inner one and one outer one, must be replaced during installation.

The installation is a reversal of the removal procedure, noting the tightening torques already given during the removal instructions. Tighten the Torx-head bolts (2) to 0.8 kgm. First tighten all bolts finger-tight and then to the given torque.

Removal and installation of oil filler neck

The oil filler neck has been modified in the case of vehicles built before September 2000. Fig. 1.12 shows this version. On engines before the given date, the oil filler is connected to the crankcase ventilation as shown in Fig. 1.13. Remove the version in question as follows:

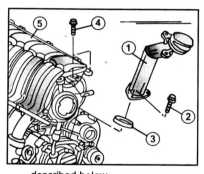

Fig. 1.12 – Removal and installation of the oil filler neck after Sept. 2000.
1   Oil filler neck
2   Tory-head bolt
3   Sealing ring
4   Torx-head bolt
5   Cylinder head cover

To end of August 2000 – See Fig. 1.13

- Remove the cooling system expansion tank and place it to one side, with the cooling hoses connected.
- Remove the suction module (6) and in this connection the mixture chamber as described below.

- Disconnect the air intake hose and the ventilation hose (4) connected to the filler neck (1).

Fig. 1.13 – Oil filler neck with crankcase ventilation to end of August 2000.
1   Oil filler neck
2   Torx-head bolt
3   Sealing ring
4   Ventilation hose
5   Torx-head bolt
6   Intake module
7   Connector plug
8   Connector plug

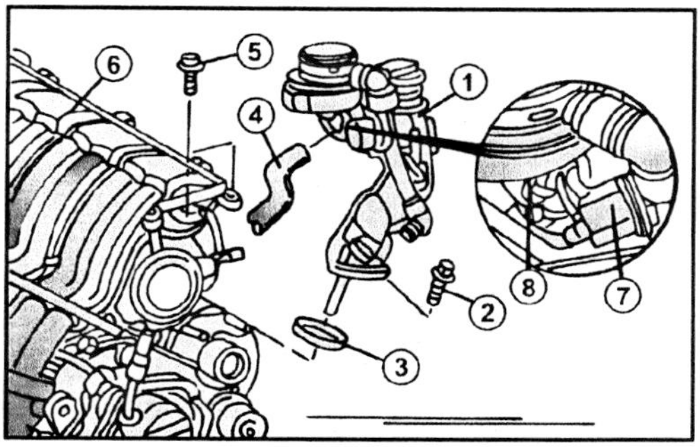

- Withdraw two plug connectors (7) and (8) from the oil filler neck and unscrew the filler neck from the cylinder head cover and remove towards the top.

The installation is a reversal of the removal procedure. The sealing ring underneath the oil filler neck must always be replaced.

From beginning of September 2000 – See Fig. 1.12

As shown in the illustration there are no problems to remove the oil filler neck on the later models. After removal of the coolant expansion tank, separate the air intake hose with the connected hoses and push the assembly to one side. Remove the Torx-head bolts (4) out of the cylinder head cover (5) and remove the bolts (2) to release the filler neck (1). Remove the neck in an upward direction. The installation is a reversal of the removal procedure.

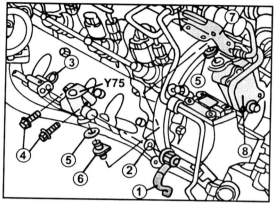

Fig. 1.14 – Details for the removal and installation of the electric shut-off valve.

1	Fuel pipe
2	Sealing ring
3	Plug connector for valve
4	Torx-head bolts
5	Sealing rings
6	Connecting piece
7	Retaining bracket
8	Pre-delivery pump

Removal and Installation of the electric Shut-off Valve

The valve is fitted above the pre-delivery pump as shown in Fig. 1.14 to the cylinder head and is shown in the illustration with "Y75". As a fuel line must be disconnected take the necessary precautions during the following operations.

- Disconnect the fuel line (1) from the side of the valve. Some fuel may run out and should be collected with a suitable rag. The pipe is connected with a locking arm which must be set to the release position to separate the fuel line. For technical reason you must, however, return the arm back to its original position. The seal (2) must always be replaced during installation.
- Remove the plug connector (3) from the other side of the valve.
- Unscrew the shut-off valve from the bracket (7). It is secured with 4 bolts. Remove the valve from the pre-delivery pump (8).
- Carefully detach the connecting piece (6) from the pre-delivery pump, replace the sealing ring (5) and refit the connecting piece.

The installation is a reversal of the removal procedure. Tighten the bolts on the bracket and the cylinder head cover to 0.9 kgm. Refit the fuel line with a new sealing ring (2). Check that the fuel line is securely fastened.

Removal and Installation of the Intake Module

The intake module (intake manifold) is fitted at the top of the cylinder head and is shown in Fig. 1.2 with (13). The removal (and the installation) is rather complicated as it will also be necessary to remove the mixing chamber (described below). Some references are made to Fig. 1.2 during the following description.

- Disconnect the air intake hose (2).
- Remove the mixing chamber (see below).
- Detach the full-flow filter (15) at the intake module and place it to one side without disconnecting the fuel lines (6) and (7).
- Detach the vacuum line for the brake servo unit on the R.H. side of the intake module. A quick fastener is used to secure the line, which must be pressed together and withdrawn at the same time.

- Remove the coolant thermostat (6) at the position shown. In section "Cooling System" you will find details of the removal.
- Remove both camshafts (7) and (8) as described in the section dealing with the timing gear.

Fig. 1.19 – Removal and installation of the cylinder head.

1 Cylinder head
2 Torx-head bolt
3 Cylinder head bolt
4 Cylinder head gasket
5 Guide rail pin
6 Exhaust manifold

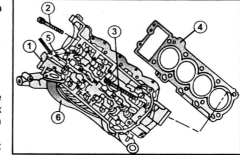

- Remove the two valve operating levers (4). Mark their position to refit them in the same position.
- Mark the camshaft sprocket (2) and the timing chain (3) on opposite points with a spot of paint (allow the paint to dry) and then remove the camshaft sprocket.
- Disconnect the coolant hose (5) at the side of the cylinder head (1) after slackening of the hose clamps.
- Detach the engine mount (10) from the engine support (11). To make sure that the engine mounting is not under tension place a mobile jack with a suitable wooden block underneath the engine and lift the engine until you are sure that there is no more pressure on the mounting. The bolt (9) is tightened to 5.5 kgm (40 ft.lb.) during installation.
- Unscrew the Torx-head bolts (2) in Fig. 1.19,
- Slacken the cylinder head bolts (3) in several stages in reverse to the order shown later on until they are slack and can be removed. Immediately check the length of the cylinder head bolts. Any bolt longer than 188 mm (new 186 mm) must be discarded. We must repeat once more, the engine must be cold.
- Lift off the cylinder head. If necessary use a soft-metal mallet to free the head. Note that the head is guided on dowel pins on the L.H. and R.H. side. Remove the cylinder head gasket (4).

The installation is a reversal of the removal procedure. Note the following points:

- Thoroughly clean the cylinder block and cylinder head sealing faces. Make sure all old gasket material (if present) is removed. The faces must be free of water and oil.
- Place the new cylinder head gasket the correct way round over the cylinder block face, dowel pins engaged, and tap it in position with a soft-faced mallet. When installing the head guide the guide pins (5) in the cylinder head must engage with the slide rail at the position shown by the arrow in Fig. 1.19.
- Lubricate the thread of the cylinder head bolts and the underside of the bolt heads with engine oil and screw the bolts in position without torque wrench until fairly tight. Tighten the cylinder head by referring to Fig. 1.20. Note that the bolts (11) and (12) are tightened last.
- **First Stage:** Tighten all bolts in the order shown to 3.5 kgm (25 ft.lb.).
- **Second Stage:** Tighten all bolts in the order shown without torque wrench by a further quarter of a turn (90°).

Mixing Chamber with Exhaust Gas Re-circulation Valve – Removal and Installation

The mixing chamber fitted to all engines is shown in Fig. 1.17. It is fitted to the end of the intake module (inlet manifold) and must be removed if the module is removed for any reason, as for example during the operations described above. Remove as follows:

- Disconnect the vacuum hose (1) from the EGR valve (10).

Fig. 1.17 – Details for the removal and installation of the mixing chamber and the exhaust gas re-circulation valve.

1　Vacuum hose
2　Charge air hose
3　Mixing chamber
4　Torx-head bolts
5　EGR re-circulation pipe
6　Gasket
7　Sealing ring
8　Torx-head bolt

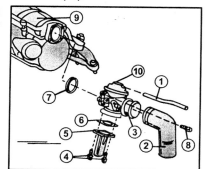
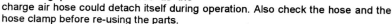
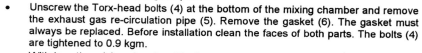

- Disconnect the charge air hose (2) from the mixing chamber (3). Before re-connecting the hose clean the connecting points of the hose as the charge air hose could detach itself during operation. Also check the hose and the hose clamp before re-using the parts.

- Unscrew the Torx-head bolts (4) at the bottom of the mixing chamber and remove the exhaust gas re-circulation pipe (5). Remove the gasket (6). The gasket must always be replaced. Before installation clean the faces of both parts. The bolts (4) are tightened to 0.9 kgm.

- Withdraw the mixing chamber (3) after removal of the Torx-head bolts (8) from the intake module (9). Again clean the joining faces of both parts. Tighten the bolts (8) to o.9 kgm.

Cylinder Head – Removal and Installation

Again you will find some operations described which will have to be carried out before the cylinder head can be removed. Fig. 1.18. Remove as follows:

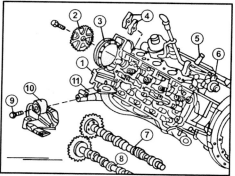

Fig. 1.18 – Details for the removal and installation of the cylinder head. Shown are the items which must be removed.

1　Cylinder head
2　Camshaft timing sprocket
3　Timing chain
4　Rocker levers
5　Coolant hose
6　Thermostat housing
7　Inlet camshaft
8　Exhaust camshaft
9　Collar bolt
10　Engine mount
11　Engine mounting support

- Disconnect the battery earth cable.
- Drain the cooling system. Only open the expansion tank when the engine is cold.
- Remove the bottom part of the noise encapsulation at the front as described later on in this section.

24

Cover on rear of the cylinder head

To remove the rear cover, the attachment of which is shown in Fig. 1.22, the pre-delivery pump and the high pressure pump must be removed. Removal and installation are covered in section "Diesel Injection System". After removal of the cylinder head cover (already covered) remove the bolts (1) securing the cover (2) and remove the cover from the cylinder head. A rubber mallet can be used to tap the cover off.

Before installation clean the sealing faces of cover and cylinder head. Coat the sealing face of the cylinder head with "Loctite 5970" sealing compound. Fit the cover, making sure that the dowel pins (3) engage. If a new cover is fitted it must be fitted without using the dowel pins, i.e. remove the fitted dowel pins. The additional points must in this case be observed:

- Fit the cover (2) to the end of the inlet camshaft (4) and push against the cylinder head.
- Align the L.H. upper end of the cover flush with the cylinder head face (arrow).
- Tighten the bolts (1) to 0.9 kgm.
- Coat the R.H. upper end of the repair set cover with the sealing compound mentioned above.

1.3.0.2. Cylinder Head - Dismantling

The following description assumes that the cylinder head is to be replaced. If only a top overhaul is asked for, ignore the additional instructions. The cylinder head must be removed.

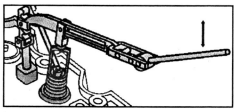

Fig. 1.23 – A valve lifter is used in the manner shown. Any suitable valve lifter can be used.

The valve stem oil seals can be replaced with the cylinder head fitted, but we recommend to have the replacement carried out in a workshop, as the valves must be kept in their fitted position when the seals are replaced. The replacement of the valve guide seals with the cylinder head removed is described, however, in the section dealing with the overhaul of the head. Signs of worn oil seals are blue exhaust smoke when the vehicle is coasting (gear engaged), when the engine is accelerated after idling for a while or blue smoke when starting the cold engine. If the oil consumption has reached 1 litre per 600 miles, replace the valve stem oil seals as described under a separate heading.

Proceed as follows during dismantling:

- Remove all auxiliary parts from the cylinder head, including the exhaust manifold.
- Remove the camshafts as described under a separate heading.
- A valve spring compressor is required to remove the valves. Valves are held in position by means of valve cotter halves. Compress the springs and remove the valve cotter halves with a pair of pointed pliers or a small magnet. Various valve spring compressors are suitable. Fig. 1.23 shows the one used in a Mercedes-Benz workshop.
- If a valve spring compressor is not available, it is possible to use a short piece of tube to remove the valve cotter halves. To do this, place the tube over the upper valve spring collar and hit the tube with a blow of a hammer. The valve cotter

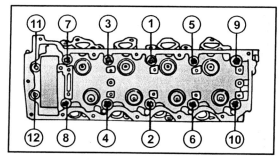

Fig. 1.20 – Tightening sequence for the cylinder head bolts. Bolts (11) and (12) are tightened after the remain bolts have been tightened to the correct torque setting.

• **Third Stage:** Tighten all bolts in the order shown without torque wrench by a further quarter of a turn (90°).

• Tighten the bolts (3) in Fig. 1.19 (11 and 12 in Fig.

1.20) to 2.0 kgm (14.5 ft.lb.).

Removal and installation of front and rear cylinder head cover

One cover is fitted underneath the vacuum pump, the other cover on the opposite end. Remove the cover in question as follows:

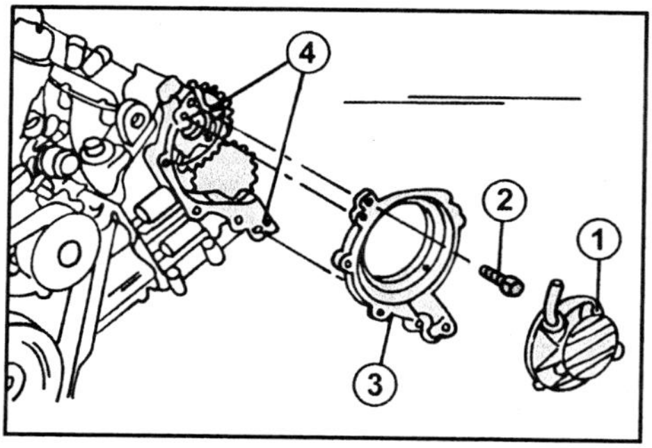

Fig. 1.21 – Details for the removal and installation of the front cover on the cylinder head.
1   Vacuum pump
2   Torx-head bolt
3   Front cover
4   Dowel pins

Cover on the side of the vacuum pump

The operations are carried out with the help of Fig. 1.21.

• Remove the cylinder head cover as described earlier on and remove the vacuum pump (section "Brakes").

• Remove the Torx-head bolts (2) securing the front cover from the cylinder head (tightening torque 0.9 kgm) and remove the cover (3). A rubber mallet will facilitate the removal. The cover is guided by the two dowel pins (4).

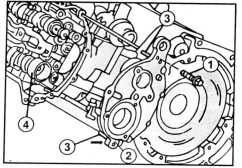

Fig. 1.22 – Details for the removal and installation of the rear cover on the cylinder head.
1   Torx-head bolt, 0.9 kgm
2   Rear cover
3   Dowel pins (standard cover)
4   Inlet camshaft (only to be observed when repair cover is fitted).

• Before installation clean the sealing faces of cover and cylinder head. Coat the sealing face of the cylinder head with "Loctite 5970" sealing compound. Fit the cover so that the dowel pins (4) engage. Evenly tighten the bolts (2) to the torque value given above.

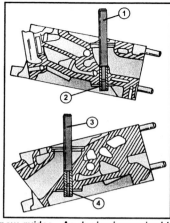

Fig. 1.25 – Removal of valve guides. The mandrels (2) and (4) have a different diameter, depending on the type of valve.

1   Press mandrel, 7 mm diameter
2   Exhaust valve guide
3   Press mandrel, 6 mm diameter
4   Inlet valve guide

Guides are removed with a shouldered mandrel from the combustion chamber side of the cylinder head. As the guides are pressed in at an angle you will have to support the cylinder head as shown in Fig. 1.25. The upper view shows the removal of an exhaust valve guide, the lower view shows the removal of an inlet valve guide. If guides with nominal dimension 1 can be used, drive them in position. If repair size guides are fitted, the locating bores in the cylinder head must be reamed out to take the new guides. As dry ice is required to fit the new valve guides, we recommend to have the work carried out in a workshop.

Before a valve guide is replaced, check the general condition of the cylinder head. The guides must be reamed after installation, and after the cylinder head has cooled down, if applicable, to their correct internal diameter. Again this may be better in the hands of an engine shop.

Valves must always be replaced if new valve guides are fitted. The valve seats must be re-cut when a guide has been replaced. If it is obvious that seats cannot be re-ground in the present condition, new valve seat inserts must be fitted.

Again this is an operation for a specialist and the work should be carried out in a workshop.

Valve Seats: If the camshaft bearings are excessively worn, fit a new or exchange cylinder head. In this case there is no need to renovate the valve seats.

Check all valve seats for signs of pitting or wear. Slight indentations can be removed with a 45° cutter. If this operation is carried out properly, there should be no need to grind-in the valves. Use correction cutters to bring the valve seating area into the centre of the valve seat. This again is achieved by using cutters of different angles (for example 15° and 60°). Valve seat inserts can be fitted to the cylinder head. Replacement of valve seat inserts will require that the old seat insert is removed by machining. The machining must not damage the bottom face of the head recess. As this is a critical operation,- we advise you to bring the cylinder head to your Mercedes Dealer who has the necessary equipment and experience to do the job. It may be possible to obtain a reconditioned cylinder head in exchange for the old one to avoid time delay. In this case remove all ancillary parts from the old head and refit them to the new head.

Valves can be ground into their seats in the conventional manner.

Valves: The stems of inlet valves and exhaust valves have been specially treated, i.e. the ends of the valve stems must not be ground off.

Valves can be cleaned best with a rotating wire brush. Check the valve faces for wear or grooving. If the wear is only slight, valves can be re-ground to their original angle in a valve grinding machine, but make sure that there is enough material left to have an edge on the valve head. The valve head thickness must be 0.5 - 0.7 mm in the case of the inlet valves and 0,5 - 0.6 mm in the case of the exhaust valves.

halves will collect in the inside of the tube and the components can be removed. The valve head must be supported from the other side of the cylinder head. Keep the hammer in close contact with the tube to prevent the cotter halves from flying out.

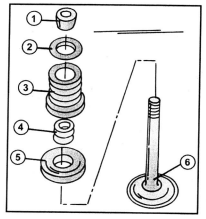

Fig. 1.24 – Valve together with component parts. Both types of valve are fitted the same parts.

1   Valve cotter halves
2   Upper valve spring cup
3   Valve spring
4   Valve stem oil seal
5   Lower valve spring cup
6   Valve

• Remove the valve spring collar and the valve spring. The valve springs (one spring per valve) are identified with a paint spot and only a spring with a paint spot of the same colour must be fitted. A thrust ring is fitted underneath each valve spring and can be removed. Fig. 1.24 shows the individual parts on each valve.

• Remove valve stem oil seals carefully with a screwdriver or a pair of pliers.

• Remove the valves one after the other out of the valve guides and pierce them in their fitted order through a piece of cardboard. Write the cylinder number against each valve if they are to be re-used.

1.3.0.3. Cylinder Head - Overhaul

The cylinder head must be thoroughly cleaned and remains of old gasket material removed. The checks and inspections are to be carried out as required.

Valve Springs: If the engine has a high mileage, always replace the valve springs as a set. To check a valve spring, place the old spring and a new spring end to end over a long bolt (with washer under bolt head) and fit a nut (again with a washer). Tighten the nut until the springs are under tension and measure the length of the two springs. If the old spring is shorter by more than 10%, replace the complete spring set. When a spring tester is available.

The springs must not be distorted. A spring placed with its flat coil on a surface must not deviate at the top by more than 2 mm (0.08 in.).

Valve Guides: Valve guides for inlet and exhaust valves are made of cast iron and have not the same outer diameter.
Clean the inside of the guides by pulling a petrol-soaked cloth through the guides. Valve stems can be cleaned best by means of a rotating wire brush. Measure the inside diameter of the guides. As an inside micrometer is necessary for this operation, which is not always available, you can insert the valve into its guide and withdraw it until the valve head is approx. level with the cylinder head face. Rock the valve to and fro and check for play. Although no exact values are available, it can be assumed that the play should not exceed 1.0 - 1.2 mm (0.04 -0.047 in.). Mercedes workshops use gauges to check the guides for wear.

installation of the valve stem seals.

- Fit the valve springs with the paint spot towards the bottom, fit the upper spring cup and compress the springs until the valve cotter halves can be inserted. Make absolutely sure that the cotter halves have properly engaged before the crankshaft is rotated.

Note: Operate the valve spring compressor very slowly, as valve cotter halves sometimes stick to the valve stems. Observe the valve spring during compression. Only the spring should move, not the valve. Prevent by all means that the valve can press against the piston.

1.3.0.4. Cylinder Head - Assembly

The assembly of the cylinder head is a reversal of the dismantling procedure. Note the following points:

- Lubricate the valve stems with engine oil and insert the valves into the correct valve guides.
- Fit the valve stem seals as described above. The repair kit contains fitting sleeves and these must be used to fit the seals. The sleeves are fitted over the valve stem before the seal is pushed in position
- Fit the valve spring and valve spring collar over the valve and use the valve lifter to compress the spring. Insert the valve cotter halves with a pair of pointed pliers and release the valve spring lifter. Make sure that the cotter halves are in position by tapping the end of the valve stem with a plastic mallet. Place a rag over the valve end - just in case. The order of fitting is shown in Fig. 1.22.

1.3.1. TIMING MECHANISM (timing chain, sprockets, tensioner)

The following operations may be necessary on the timing mechanism, i.e. timing chain, timing chain tensioner, camshaft, etc.

1.3.1.0. Checking the basic position of the camshaft

The operation is for example necessary before the installation of the cylinder head. The cylinder head cover must be removed before the camshaft and crankshaft setting can be checked.

- Rotate the engine on the pulley end and check the TDC marking on the pulley. The "OT" mark (top dead centre mark) on the pulley must be opposite the pointer on the timing cover, as shown in Fig. 1.27 with the arrow.
- In this position of the crankshaft pulley check the basic position of the camshaft. Looking at the camshaft check that the marks in Fig. 1.27 on the camshaft bearing cap and the camshaft sprocket are opposite each other.

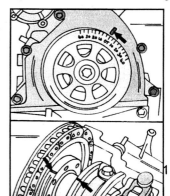

Fig. 1.27 – The upper vie shows the position of the crankshaft pulley. The marking "OT" (TDC) must be opposite the pointer on the timing case cover (arrow).

The lower vie shows the alignment of the camshaft sprocket and the camshaft bearing cover (arrrows).

- If this is the case, the cylinder head can be fitted. Also all other operations which require the camshaft in the basic position can be carried out.

Note that the exhaust valves are filled with sodium. Do not dispose of them by ordinary means, but take them to the workshop where they can be disposed of in line with the safety laws-

Check the valve stem diameters and in this connection the inside diameters of the valve guides. If there is a deviation from the nominal values, it may be necessary to replace the valve guides (see above). Also check the end of the valve stems. There should be no visible wear in this area.

Sometimes it is only required to replace the exhaust valves, if these for example are burnt out at their valve head edges.

Cylinder Head: Thoroughly clean the cylinder head and cylinder block surfaces of old gasket material and check the faces for distortion. To do this, place a steel ruler with a sharp edge over the cylinder head face and measure the gap between ruler and face with feeler gauges. Checks must be carried out in longitudinal and diagonal direction and across the face. If a feeler gauge of more than 0.10 mm (0.004 in.) can be inserted, when the ruler is placed along or across the cylinder head, have the cylinder head face re-ground.

Fig. 1.26 – Checking a camshaft for run-out.

Camshafts: Place the camshafts with both end journals into "V" blocks or clamp the shaft between the centres of a lathe and apply a dial gauge to the centre journal, as shown in Fig. 1.26. Slowly rotate the shaft to check for run-out. If the dial gauge reading exceeds 0.01 mm, fit a new shaft. The following points must be observed when replacing the camshaft: Make sure to fit the correct shaft if the shaft is to be replaced. Check the identification number when ordering a new shaft.

Replacing Valve Stem Oil Seals (Cylinder Head fitted): Valve stem oil seals are available in repair kits. Included in the repair kits are protective sleeves which must be pushed over the valves during installation of the seals..

Normally a special tool is used to fit the seals, but a well fitting piece of tube of suitable diameter can be used. Take care not to damage the sealing lip and the spring.

• Remove the valve cotter halves of the first cylinder as described in Section 1.3.0.2.

• Use a pair of pliers or a screwdriver to remove the valve stem seals, without damaging the valve stems.

Fig. 1.27 – Installation of valve stem seals.
1 Pliers to remove old seal
2 Mandrel to fit new seal
3 Protective sleeve
4 Valve stem seal

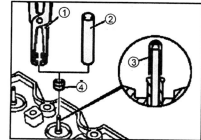

• Coat the new seals with engine oil and carefully push them over the valve stems. The protective sleeve must be used for the inlet valves. Push the seals over the valve guides until properly in position. Fig. 1.27 demonstrates the installation of the valve stem seals.

- Fit the valve springs with the paint spot towards the bottom, fit the upper spring cup and compress the springs until the valve cotter halves can be inserted. Make absolutely sure that the cotter halves have properly engaged before the crankshaft is rotated.

Note: Operate the valve spring compressor very slowly, as valve cotter halves sometimes stick to the valve stems. Observe the valve spring during compression. Only the spring should move, not the valve. Prevent by all means that the valve can press against the piston.

1.3.0.4. Cylinder Head - Assembly

The assembly of the cylinder head is a reversal of the dismantling procedure. Note the following points:

- Lubricate the valve stems with engine oil and insert the valves into the correct valve guides.
- Fit the valve stem seals as described above. The repair kit contains fitting sleeves and these must be used to fit the seals. The sleeves are fitted over the valve stem before the seal is pushed in position
- Fit the valve spring and valve spring collar over the valve and use the valve lifter to compress the spring. Insert the valve cotter halves with a pair of pointed pliers and release the valve spring lifter. Make sure that the cotter halves are in position by tapping the end of the valve stem with a plastic mallet. Place a rag over the valve end - just in case. The order of fitting is shown in Fig. 1.22.

1.3.1. TIMING MECHANISM (timing chain, sprockets, tensioner)

The following operations may be necessary on the timing mechanism, i.e. timing chain, timing chain tensioner, camshafts, etc.

1.3.1.0. Checking the basic position of the camshafts

The operation is for example necessary before the installation of the cylinder head. This will set the piston of No. 1 cylinder to the top dead centre position of its compression stroke. The cylinder head cover must be removed before the camshaft and crankshaft setting can be checked.

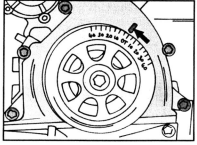

Fig. 1.28 – The position of the crankshaft pulley. The marking "OT" (TDC) must be opposite the pointer on the timing case cover (arrow).

- Rotate the engine on the pulley end and check the TDC marking on the pulley. The "OT" mark (top dead centre mark) on the pulley must be opposite the pointer on the timing cover, as shown in Fig. 1.28 with the arrow in the upper view.
- In this position of the crankshaft pulley check the basic position of the camshafts by referring to Fig. 1.29. You must be able to insert two cylindrical pins of 6 mm diameter (1) through the bores of the inlet

31

camshaft (2) and the exhaust camshaft (3), The pins must contact the cylinder head.

Fig. 1.29 – Checking the position of the basic position of the camshafts. The cylindrical drifts (1) must be inserted into the inlet camshaft (2) and the exhaust camshaft (3). If not possible refit the camshaft position.

• If this is the case, the cylinder head can be fitted. Also all other operations which require the camshaft in the basic position can be carried out.

1.3.1.1. Setting the Camshaft to the basic position

The operation must be carried out if the alignment shown in Fig. 1.28 and Fig. 1.29 cannot be obtained or the engine has been completely dismantled and is being assembled. The two camshafts must be removed as described later on.
• Insert the two 6 mm cylindrical drifts shown in Fig. 1.29 through the bores in inlet camshaft (2) and exhaust camshaft (3) and push them to their stop against the cylinder head. If necessary rotate the camshaft(s) to insert the drifts.
• Check that the TDC mark on the crankshaft pulley is aligned as shown in Fig. 1.28.
• Refit the camshafts as described below and rotate the crankshaft by two complete revolutions in the direction of rotation. Re-check the camshaft position.

1.3.1.2. Removal and Installation of the Chain Tensioner

The chain tensioner is fitted at the position shown in Fig. 1.30. Before removal rotate the engine until the No. 1 cylinder is at top dead centre in the compression stroke, to be checked with Fig. 1.28. Unscrew the chain tensioner (1) out of the cylinder head.

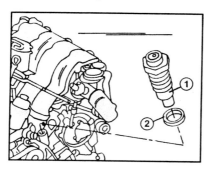

Fig. 1.30 – Details for the removal and installation of the chain tensioner (1). The sealing ring (2) must always be replaced.

If you find difficulties to reach the chain tensioner it is possible to disconnect the coolant hose (drain coolant, of course). Replace the sealing ring (2) during installation. The chain tensioner is tightened to 8.0 kgm (58 ft.lb.).

1.3.1.3. Removal and Installation of the Timing Case Cover

Important note before commencing removal: The engine must be removed together with the front axle carrier and the engine separated from the carrier as described later on. You have been warned.

If you intend to remove the cover refer to Fig. 1.31. The illustration shows a petrol engine, but for these engines you can ignore the removal of the water pump pulley (2) and the disconnection of the crankcase ventilation hose (4). The following description assumes that the engine has already been separated from the front axle carrier.

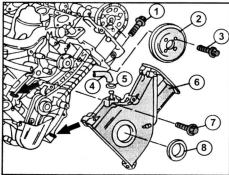

Fig. 1.31 – Details for the removal and installation of the timing case cover.
1   Bolts inserted from above
2   Water pump pulley
3   Pulley bolts, 0.8 kgm
4   Crankcase ventilation hose
5   Hose clamp
6   Timing case cover
7   Bolts in timing case cover
8   Oil seal in timing case cover

• In the following order remove the cylinder head cover, the vacuum pump, the front cylinder head cover (already described), the oil sump (section "Lubrication System"), the crankshaft pulley with the vibration damper (see below). The parts to be removed are shown in Fig. 1.31.

• Remove the Torx-head bolts (1). The bolts are located next to the camshaft sprocket on one side. Tighten the bolts to 2.0 kgm (4.5 ft.lb.) during installation.

• Remove the Torx-head bolts (7) securing the timing case cover (6) to the crankcase. Note that bolts have a different length. Mark their position.

• Remove the timing case cover, if necessary using a soft-face mallet. Dowel pins are used at the positions shown by the arrows.

• Carefully remove the oil seal (8) out of the timing case cover bore, using a screwdriver.

• Thoroughly clean the sealing faces of cover and crankcase and coat them with "Loctite". The outer diameter and the sealing lip of the seal must be lubricated with engine oil.

The installation is a reversal of the removal procedure, observing the points already mentioned above.

1.3.1.4.   Removal and Installation of Crankshaft Sprocket

After removal of the timing case cover in the manner described above position the piston of No. 1 cylinder to the TDC position (also already described), remove the cylinder head cover, the oil pump (section "Lubrication System") and the chain tensioner (already described). The removal of the sprocket requires a suitable two- or three arm puller.

• Remove the inlet camshaft sprocket (the R.H. shaft looking at the two camshaft sprockets). Mark the timing chain and the camshaft sprocket with a spot of paint (allow the paint to dry or use quick-drying paint). Remove the bolts, but note that they should be replaced. Lift the chain from the other sprocket, and lower it until it can be disengaged from the crankshaft sprocket. The tensioning arm for the oil pump drive chain must be pushed to one side and the oil pump drive chain lifted off the sprocket.

• The sprocket can now be withdrawn from the end of the crankshaft, using the puller. Fig. 1.32 shows the parts on the end of the crankshaft.

During installation align the Woodruff key (1) in the end of the crankshaft with the groove in the crankshaft sprocket. If necessary the sprocket can be heated up in hot (boiling) water.

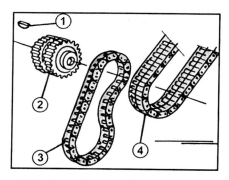

Fig. 1.32 – The drive chains on the end of the crankshaft sprocket.
1   Woodruff key
2   Crankshaft sprocket
3   Oil pump drive chain
4   Timing chain

The installation is a reversal of the removal procedure, noting the points already given above. Finally rotate the crankshaft by two full revolution and check that the camshafts are in their basic position, as described earlier on.

1.3.1.5. Removal and Installation of Crankshaft Pulley

The crankshaft pulley identified with (1) in Fig. 1.33 is only fitted to one of the petrol engines (1.3 litre). All other engines have a pulley with vibration damper, in Fig. 1.33 shown by (3).

As already described earlier on, the engine must be removed together with the front axle carrier and the engine detached from the carrier, i.e. a complicated operation. Then proceed as follows:

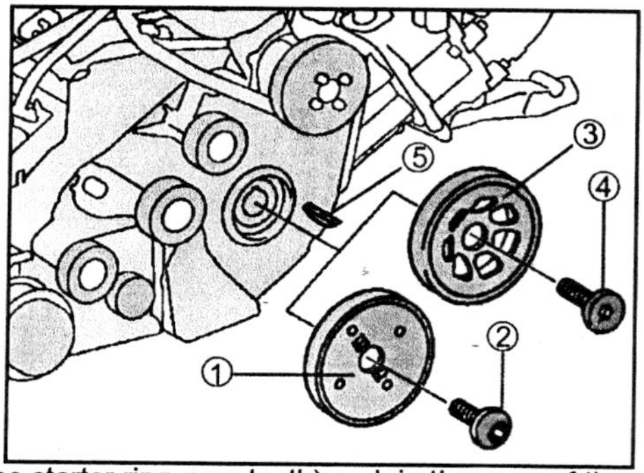

Fig. 1.33 – Removal and installation of the crankshaft pulley with and without vibration damper.
1   Pulley for 1.4 litre petrol engine
2   Bolt, 20 kgm + 90°
3   Pulley with vibration damper
4   Bolt, 20 kgm + 90°
5   Woodruff key

- Remove the Poly drive belt as described under separate heading.
- Prevent the crankshaft from rotating in suitable manner (if necessary remove the starter motor and insert a tyre lever into the starter ring gear teeth) and, in the case of the diesel engine remove the bolt (4). Remove the pulley with the vibration damper (3) from the end of the crankshaft.

The installation is a reversal of the removal procedure. Make sure that the Woodruff key (5) engages with the groove in the pulley. The bolt (4) is tightened to 20.0 kgm (144 ft.lb.) and from the final position a further quarter of a turn. The crankshaft must be prevented from rotating.

1.3.1.6. Removal and Installation of Camshafts

The installation of the camshafts is shown in Fig. 1.34. Remove the camshafts by referring to the illustration.

- Remove the cylinder head cover (already described).
- Rotate the crankshaft in direction of rotation until the top dead centre position has been obtained. Refer to Fig. 1.28 for details. Check on crankshaft pulley and camshafts.
- Remove the plastic cover over the exhaust camshaft sprocket.

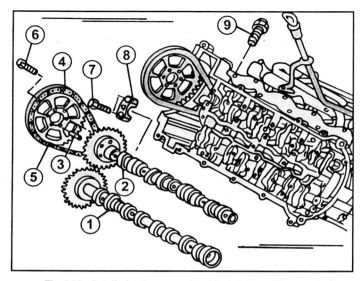

Fig. 1.34 – Details for the removal and installation of the camshafts.

1	Exhaust camshaft
2	Inlet camshaft
3	Dowel pin
4	Camshaft sprocket
5	Timing chain
6	Torx-head bolt for sprockets, 1.8 kgm
7	Torx-head bolt for camshaft bearing caps, 0.9 kgm
8	Camshaft bearing caps note sequence during removal and installation of bolts)

- Remove the front and rear cover from the cylinder head as already described above.
- Prevent the crankshaft from rotating in suitable manner (if necessary remove the starter motor and insert a tyre lever into the flywheel ring gear teeth).
- Mark the camshaft sprocket (4) and the timing chain (5) in relation to each other, using a spot of paint (allow it to dry). Make sure that the markings are opposite each other when the parts are refitted. After installation check the basic position of the camshafts and if necessary adjust. Both operations have already been described.
- Remove the chain tensioner (already described).
- Remove the Torx-head bolts (6) from the inlet camshaft sprocket (2) and lift off the timing chain (5). Withdraw the sprocket from the end of the camshaft. The sprocket is guided by means of a dowel pin (3). The bolts (6) must always be replaced. Tighten the bolts to 1.8 kgm (13 ft.lb.). The sprocket is fitted together with the mounted timing chain (5).
- Slacken and remove the camshaft bearing cap bolts (8) evenly across and lift off the caps as soon as they are free. The slackening of the bearing cap bolts must be carried out in a certain sequence which is shown in Fig. 1.35. The bolts are slackened by half a turn at a time. First slacken bolts 1, 3, and 5 and also 6, 8 and 10 in the upper view and lift off the covers marked with the arrows. Then slacken the bolts 2, 4, 7 and 9 in the lower view and then remove the covers marked with

the arrows. The camshafts must not be rotated when the bearing caps are removed in the sequence given. As the bearing caps must be refitted in their original position mark each cap in suitable manner.

- Remove the camshafts (1) and (2).

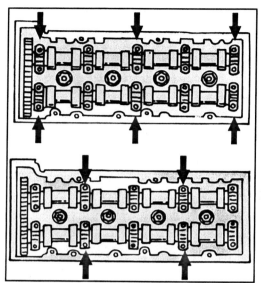

Fig. 1.35 – Slacken and tighten the camshaft bearing caps in accordance with the arrows in the order shown as explained in the text.

The installation is a reversal of the removal procedure. In addition to the special points already mentioned, also note the following:

- Insert the two camshafts so that the two 6 mm pins shown in Fig. 1.29 can be inserted into the two bores of the camshaft sprockets. The two sprockets must be fitted provisionally. Use the old bolts. Push the pins against the cylinder head.
- The camshaft are sensitive to distortion and must be handled with care and fitted free of tension. If a new camshaft is fitted make sure to fit the correct shaft as they are different for the various engines (not all engines have the same valve timing).

Fig. 1.36 – The position of the camshaft bearing caps. In the upper view for the inlet camshaft, in the lower view for the exhaust camshaft.

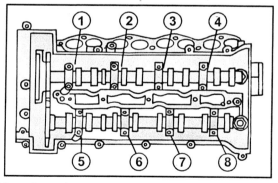

- Fit the camshaft bearing caps in accordance with the marks made during removal. Fig. 1.36 shows the marking of the bearing caps. In the case of the inlet camshaft the marking commences at the front from 1 to 4, in the case of the exhaust camshaft from 5 to 8. Make absolutely sure that the caps are fitted to their original position. All bolts are tightened evenly to 0.9 kgm (7 ft.lb.).
- Refit the camshaft sprockets to the camshafts. The bolts (6) must always be replaced. Make sure that the dowel pins engage.
- Refit the chain tensioner (previously described).

- Check the basic position of the camshafts and if necessary adjust (described earlier on). Make sure that the top dead centre on camshafts and crankshaft pulley have been obtained.
- All other operations are carried out in reverse order.

1.3.1.7.   Timing Chain – Removal and Installation

Although it would be possible to replace the timing chain with the engine fitted to the vehicle, it is practically impossible to replace the chain outside a Mercedes dealer, as a complete special tool set is required to remove a chain link and the new link must be riveted to the new chain. The chain can be replaced with the engine removed (although the power unit must be lowered together with the front axle carrier) by following the various operations already described above. It should be noted that the double roller chain, fitted to a certain date, has been replaced by a single roller chain during the production of later models. If a new chain is fitted, you will have to know that. Quote the engine type and the model year to prevent mistakes.

1.3.1.8.   Tensioning Rail and Slide Rail – Removal and Installation

Both rails are fitted to the timing case cover. Fig. 1.37 shows the tensioning rail. Removal of the two rails are carried out in the same manner.

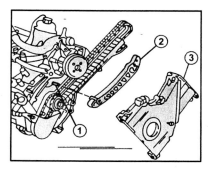

Fig. 1.37 – Removal and installation of the tensioning rail inside the timing case/timing cover. The slide rail is attached in the same manner.
1   Bearing pin
2   Tensioning rail
3   Timing case cover

- Remove the cylinder head and the timing case cover as already described.
- Withdraw the tensioning rail or the slide rail from the bearing pin (1).
- Refit the part in question in reverse order.

1.3.1.7.   Detaching and Attaching Engine from the Front Axle Carrier

First requirement is the availability of a suitable hoist and chains to lift the engine from the front axle carrier. The engine must be in a horizontal position, the chains must be attached as shown in Fig. 1.38. The engine must be lifted until the weight of the engine is no longer resting on the engine mountings. Fig. 1.39 on the next page shows the removed front axle carrier with some of the attachments to be removed in the case of a petrol engine, but similar operations apply to a diesel engine. The necessary tightening torques are given during the removal instructions.
- Remove the bolts (1) and (2). Tighten to 5.5 kgm (40 ft.lb.) during installation.
- Using a suitable screwdriver press the L.H. drive shaft (6) out of the gearbox.
- Detach the bearing bracket (4) of the intermediate shaft (5) on the engine side and, using a suitable screwdriver, press the intermediate shaft (5) out of the gearbox. The bolt (3) is tightened to 2.0 kgm (14.5 ft.lb.).
- Lift the engine and transmission out of the front axle carrier as shown in Fig. 1.38. During this operation guide the L.H. drive shaft (6) and the intermediate shaft (5) carefully out of the transmission. Inspect the condition of the circlip at the end of

the shaft and replace if necessary. During installation insert the L.H. drive shaft (5) and the intermediate shaft (6) carefully into the splines in the gearbox until the circlips snap into place.

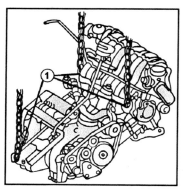

Fig. 1.38 – The engine is attached with chains at the positions shown to lift it off the front axle carrier.

- Remove the starter motor. The bolts are tightened 2.0 kgm (14.5 ft.lb.).
- Detail the gearbox from the engine. Pay attention to the dowel sleeves between engine and gearbox. If an automatic transmission is fitted there is an additional cover fitted. During installation make sure that the dowel sleeves engage correctly. The transmission to engine bolts are tightened to 2.0 kgm (14.5 ft.lb.).

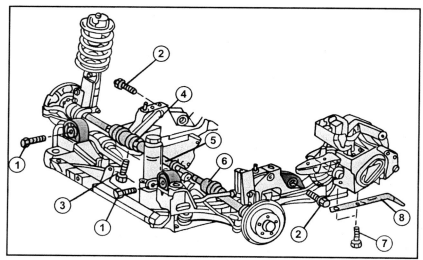

Fig. 1.39 – Details for the removal and installation of the engine from the front axle carrier. The numbers are referred to in the text.

The installation is a reversal of the removal procedure, observing then special points already mentioned above.

1.3.2.   PISTON AND CONNECTING RODS
1.3.2.0.   Technical Data

All dimensions are given in metric units.
Piston Diameter - Standard:
- A160 CDI, A170 CDI, A170 L CDI: 79.970 – 79.976 mm

38

Piston Running Clearance:
- New: 0,017 – 0,043 mm
- Wear limit: 0.12 mm

Piston pin clearance:
- In connecting rod bore: 0.018 – 0.024 mm
- In piston: 0.004 – 0.015 mm
Piston ring gaps:
- Upper rings: 0.22 – 0.42 mm
- Wear limit: 1.5 mm
- Centre rings: 0.20 – 0.40 mm
- Wear limit: 1.0 mm
- Oil control ring: 0.20 – 0.40 mm
- Wear limit: 1.0 mm
Piston ring side clearance in piston grooves:
- Upper rings: 0.12 – 0.16 mm
- Wear limit: 0.20 mm
- Centre rings: 0.050 – 0.090 mm
- Wear limit: 0.15 mm
- Oil control ring: 0.030 – 0.07 mm
- Wear limit: 0.10 mm

1.3.2.1.   Piston and Connecting Rods – Removal

Pistons and connecting rods are pushed out towards the top of the cylinder bores, using a hammer handle alter connecting rod bearing caps and shells have been removed. The engine must be removed to remove the connecting rod piston assemblies. If the piston require replacement we suggest to have the work carried out in an engine shop.

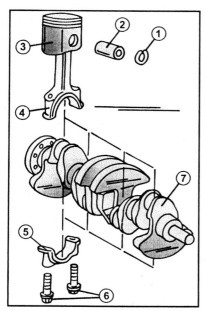

Fig. 1.38 – Exploded view of a piston and connecting rod assembly.
1   Piston pin circlip
2   Piston pin
3   Piston
4   Connecting rod and bearing shells
5   Big end bearing cap with bearing shell
6   Connecting rod bolts
7   Crankshaft

Three piston rings are fitted to each piston. The two upper rings are the compression rings, i.e. they prevent the pressure above the piston crown to return to the crankcase. The lower ring is the oil scraper ring. Its function is to remove excessive oil from the cylinder bore, thereby preventing the entry of oil into the combustion chamber. The three rings are not the same in shape. The upper ring has a rectangular section, the centre ring has a chamfer on the inside and the lower ring is chrome-plated on its outside. Only the correct fitting of the piston rings will assure the proper operation of the piston sealing.

The connection rods connect the pistons to

the crankshaft. The piston pin connects the piston to the connecting rod. Fig. 1.38 shows the parts of piston/connecting rod assemblies.

Before removal of the assemblies note the following points:

- The engine and gearbox must be removed together with the front axle carrier and the engine separated from the carrier to remove the pistons. Oil sump, oil pump and cylinder head must also be removed.
- Pistons and cylinder bores are graded in three diameter classes within specified tolerance groups and marked accordingly. The class number is stamped into the upper face of the cylinder block, next to the particular cylinder bore, as shown in Fig. 1.39 with the arrows.

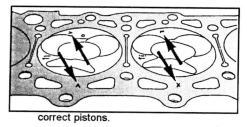

Fig. 1.39 – Identification of piston crowns and cylinder block with the piston size identification.

- The group number of the piston must always be identical with the number next to the cylinder bore. The markings you will find are I, II or III. If the cylinder block has been re-bored, you will receive the block with the correct pistons.

Fig. 1.40 – Connecting rods (1) and big end bearing caps (2) must be marked with a painted line (arrow) on the exhaust side of the engine before removal.

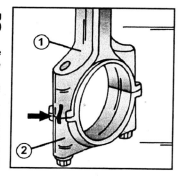

- Each piston is marked with an arrow in the piston crown. The arrow points into the direction of drive.
- Mark each piston and the connecting rod before removal with the cylinder number. This can be carried out by writing the cylinder number with paint onto the piston crown. Also mark an arrow, facing towards the front of the engine (the arrow in the piston crown will be covered by the carbon deposits).
- When removing the connecting rod, note the correct installation of the big end bearing cap. immediately after removal mark the connecting rod and the big end bearing cap on the same side. This is best done with a centre punch (cylinder No. 1 one punch mark, etc. or a spot of paint, as shown in Fig. 1.40). The marking must be on the exhaust side.

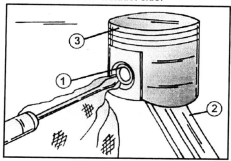

Fig. 1.41 – Removal of the piston pin circlip (1) from the piston (3) to remove the connecting rod (2).

- Mark the big end bearing shells with the cylinder number. This applies to the upper and lower shells.
- Big end bearing journals can be re-ground to four undersizes (in steps of 0.25 mm between sizes). Corresponding bearing shells are available.

- Remove the bearing caps and the shells and push the assemblies out of the cylinder bore. Any carbon deposits on the upper edge of the bores can be carefully removed with a scraper.

Fig. 1.42 – Removal or installation of piston rings.

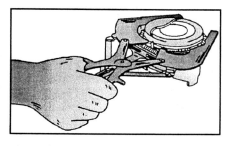

- Remove the piston pin snap rings. A notch in the piston pin bore enables a pointed drift (screwdriver) to be inserted, as shown in Fig. 1.41, to remove the rings. Place a thick piece of cloth underneath the screwdriver to prevent damage to the piston. Press the piston pins out of the pistons. If necessary heat the piston in boiling water.

- Remove the piston rings one after the other from the pistons, using a piston ring pliers if possible, as shown in Fig. 1.42. If the rings are to be re-used, mark them in accordance with their pistons and position. If no special piston ring pliers are available, use thin metal strips on opposite sides of the piston and slide them under the rings, as demonstrated in Fig. 1.43. One strip must be placed underneath the piston ring gap.

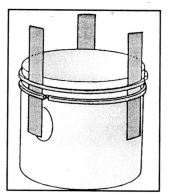

Fig. 1.43 – Piston rings can be removed by sliding metal strips underneath the rings as shown.

1.3.2.2. Measuring the Cylinder Bores

An inside caliper is necessary to measure the diameter of the cylinder bores. We strongly recommend to have the bores measured in an engine shop. If the cylinder block must be re-bored, the shop will also replace the pistons.

1.3.2.3. Checking Pistons and Connecting Rods

All parts should be thoroughly inspected. Signs of seizure, grooves or excessive wear requires the part to be replaced. Check the pistons and connecting rods as follows:

Fig. 1.44 – Checking the side clearance of the piston rings in the grooves of the piston.

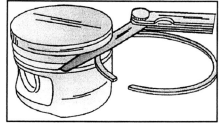

- Check the side clearance of each piston ring in its groove by inserting the ring together with a feeler gauge, as shown in Fig.

1.44. The grooves must be thoroughly cleaned before the check. If the wear limit given in the technical data exceed the values in the technical data is reached, either the rings or the piston are worn.

• Check the piston ring gap by inserting the ring from the bottom into the cylinder bore. Use a piston and carefully push the piston ring approx. 1 in. further into the bore. This will square it up. Insert a feeler gauge between the two piston ring ends to check the ring gap, as shown in Fig. 1.45. Refer to Section 1.3.2.0. for the wear limits. Rings must be replaced, if these are exceeded. New rings should also be checked in the manner described.

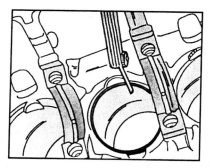

Fig. 1.45 – Checking the piston ring gaps, using a feeler gauge. The gap "A" must be measured.

• Piston pins and small end bushes must be checked for wear or seizure. One individual connecting rod can be replaced, provided that a rod of the same weight group is fitted. Connecting rods are marked with either one or two punch marks (Fig. 1.40), indicating the weight category, and only a rod with the same mark must be fitted. The difference of the connecting rod weight in one engine must not exceed 5 grams. The bushes in the connecting rod small ends can be replaced, but we recommend to take the set to an engine shop.

• Before re-using the connecting rod bolts check their length between the underside of the bolt head and the end of the thread. Any bolt longer than 38.4 mm must be replaced. New bolts have a length of 38.00 mm.

• Connecting rods should be checked for bend or twist, particularly when the engine has covered a high mileage. A special jig is necessary for this operation and the job should be carried out by an engine shop.

The following information concern the connecting rods:

• Connecting rods which were over-heated due to bearing failure (bluish colour) must not be refitted.

• Connecting and bearing caps are matched to each other and must be fitted accordingly.

• New connecting rods are supplied together with the small end bearing bush and can be fitted as supplied.

• If the piston pin has excessive clearance in the small end bush, a new bush must be fitted. Again this is best left to an engine shop, as the bush must be reamed out to the correct diameter to obtain the correct running clearance for the piston pin.

1.3.2.4. Piston and Connecting Rods - Assembly

Fig. 1.38 shows the component parts of a piston and a connecting rod and can be referred to during the assembly. Also note the following:

• If new pistons are fitted, check the piston crown markings to ensure the correct pistons are fitted, if the original pistons are fitted, arrange them in accordance with the cylinder number markings.

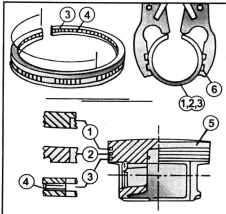

Fig. 1.46 – Sectional view of a piston with the location of the piston rings. Note the sectional view and the arrangement of the ring gaps during installation. The view at the upper R.H. corner shows how the rings are gripped during installation.

1   Plain compression ring
2   Chamfered compression ring
3   Oil scraper (control) ring
4   Coil spring
5   Piston
6   Piston ring pliers

• Insert the connecting rod into the piston and align the two bores. Make sure that the arrow in the piston crown is facing the front of the engine.

• Generously lubricate the piston pin with engine oil and insert it into the piston and connecting rod, using thumb pressure only. Never heat the piston to fit the piston pin. Fit the circlips to both sides of the piston, making sure of their engagement around the groove.

• Using a pair of piston ring pliers, as shown in Fig. 1.42, fit the piston rings from the top of the piston, starting with the bottom ring. The two compression rings could be mixed up. Under no circumstances mix-up the upper and lower compression rings. Fig. 1.46 shows a sectional view of a piston and the piston rings and the rings must be fitted accordingly. Rings 1 to 3 are marked with "Top" or a paint mark, which must face towards the piston crown. The compression ring gaps must be arranged at 120° to each other. The oil scraper ring gap must be arranged as shown top left in the illustration.

1.3.2.5.   Pistons and Connecting Rods – Installation

• Generously lubricate the cylinder bores with oil. Markings on connecting rods and bearing caps must be opposite each other (see Fig. 1.41). The arrows in the piston crowns must face towards the front of the engine, the markings on con rods and bearing caps on the exhaust side.

• Arrange the piston rings at equal spacing of 120° around the circumference of the piston skirt. The spring (4) in the oil scraper ring (3) in Fig. 1.46 must be offset by 180° in relation to the ring gap.

Fig. 1.47 – Fitting a piston (1) with a piston ring compressor (2). Push the piston into the bore with a hammer handle.

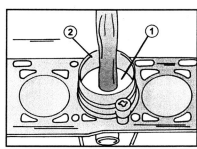

• Use a piston ring compressor and place it around the piston rings as can be seen in Fig. 1.47 and push the rings into their grooves. Check that all rings are fully pushed in. Check that the marking "Top" or the name of the manufacturer can be read from above after installation. Make sure that all rings are fitted as shown in Fig. 1.46.

• Rotate the crankshaft until two of the crankpins are at the bottom.

- Insert the connecting rod and the piston from above into the cylinder bore and push the piston into the bore as shown in the illustration. The cylinder block can be placed on its side to guide the connecting rod. The big end bearing shell must be in the connecting and in the big end bearing.
- Insert the second bearing shell into the connecting rod bearing cap, with the locating tab and fit the assembly over the connecting rod. Use a soft-metal hammer and carefully tap the cap in position. Both bearing shells must be well lubricated. Do not interchange upper and lower bearing shells. Check that connecting rod/cap marks are facing each other.
- Coat the contact areas for the cap bolts with engine oil and fit and tighten the bolts to 0.5 kgm and then again to 1.5 kgm (11 ft.lb.) in several stages. From this position tighten each bolt by a further 90° (1/4 of a turn) without using the torque wrench. It is assumed that the stretch bolts have been measured as previously described.
- Rotate the crankshaft until the two remaining crankpins are at bottom dead centre and fit the two other piston/connecting rod assemblies in the same manner.
- Check the pistons and connecting rods once more for correct installation and that each piston is fitted to its original bore, if the same parts are refitted.
- With a feeler gauge measure the side clearance of each big end bearing cap on the crankpin. The wear limit is 0.50 mm (standard clearance 0.11 to 0.23).
- The remaining installation is a reversal of the removal procedure, i.e. fit the oil pump, the oil sump and the cylinder head as describer in the relevant sections. Finally refit the engine to the front axle carrier and the front axle carrier with engine/transmission assembly to the vehicle.

1.3.4. CRANKSHAFT AND BEARINGS
1.3.4.0. Technical Data

All dimensions in metric units.
Machining tolerances:
Max. out-of-round of journals:: .... 0.005 mm
Max. taper of journals:: .... 0.010 mm
Max. taper of crankpins: .... 0.015 mm
Max. run-out of main journals*:
- Journals Nos. II and IV: .... 0.07 mm
- Journals No. III: .... 0.10 mm

* Crankshaft placed with Nos. I and V journals in "V" blocks.

Main Bearing Journal Diameter:
- Nominal diameter: ....54.940 – 54.975 mm
- Repair size: ....Enquire at dealer
Width of fit bearing: ....23.55 – 23.59 mm

Crankpin Diameter:
- Nominal dimension:. ....45.940 – 45.965 mm
- Repair size: ....Enquire at dealer

Width of Crankpins:
- Nominal Dimension ....22.90 - 23.10 mm

Bearing Running Clearances (all engines):
- Main bearings:..0.031 - 0.073 mm (best 0.055 mm)
- Big end bearings: ....0.031 - 0.073 mm (best 0.50 mm)
  Wear limit:.. 0.080 mm

Bearing End Float (all engines):
- Main bearings:...0.10 - 0.25 mm
- Big end bearings: .... 0.12 - 0.26 mm
- Wear limit - Main bearings: .... 0.30 mm
- Wear limit - Big end bearings:.. 0.50 mm

Connecting Rod Bolts:
- Thread: .... M7 x 1
- Max. length:... 38.4 mm
- Tightening torque: .... 0.5 kgm + 2.5 kgm + 90°

1.3.4.1.   Crankshaft - Removal and Installation

The engine and the gearbox must be removed together with the front axle carrier to remove the crankshaft. The engine is then removed with the carrier. The operations have already been described. Also remove the parts mentioned below in accordance with the instructions already given under the various headings.

Remove the following in the order given: The timing case cover, the crankshaft timing sprocket, the end cover together with the radial oil seal and the piston. The oil sump and the oil pump must be removed as described in section "Lubrication System". Fig. 1.48 shows the crankshaft together with the bearings and can be referred to during the removal.

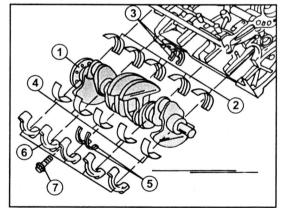

Fig. 1.48 – The crankshaft together with main bearing shells and thrust washers.
1 Crankshaft
2 Main bearing shells in crankcase
3 Thrust washers in crankcase
4 Main bearing shells in bearing caps
5 Thrust washers in caps
6 Main bearing caps
7 Main bearing cap bolts, 4.0 kgm + 90°

- Remove the transmission from the engine. Take care not to distort the clutch shaft.

- Counterhold the flywheel in suitable manner and evenly slacken the clutch securing bolts. Use a centre punch and mark the clutch and flywheel at opposite points. Lift off the clutch plate and the driven plate. Immediately clean the inside of the flywheel and unscrew the flywheel.

- Remove the flywheel. To prevent the flywheel from rotating you can refer to Fig. 1.49. Use a piece of metal bar, drill two holes in it and bolt it to the flywheel as shown. The engine must be supported well. Remove the flywheel bolts and take off the flywheel. Remove the drive plate for a torque converter of an automatic transmission in the same manner.

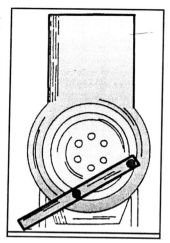

Fig. 1.49 – A piece of metal bar can be bolted to the flywheel to prevent it from rotation. Move the bar to the other side when the bolts are tightened.

- From the front end of the engine remove the bolt securing the crankshaft pulley or the pulley with the vibration damper as long as the flywheel is locked.

- The crankshaft end float should be checked before the crankshaft is removed. To do this, place a dial gauge with a suitable holder in front of the cylinder block and place the gauge stylus against the end flange of the crankshaft, as shown in Fig. 1.50. Use a screwdriver to push the crankshaft all the way to one end and set the gauge to "0" ' Push the shaft to the other side and note the dial gauge reading. The resulting value is the end float. If it exceeds 0.30 mm (0.012 in.) replace the thrust washers on the centre bearing (3 and 5 in Fig. 1.48) during assembly, but make sure to fit washers of the correct width. These are located left and right at the centre bearing. Note that only two washers of the same thickness must be fitted.

- Unscrew the oil seal flange from the rear of the cylinder block.

- Unscrew the main bearing bolts (7) evenly across. The bearings caps (6) are marked with the numbers 1 to 5. The numbers are stamped into the centre of the caps. No. 1 cap is located at the crankshaft pulley side.

Fig. 1.50 – Checking the crankshaft end float.

- Remove the bearing shells (4) from the bearing journals (they could also stick to the caps) and immediately mark them on their back faces with the bearing number. Also remove the thrust washers (5).

- Lift the crankshaft (1) out of the cylinder block and remove the remaining thrust washers (3) from the centre bearing location and the remaining bearings shells (2). Keep the shells together with the lower shells and the bearing caps. These shells have an oil bore and a groove and must always be fitted into the crankcase when the crankshaft is installed.

1.3.4.2. Inspection of Crankshaft and Bearings

Main and crankpin journals must be measured with precision instruments to find their diameters. All journals can be re-ground four times and the necessary bearing shells are available, i.e. undersize shells can be fitted.

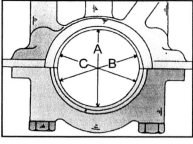

Fig. 1.51 – Measuring the inside diameter of the crankshaft basic bore in the crankcase.

Place the crankshaft with the two end journals into "V" blocks and apply a dial gauge to the centre main journal. Rotate the crankshaft by one turn and read off the dial gauge. If the reading exceeds 0.06 mm, replace the crankshaft.

Check the main bearing running clearance as follows:

• Bolt the main bearing caps without shells to the crankcase, oil the bolt threads and fit each cap. Tighten the

bolts to 4.0 kgm (29 ft.lb.) and then angle-tighten them a further 90 °. Bearing caps are offset and can only be fitted in one position.

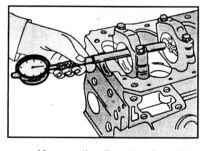

Fig. 1.52 – Measuring the inside diameter of the fitted bearing shells.

• Referring to Fig. 1.51 measure the bearing bores in directions A, B and C and write down the results. If the basic diameter is exceeded (see Section 1.3.4.0.), the bearing cap and/or the cylinder block must be replaced.

• Remove the bearing caps and refit them, this time with the well cleaned bearing shells. Re-tighten the bolts as specified.

• Measure the diameter of each bearing in accordance as shown in Fig. 1.52 and write down the results. Deduct the journal diameter from the bearing diameter. The resulting difference is the bearing running clearance, which should be between 0.031 - 0.073 mm, with a wear limit of 0.080 mm.

• Check the big end bearing clearances in a similar manner, but bolt the bearing caps to the connecting rods. Tighten the nuts to the value given in the technical data and angle-tighten as above. The bearing clearance should be between 0.031 - 0.073 mm, with the same wear limit.

Fig. 1.53 – Correct fitting of the crankshaft thrust washers.

Selection of bearing shells is rather complicated, and we advise you to take the cylinder block to an engine shop, if the above measurements have revealed that new bearing shells are necessary.

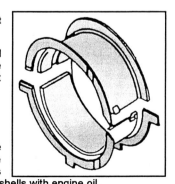

1.3.4.3. Crankshaft - Installation

• Thoroughly clean the bearing bores in the crankcase and insert the shells (2) with the drillings into the bearing bores, with the tabs engaging the notches. Generously lubricate the shells with engine oil.

• Fit the thrust washers (3) in Fig. 1.47 to the centre bearing, with the oil grooves towards the outside, as shown in Fig. 1.53. Use the two forefingers as shown in

Fig. 1.54 to hold the thrust washers against the bearing cap and fit the cap in position.

Fig. 1.54 – Fitting the main bearing cap together with the thrust washer.

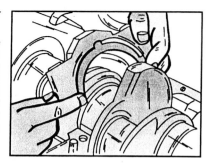

- Lift the crankshaft in position and fit the bearing caps with the inserted shells (4) – again shells well oiled and locating tabs in notches. Fig. 1.55 shows the arrangement of the bearing shells and the thrust washers. The numbers refer to Fig. 1.48. Parts shown with A"" are in the crankcase, parts shown with "B" are fitted to the main bearing caps.

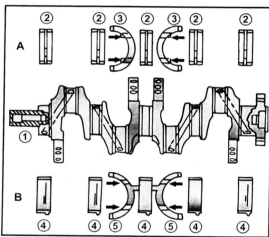

Fig. 1.55 – Crankshaft together with fitting position of main bearing shells and thrust washers. The numbers are the same as given in Fig. 1.47.
A In crankcase
B In main bearing caps

- Fit the two thrust washers (5) to the centre bearing cap, again with the oil groove towards the outside. Place this cap in position, guiding the two thrust washers in order not to dislodge them. Use the forefingers to hold the washers as shown in Fig. 1.54. Use a mallet to tap the caps in position. Check the numbering of the bearing caps and fit the well oiled bolts. The number "1" in the crankcase shows where bearing cap "1" must be fitted, i.e. you follow Fig. 1.56 to fit the bearing caps correctly.

Fig. 1.56 – Marking of main bearing caps (1). Cap and cylinder block are marked accordingly.

Important Note when fitting the Main Bearing Caps

Main bearing caps can be fitted in one position only. If the caps have been fitted incorrectly, you will see the lug, shown in Fig. 1.57 with the arrow, facing towards the rear (against the direction of drive). The main bearing caps are machined together with the crankcase and must therefore not be interchanged. As already mentioned the No. 1 cap is located on the timing side of the engine.

- Tighten the bolts from the centre towards the outside in several steps to a torque reading of to 4.0 kgm (29 ft.lb.) and from this position a further 90° (quarter of a turn).
- Rotate the crankshaft a few times to check for binding.
- Re-check the crankshaft end float as described during removal. Attach the dial gauge to the crankcase as shown in Fig. 1.49.
- Refit the pistons and connecting rods (already described).
- Refit the rear oil seal flange (see below).
- Refit the timing mechanism (already described).
- The remaining operations are carried out in reverse order to the removal procedure. The various sections give detailed description of the relevant operations, i.e. flywheel and clutch or drive plate, oil pump, oil sump and cylinder head.

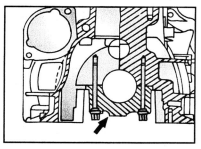

Fig. 1.57 – Correct installation of the main bearing caps. The parts of the cap marked with the arrow must be located as shown.

1.3.4.4. Rear Crankshaft Oil Seal and Oil Seal Carrier

The rear crankshaft oil seal is located inside a flange, which is bolted to the rear of the crankcase. Two dowels, one on each side of the cover, locate the flange correctly in relation to the crankshaft centre. The flange is secured by means of six bolts, as shown in Fig. 1.58 and is fitted with sealing compound ("Loctite"). The cover is supplied with the oil seal as an assembly and longer hexagonal head bolts and pre-mounted fitting sleeves. Originally Torx-head bolts were used during manufacture.

The replacement of the oil seal carrier is carried out as follows:

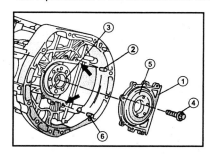

Fig. 1.58 – Details for the removal and installation of the rear oil seal carrier. The dowel sleeves are fitted at the points shown by the arrows.
1 Carrier with oil seal (die cast carrier as replacement part)
2 Torx-head bolt (longer hexagonal head bolts in repair kit)
3 Dowel pins
4 Assembly sleeve (pre-fitted to carrier)

- Remove the oil filter.
- Remove the manual transmission or the automatic transmission.
- Remove the bolts (2) securing the oil seal carrier (1) on the outside and remove the cover with the oil seal. Immediately check the dowel pins for good condition and new ones if in doubt. As already mentioned the new oil seal carrier is supplied with a new oil seal and a pre-mounted fitting sleeve and the longer hexagonal head bolts.

- Clean the carrier (if the original cover is refitted) and crankcase faces. The running area of the crankshaft must be cleaned with a clean rag.
- Coat the carrier face with sealing compound mentioned where is contacting the oil sump gasket (arrows) above and fit it to the block. Fit the carrier with the fitted mounting sleeve (4) carefully flush against the cylinder block and remove the fitting sleeve. The sealing ring must be resting against the crankshaft.
- After installation drive the dowel sleeves (3) in position.
- Fit the bolts (2) and tighten them to 0.8 kgm (6 ft.lb.).
- Carry out all other operations in reverse order, i.e. fit the flywheel or the drive plate (automatic), fill the engine with oil and refit the oil filer.

1.3.4.5. Front Crankshaft Oil Seal

The front crankshaft oil seal is located in the timing case cover. Oil leaks at this position can also be caused by a leaking timing cover gasket. Check before replacing the oil seal. The crankshaft pulley or the pulley together with the vibration damper must be removed to replace the oil seal.

Fig. 1.59 – Removal of the oil seal in the front cover. Protect the screwdriver blade s shown.

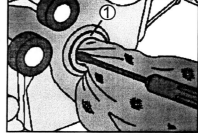

The seal (1) can be carefully removed with a screwdriver as shown in Fig. 1.59. In order not to damage the crankshaft or the mounting bore for the seal during removal, use a clean rag and place it under the screwdriver blade as shown. Otherwise screw a self-tapping screw into the outside of the seal and apply the screwdriver blade under the screw head.

Thoroughly clean the surrounding parts. Burrs on the timing cover bore can be removed with a scraper. Fill the space between sealing lip and dust protection lip with grease and carefully drive a new oil seal into the timing cover and over the crankshaft until the ring outer face is flush. If oil leaks were the reason for replacement it is possible to drive the seal in a little further, but not more than by 0.7 mm, to give the sealing lip a new running area. Refit the vibration damper and pulley or the pulley as described earlier on.

1.3.4.6. Flywheel or Drive Plate (Automatic)

The flywheel is the same on all engines, as all engines are fitted with a dual-mass flywheel. The flywheel or the drive plate for an automatic transmission model can be removed without removal of the crankshaft.

Remove the part in question as follows:

- Remove the transmission (Section 3.1.) or the automatic transmission. Remove the clutch in the case of a manual transmission.
- Counterhold the flywheel in suitable manner and remove the clutch after having marked its relationship to the flywheel. Remove the drive plate in a similar manner. 8 bolts (3) or (5) are used to secure the flywheel. A dowel pin is fitted into the crankshaft flange to guide the flywheel or driven plate during installation. During installation of the flywheel (4) or the driven plate (1) it will be necessary to engage the dowel pin with the hole in the crankshaft flange. Fig. 1.60 shows the location of the hole in the case of a driven plate. The flywheel has a similar hole as can be seen in the R.H. view.

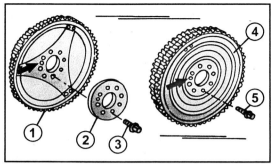

Fig. 1.60 – Removal and installation of the driven plate on the left and the flywheel on the right. The arrows show where the dowel pin must engage.
1   Driven plate
2   Washer
3   Bolt, 4.5 kgm + 90°
4   Flywheel
5   Bolt, 4.5 kgm + 90°0

• Remove the flywheel or the drive plate. A distance washer (2) is used in the case of the drive plate, which can also be removed. The securing bolts can be discarded, as they must be replaced.

• If the flywheel or the starter ring looks worn, take the wheel to your dealer to have the flywheel re-machined and/or the ring gear replaced.

Fit the flywheel or drive plate as applicable. Always use new flywheel bolts.

• Fit the flywheel or the drive plate to the crankshaft flange and rotate it until the two alignment holes are in line and push the flywheel or plate over the dowel pin. Refer to Fig. 1.60. In the case of a driven plate place the washer (2) over the plate.

• Fit new bolts (3) or (5) and tighten them evenly across to 4.5 kgm (32.5 ft.lb.). An Allen key will be necessary. From this position tighten the bolts a further 90° (quarter of a turn).

1.4.   Poly V-Belt
1.4.1.   REMOVAL AND INSTALLATION

A single drive belt is used to drive the units at the front of the engine, but a different layout is used on models with and without air conditioning system. The compressor, if fitted (A/C) is also driven by the same belt. The same drive belt layout is fitted to all engines and the belt is tensioned by an automatic tensioning device. The length of the belt is different, i.e. 1290 mm without air conditioning system or 1750 mm with air conditioning system (all engines).

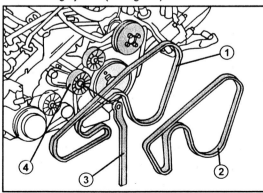

Fig. 1.61 – Removal and installation of the Poly drive belt.
1 Belt without air conditioning
2 Belt with air conditioning system
3 Assembly lever
   (166 589 00 03 00)
4 Tensioning pulley

If a new belt is purchased you will have to mention it.
The belt can be removed by referring to Fig. 1.61. The workshop uses a special lever (3) which is applied to the tensioning pulley as shown. Remove the belt as

follows:

Fig. 1.62 – Layout of the Poly drive belt. In the upper view for models without air conditioning system, in the lower view with compressor.

1   Crankshaft pulley
2   Water pump pulley
3   Guide pulley, with A/C system
4   Guide pulley, lower view with compressor
5   Alternator pulley
6   Belt tensioning pulley
7   Guide pulley

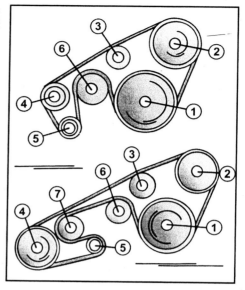

- Slacken the drive belt by tuning the tensioning pulley (4) with the special lever (3) in a clockwise direction (arrow) until the belt is no longer under tension and can be lifted off.
- Check the removed belt for visible damage. The following damage can have occurred: The sides of the belt can be worn, wear has taken place on the inside of the belt grooves, cuts in the belt, the rubber layer has come off the rear of the belt, dirt or other foreign matter can be seen in the belt. In each case a new belt must be fitted.

The installation of the belt is carried out as follows:
- Place the Poly drive belt (1) or (2) over the various pulleys. First place the belt over the tensioning pulley. Then route the belt, depending on the fitted units, over the remaining pulleys as shown in Fig. 1.62.

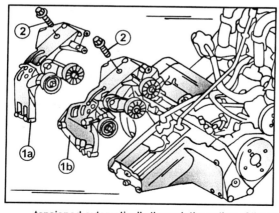

Fig. 1.63 – Details for the removal and installation of the drive belt tensioning device.

1a Carrier with tensioning device, without A/C system
1b Carrier with tensioning device, with A/C system
2   Torx-head bolts, 2.0 kgm

- The belt is now tensioned by referring to Fig. 1.61, i.e. use the special lever (3) and rotate the pulley in clockwise direction. Make sure that the belt has engaged with all pulley grooves and slowly release the lever. The belt will now be tensioned automatically through the action of the spring.
- Rotate the crankshaft a few times and check the belt for correct engagement in the centre of the pulleys.

1.4.1.   POLY BELT TENSIONING DEVICE

The engine must be lowered together with the front axle carrier (not removed) until access is possible to the parts shown in Fig. 1.63. Removal and installation is carried out as follows, but will only be necessary in very rare cases:

- Remove the alternator (generator) as described in section „Electrical System".
- Refer to the illustration and remove the carrier for the tensioning device from the crankcase after removal of the bolts (2). As you can see different parts are fitted. On models without air conditioning system the carrier is shown with (1a), on models with air conditioning system with (1b). Pull the carrier downwards to take it off.

The installation is a reversal of the removal procedure. If a new carrier is fitted also fit a new guide pulley. Tighten the bolts (2) to 2.0 kgm (14.5 ft.lb.).

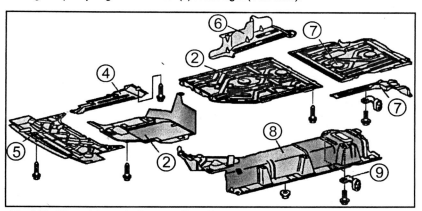

Fig. 1.64 – View of the underfloor panelling. The numbers are explained in the text. Panels (1) to (7) can be removed separately.

Removal and Installation of bottom Engine Compartment Panelling

Fig. 1.64 shows the individual parts underneath the vehicle which must be removed to carry out certain operations. The underfloor panel (8) can only be removed after the exhaust system has been removed. Note the following when a panel is removed.

- The panel (1) is the rear underfloor panelling. Can be removed separately.
- The panel (2) is the centre panelling. Can be removed separately.
- The panel (3) is fitted at the L.H. front of the engine compartment. Can be removed separately.
- The panel (4) is fitted at the R.H. front of the engine compartment. Can be removed separately.
- The panel (5) is fitted at front of the engine compartment. Can be removed separately.
- The panel (6) is fitted at the R.H. rear of the vehicle. The panel (4) is fitted at the R.H. front of the engine compartment. Can be removed separately.
- The panel (7) is fitted at the L.H. rear of the vehicle. The panel (4) is fitted at the R.H. front of the engine compartment. Can be removed separately.

- The exhaust underfloor panelling (4). The rear underfloor panelling (1) and the centre underfloor panelling (2) engage in the exhaust system underfloor panelling (8).
- The brackets (9) – 2 brackets – must be removed. Unscrew the bolts and take off the bracket. The nut with washer must be removed at the fuel tank. Tighten the nut to 3.0 kgm (22 ft.lb.).

1.5.   Tightening Torque Values

The tightening torques only refer to the major component parts. All other tightening torques, when applicable, are given during the installation instructions of the various parts.

Cylinder Head Bolts (refer to tightening sequence, Fig. 1.20:
- 1st stage: ....3.5 kgm (25 ft.lb.)
- 2nd stage ....90° angle-tightening
- 3rd stage: ....90° angle-tightening
- 4th stage: .... Tighten bolts (11) and (12) to 2.0 kgm (14.5 ft.lb.)
Cylinder head cover: ....0.8 kgm (6 ft.lb.)
Intake module: ....1.4 kgm (10 ft.lb.)
Camshaft timing sprockets to camshaft: ....1.8 kgm (13 ft.lb.)
Engine mounting carrier: ....5.5 kgm (40 ft.lb.)
Oil sump drain plug (automatic transmission): ....2.2 kgm (16 ft.lb.)
Fluid pipe (automatic) to radiator: ....2.5 kgm (18 ft.lb.)
Clamp bolt, steering universal joint: ....2.0 kgm (14.5 ft.lb.)
Support strut to front axle carrier: ....6.0 kgm (43 ft.lb.)
Front axle carrier to body: ....12.0 kgm (86.5 ft.lb.)
Chain tensioner bolts: ....8.0 kgm (58 ft.lb.)
Water pump pulley bolts: ....0.8 kgm (6 ft.lb.)
Timing case cover to engine: ....2.0 kgm (14.5 ft.lb.)
Crankshaft pulley/vibration damper bolt: ....20.0 kgm (144 ft.lb.)
Starter motor bolts: ....2.0 kgm (14.5 ft.lb.)
Connecting Rod Bearing Caps:
- 1st stage: ....0.5 kgm (3.5 ft.lb.)
- 2nd stage: ....1.5 kgm (11 ft.lb.)
- 3rd stage ....Angle-tighten 90°
Main Bearing Cap Bolts:
− 1st stage ....4.0 kgm (29 ft.lb.)
− 2nd stage ....Angle-tighten 90°
Flywheel or driven plate:
- 1st stage: ....4.5 kgm (32.5 ft.lb.)
- 2nd stage ....Angle-tighten by 90°
Tensioning device for Poly belt: ....2.0 kgm (14.5 ft.lb.)
Inlet manifold/exhaust manifold to cylinder head: ....2.5 kgm (18 ft.lb.)
Oil drain plug in sump: ....2.5 kgm (18 ft.lb.)
Oil pump: ....Refer to "Lubrication System"
Oil filter: ....Refer to "Lubrication System"

1.6.   Lubrication System

The lubrication system used in the engines is a pressure-feed system. A gear-type oil pump is driven via the crankshaft by means of a separate chain. The chain has its own tensioner.

The oil pump can be removed after removal of the oil sump. The pump cannot be serviced or repaired and must be replaced in case of malfunction.

A warning light in the instrument panel will light up, when the oil level is approaching the lower limit of the oil dipstick. At least 1 litre of oil should be filled in as soon as possible.

Oil pressure indication is electrically by means of a contact switch. Increased oil pressure increases the resistance in the switch and changes the reading in the instrument accordingly. The oil filter is fitted in upright position to the cylinder block. The oil flows through the filter element from the outside to the inside. A return shut-off valve prevents oil from flowing back through the oil pump into the oil sump when the engine is switched off. A by-pass valve opens when the pressure differential between the dirty and the clean end the filter exceeds a certain value. The oil is then directed to the oil gallery without being cleaned. It should be noted that the oil filter element must be changed after 600 - 1000 miles if the engine has been overhauled.

An oil cooler is fitted to all diesel models.

1.6.0.   TECHNICAL DATA

Oil capacity (with filter): ....4.5 litre
Oil pressure:
- at 80° C and 760 rpm:.. 0.7 bar
- at 80° C and 1200 rpm:... 1.2 bar
- at 80° C and 2800 rpm:... 2.8 bar
- at 80° C and 4400 rpm:... 3.0 bar
Measuring point for oil pressure:.. On oil filter

1.6.1.   OIL SUMP - REMOVAL AND INSTALLATION

The removal of the oil sump is not a straight forward operation, as the engine must be lifted out of its mountings. The engine must therefore be lifted by means of a jack or a suitable hoist (hand crane) to reach various parts. Fig. 1.65 shows details of the oil sump removal and installation and should be referred to when required. The illustration shows the oil sump as fitted to a petrol engine, but also valid for the diesel:

• Place the front end of the vehicle on chassis stands.

• Place a container underneath the area of the oil sump (capacity approx. 5 litres) and drain the engine oil. The oil filler cap should be removed to speed-up the operation. After the oil has been drained, refit the drain plug with a new sealing ring and tighten to 2.5 kgm (18 ft.lb.).

• Drain the cooling system.

• Remove the front exhaust system. Instructions can be found in section "Exhaust System".

• Remove the oil dipstick guide tube as described later on in this section.

• Remove the bracket together with the Poly V-belt as described at the end of the engine section.

• Remove the bracket together with the Poly V-belt tensioning device as described .

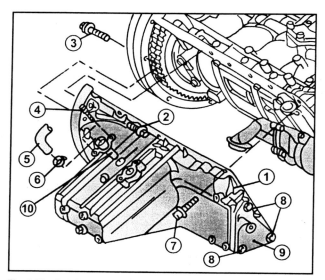

Fig. 1.65 – Details for the removal and installation of the oil sump.

1 Oil sump	5 Crankcase ventilation hose	9 Engine support
2 Bolt, flywheel end, 1.4 kgm	6 Hose clamp	10 Flange
3 Bolt, 1.4 kgm	7 Oil sump bolts, 2.4 kgm	11 Sealing ring
4 Flange bolt	8 Bolt, 2.0 kgm	

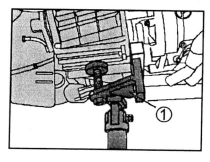

Fig. 1.66 – The transmission is lifted with a suitable support. Shown is the lifter used in a workshop.

• Slacken the hose clamp (6) and withdraw the crankcase breather hose (5) from the flange connection (10) on the oil sump (1). The condition of the clamp (6) must be checked before it is re-used during installation.

• Unscrew the oil pump bolts (2) at the transmission end of the oil sump.

Fig. 1.67 – Removal and installation of the engine mounting support.

1   Engine support at oil sump
2   Engine mount
3   Bolt, 5.5 kgm

• The transmission in lifted in the workshop as shown in Fig. 1.66. Otherwise use a jack lift the engine by means of a jack or a hoist until the weight of the engine is taken off the rear engine mounting. The mounting in question is shown in Fig. 1.67. Remove the bolt (3) out of the engine mounting (2).

56

- You will now need a wooden block which can be inserted between the timing cover and the front axle carrier. The wooden block must be slightly wider than the existing gap. The engine must be pushed to one side, using a tyre lever, and the block inserted as described above. The lever must, however, not be applied to the crankshaft pulley.
- Unscrew the bolts (7) securing the oil sump evenly around the circumference and carefully detach the oil sump from the crankcase (cylinder block) towards the bottom. A soft-faced mallet can be used to tap off a sticking oil sump.
- If the oil sump must be replaced (very unlikely) remove the bolts (8) and remove the engine support (9) from the oil sump. In Fig. 1.67 you can see the mounting, identified by (1). In this case also remove the flange (10) after unscrewing the bolts (4).

The installation is a reversal of the removal procedure, but the following points must be noted:

- Thoroughly clean the sealing faces of oil sump and cylinder block and coat the oil sump face with "Loctite" 5970 sealing compound.
- Place the sump in position and evenly tighten the bolts until the bolt heads contact the oil sump. Tighten the bolts (2) to 2.0 kgm (14.5 ft.lb.) and the bolts (7) to 1.4 kgm (10 ft.lb.).
- If the engine support (9) has been removed, tighten it to 2.0 kgm (14.5 ft.lb.) on the oil sump. The bolt (3) in Fig. 1.67 is tightened to 5.5 kgm (40 ft.lb.) after the engine has been lowered back onto its mountings.
- If the flange (10) has been removed, replace the oil seal (11). Tighten the bolts (4) to 0.8 kgm (6 ft.lb.).
- All other operations are carried out in reverse order. Finally fill the engine with oil and start the engine. Check around the oil sump/crankcase faces for possible oil leaks.

1.6.2. OIL PUMP - REMOVAL AND INSTALLATION

Fig. 1.68 shows details for the removal and installation of the oil sump. The pump removal is the same on all models. Remove the pump as follows:

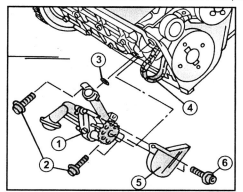

Fig. 1.68 – Details for the removal and installation of the oil pump.
1   Oil pump
2   Torx-head bolts, 1.4 kgm
3   Oil pump sealing ring
4   Oil pump drive chain
5   Cover panel
6   Allen-head bolt

- Remove the oil sump as described in the last section.
- Remove the cover panel (5) from below. Tighten the Torx-head bolts to 1.4 kgm during installation.
- Remove the oil pump (1) from the crankcase (remove bolts (2).

Underneath the pump you will find a sealing ring (3) which must always be replaced. The oil pump drive chain (4) must be disengaged from the drive sprocket as the pump is removed. Immediately clean the oil pump strainer if the pump is to be refitted.

The installation is a reversal of the removal procedure. Fill the pump with engine oil before installation to supply the oil immediately when the engine is started. Tighten the bolts (2) to 1.4 kgm(10 ft.lb.). After installation start the engine and check the area crankcase/oil sump for possible leaks.

1.6.3. OIL PUMP - REPAIR

As already mentioned there is no provision to service or repair the oil pump. If a new pump is fitted also check the drive chain and the drive sprocket as worn parts should not be used with a new pump.

1.6.4. OIL LEVEL SENSOR – REMOVAL AND INSTALLATION

The oil level sensor is fitted to the upper side of the oil sump as can be seen in Fig. 1.69 (identified with "S43"). We must point out that the engine must be lowered to gain access to the sensor. The remaining operations are easy.

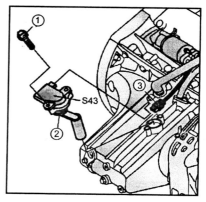

Fig. 1.69 – Removal and installation of the oil level sensor from the oil sump.
1   Bolt, 0.8 kgm
2   Oil level sensor sealing ring
3   Plug connector
S43 Oil level sensor

Withdraw the connector plug from the sensor and remove the securing bolts. The sensor is simply withdrawn from the oil sump. The oil seal underneath the sensor should always be replaced. Tighten the bolts to 0.8 kgm (6 ft.lb.).

1.6.5. DIPSTICK GUIDE TUBE – REMOVAL AND INSTALLATION

The oil dipstick guide tube must be removed to gain access to certain parts, but it should be noted that the dipstick and mounting bracket is not the same on all engines. By referring to Fig. 1.70 you will, however, be able to quickly to see the type fitted to your particular engine, but note that some parts are only fitted to diesel engines. The removal and installation can be carried out by referring to the illustration, but we do not suggest that this is an easy operation.

* The front axle carrier and the engine must be lowered to gain access to all parts, as the guide tube is attached to the upper end of the oil sump.
* Remove the racket (3a) or (3b) to detach the tube from the intake manifold.
* Remove the oil level sensor as already described above.
* Unscrew the guide tube (2a), (2b) or (2c) from the oil sump. The tube must be rotated to one side so it can be removed.

The installation is a reversal of the removal procedure. The sealing ring (5) must always be replaced. Tighten the bolts (4) or (6) to 0.8 kgm (6 ft.lb.).

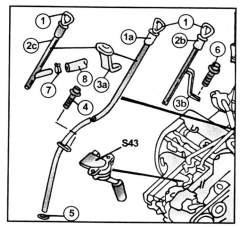

Fig. 1.70 – Details for the removal and installation of the oil dipstick guide tube. Depending on the engine the tube and the bracket will be different.
1 Oil dipstick
2a Guide tube
2b Guide tube
2c Guide tube
3a Securing bracket
3b Securing bracket
4 Torx-head bolt, 0.8 kgm
5 Sealing ring
6 Torx-head bolt, 0.8 kgm
7 Hose clamp (diesel)
8 Ventilation hose (diesel)
S43 Oil level sensor

Fig. 1.71 – Partially removed oil filter.
1   Screw cap, 2.5 kgm
2   Sealing ring under cap
3   Filter element

1.6.6.   OIL FILTER

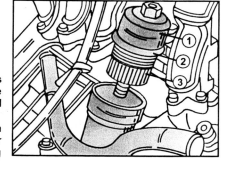

Fig. 1.71 shows where the oil filter is located. To remove the screw cap at the top of the filter a 27 mm A/F socket and extension is required.

- Remove the screw cap together with the filter insert (3) out of the filter housing and remove the sealing ring.

- Insert the new filter insert (3) into the screw cap and fit the cap over the filter housing. Use the socket and a torque wrench and tighten the cap to 2.5 kgm (18 ft.lb.).

- Check the oil level, if only the filter insert has been replaced. Otherwise fill the engine with oil. Start the engine and check for oil leaks in the immediate surrounding of the filter.

1.6.7.   ENGINE OIL CHANGE

The engine oil should be changed every 10000 miles. Remember that there are a few litres of engine oil to handle and the necessary container to catch the oil must be large enough to receive the oil. Dispose of the old oil in accordance with the local laws. You may be able to bring it to a petrol station. **Never discharge the engine oil into a drain.** Drain the oil as follows, when the engine is fairly warm:

- Jack up the front end of the vehicle and place the container underneath the oil sump. Unscrew the oil drain plug (ring spanner or socket). Take care, as the oil will "shoot" out immediately. Remove the oil filler cap to speed-up the draining.

- Check the plug sealing ring and replace if necessary. Clean the plug and fit and tighten to 2.5 kgm (18 ft.lb.).
- Replace the oil filter if necessary.
- Fill the engine with the necessary amount of oil.
- Refit the oil filler cap and drive the vehicle until the engine operating temperature is reached. Jack up the vehicle once more and check the drain plug area for oil leaks.

1.6.8. ENGINE OIL PRESSURE

The oil pressure can only be checked with an oil pressure gauge, which is fitted with a suitable adapter in place of the oil pressure switch. We recommend to leave the oil pressure check to a workshop. Low oil pressure can also be caused through a low oil level in the sump.

1.7. Cooling System
1.7.0. TECHNICAL DATA

Type of system	Sealed with expansion bottle and pump assistance. System consists of expansion tank, water pump, thermostat and electrically operated fan, switched by means of switch at lower end of radiator.
Water Pump – Location and Drive:	Driven by Poly V-belt from the crankshaft.
Radiator	Aluminium cooler with header tanks. Fitted in front of engine on crossmember.
Expansion tank	If fitted, made of plastic, fitted on inner wing panel.
Opening pressure of radiator cap	1.2 bar (17 psi.), all engines, brown colour
Cooling fan	Electric operation, fitted behind radiator and actuated by switch at bottom of radiator.
Thermostat	Wax element. Opening temperature 89° C (all engines), fully open at 101° C.
Filling capacity:	6.5 litres (all models):

The water pump is fitted to the cylinder block and is sealed with an "O" sealing ring and secured by means of four bolts. It is driven by the Poly V-belt from the crankshaft pulley together with the other units. We would like to point out that the water pump can only be removed after the removal of the complete power unit together with the front axle carrier.

The thermostat is fitted inside a housing on the top of the cylinder head.

1.7.1. COOLING SYSTEM – DAINING AND REFILLING

Important Note: Only open the expansion reservoir cap shown in Fig. 1.72 when the coolant temperature is below 90° C. Slowly open the cap to allow the pressure to reduce before the cap is removed completely.

Normal tap water can be used if only a small amount is missing. Never fill in cold water when the engine is hot. Allow the engine to cool down before topping up the system. The coolant should be replaced every 40 000 miles if possible.

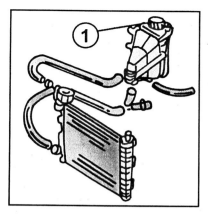

Fig. 1.72 – The coolant expansion tank is fitted inside the radiator as shown in the L.H. view. The R.H. view shows the separate expansion reservoir fitted since 1. June 1999. Both are sealed off with the filler cap (1).

Important Note: The coolant (anti-freeze solution) must be replaced if the cylinder head, the cylinder had gasket, the radiator or the heater matrix have been replaced. Otherwise you can collect the anti-freeze, provided it has not been in the system for a long time.

Drain the cooling system as follows (engine bonnet open), noting that the coolant should be collected in a suitable container to prevent contamination of surrounding areas. Fig. 1.73 shows the items mentioned below:

Fig, 1.73 – Details for the draining and refilling of the cooling system. The numbers are referred to below. The illustration also shows the filler cap (4) on older petrol models.

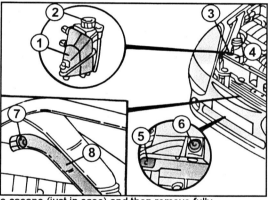

- If the engine is hot, open the filler cap slowly or on the expansion reservoir (1) in Fig. 1.72). Make sure the coolant has a temperature of less than 90° C. Rotate the cap to the first notch, allow the vapour to escape (just in case) and then remove fully.

- Jack up the vehicle, if possible at the front and rear to retain the engine in a horizontal position. Chassis stands must, however, be used.

- Place a suitable container underneath the radiator and push a small hose (5) over the drain plug (6) at the bottom of the radiator. Open the plug and allow the coolant to drain. Make sure the hose end is "aimed" for the container. Wait until all coolant has drained and check the condition of the anti-freeze. You can immediately decide if you can re-use it.

- Drain the coolant from the cylinder block. Again a small hose can be used, but in this case it is pushed over the small connector (7). The connector can be found next to one of the tubes of the inlet manifold and above the intermediate shaft of the front drive shaft. Open the plug and allow the coolant to drain. Remove the hose (8) from the connector.

- If the coolant has been in the system for a considerable time, flush the system. To do this place a mains-connected water hose into the opening of the reservoir, open the tap and allow the water to run until it emerges clear out of the radiator elbow.

The cooling system should be refilled in the following manner to avoid air locks:

- Close the radiator drain plug (0.3 kgm) and the cylinder block drain plug (1.0 kgm) and lower the vehicle onto its wheels.
- Open the expansion bottle cap and fill the system with the correct anti-freeze mixture. Fill the system slowly to avoid major air locks. The system is filled until the coolant can be seen on the outside of the reservoir. The liquid must be to the "Max" mark. Do not fit the filler cap.
- Start the engine and run at 1500 to 2000 rpm until the operating temperature is reached, i.e. the thermostat must have opened. The temperature gauge must show approx. 60 – 70° C. The upper radiator hose must be warm, the heater regulator must be to the maximum setting.
- Continue to fill the system until the coolant level is correct and fit the filler cap (both versions).
- Allow the engine to run for approx. 20 minutes with the engine speed specified above until the radiator fan cut in.
- After the engine has cooled down, check the water level once more as described.

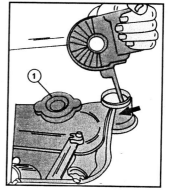

Fig. 1.74 – The strength of the anti-freeze can be checked as shown. Different types can be used.

1.7.2.   ANTI-FREEZE

Mercedes-Benz recommends a certain type of anti-freeze and this should be used when the cooling system is to be filled with anti-freeze. The cooling system is factory-filled with the mixture and should not be drained during the summer months.

The mixture strength depends on the temperatures to be expected and the following table will give you the ratios between water and anti-freeze depending on the temperature and the equipment of the vehicle. In general one can assume that a mixture of 50 % water and 50 % anti-freeze will protect the engine to most temperatures to be expected during the winter.

Total capacity:	6.5 litres
Protection to –37° C	3.25 litres anti-freeze
Protection to –45° C	3.6 litres anti-freeze

The strength of the anti-freeze can be checked with a tester. Fig. 1.74 shows a typical example, but different types are available. Important is to follow the instructions of the manufacturer in each case.

1.7.3.   RADIATOR – REMOVAL AND INSTALLATION

All models are fitted with a light-alloy radiator. The two water chambers are located on the sides of the radiator. A fluid oil cooler is fitted to the R.H. side of the radiator if an automatic transmission is fitted. At the bottom of the radiator you will find the coolant drain plug.

It is a good practice to clean the radiator core here and then from "accumulated" insects. Various sprays are available in accessory shops to clean the radiator.

Radiators with small leaks can perhaps be repaired. Enquire at a specialist dealing with radiators.

1.7.3.0. Checking the Filler Cap and Radiator for Leaks

The cooling system operates under pressure. The expansion tank cap is fitted with a spring, which is selected to open the cap gasket when the pressure has risen to value engraved in the cap. If the cap is replaced, always fit one with the same marking, suitable for the models covered.

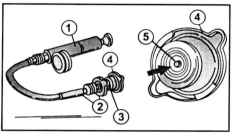

Fig. 1.75 – A radiator test pump is used to check the cooling system for leaks and the expansion tank cap for correct opening. The tools shown are, of course, special tools.
1   Test pump
2   Test cap with connecting hose
3   Connection piece, test cap
    to reservoir cap
4   Expansion reservoir filler cap
5   Vacuum valve in filler cap

To check the filler cap for correct opening, a radiator test pump is required. The pump is fitted to a test cap and the test cap is fitted to filler cap, as shown in Fig. 1.75 and operate the pump until the valve opens, which should take place near the given pressure of 1.4 – 1.5 bar (kg/sq.cm) , if the filler cap is still fairly new. A used cap must still indicate 1.3 to 1.4 bar. If this is not the case, replace the cap.

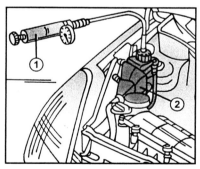

Fig. 1.76 – The test pump (1) is connected as shown directly to the expansion tank (2). On models without expansion tank connect the pump directly to the radiator filler opening..

The same pump can also be used to check the cooling system for leaks. Fit the pump to the expansion tank filler neck, as shown in Fig. 1.76. Operate the plunger until a pressure of 1.4 bar (kg/sq.cm.) is indicated. Allow the pressure in the system for at least 5 minutes. If the pressure drops, there is a leak in the system, which will be easier to detect as coolant may emerge from the leaking

point.

1.7.3.1. Radiator – Removal and Installation

Fig. 1.77 shows details of the radiator installation. The removal of the rather is a complicated operation and we suggest to read the instructions fully before commencing with the work. Some of the parts must be located before they can be removed. Proceed as follows:

• Open the engine bonnet and disconnect the battery earth cable.
• Drain the cooling system as already described. Remember not to open the cooling system unless the engine is cold.

Fig. 1.77 – Details for the removal and installation of the radiator.

1 Overflow hose
2 Retaining clamp
3 Rubber shim
4 Screw
5 Lower radiator hose
6 Upper radiator hose
7 Retaining clamp
8 Rubber grommet
9 Fluid lines (A/T)
10 Radiator
11 Condenser
12 Cover
13 Combination bolt

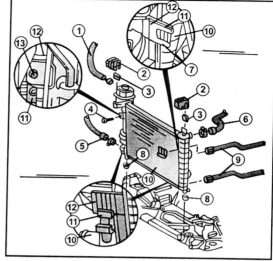

- Detach the coolant expansion tank at the R.H. front reinforcement and place it to one side with the hoses connected. Details of the reinforcement are shown in Fig. 1.78 as other operations must be carried out in this area.

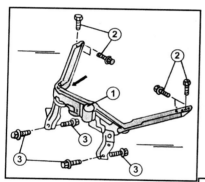

Fig. 1.78 – View of the reinforcement mentioned in the text together with the attachment on the two A door pillars and at the front end.

1 Reinforcement
2 Bolt, 1.1 kgm
3 Bolts, 2.3 kgm

- Detach the windscreen washer fluid reservoir at the L.H. front reinforcement and place it to one side with the hoses connected.
- Remove front bumper. Fig. 1.79 shows the attachment of the bumper, but it should be noted that there are some differences within the model range. The illustration shows the version to the end of February 2001.

Fig. 1.79 – Details for the removal and installation of the front bumper. The numbers are explained in the text.

- Remove the clips (4). Fit new clips if necessary during installation.
- The bumper can now be withdrawn, but two persons will be required. First unclip the bumper from the side guides (5) and then withdraw it towards the front. Specially observe the bumper at the points shown by the arrows to prevent damage

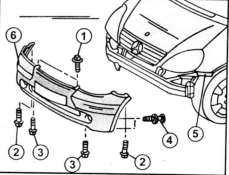

to the paint work. During installation the bumper (6) is guided into the side guides and then pushed fully in position.

- Certain models are fitted with a "Parctonic" system (PTS). In this case withdraw a plug connector from the L.H. and R.H. fog lamp and separate an electrical connection.

The installation is a reversal of the removal procedure. Check the adjustment of the fog lamps or have it checked professionally.

- Looking at the front of the vehicle remove the air intake cowl and the air intake duct on the L.H. side of the vehicle (on the R.H. side looking at the open front end).
- Remove the retaining clips (2) together with the rubber mountings (3) in Fig. 1.77.
- Remove the L.H. and R.H. headlamps as described in section "Electrical Equipment". *Remember: Headlamps must be adjusted after installation.*
- Unclip the coolant hose (1) at the R.H. front reinforcement. The arrow in Fig. 1.78 shows where the hose is attached.
- Support the bonnet in suitable manner in an upright (vertical) position.
- Detach the reinforcement in Fig. 1.78 from the A-door pillar on both sides of the vehicle. Remove bolts (3) in the illustration.
- Detach the reinforcement at the front end, take it off the front end and carefully lower it with the bonnet lock attached.
- Detach the coolant hoses (1), (5) and (6) from the radiator connecting elbows after slackening of the hose clamps. Some coolant may flow out. Replace the hose clamps if no longer in good condition. Install the hose clamp for the hose (5) so that it is accessible from the outside through the bumper eye (towing eye).
- If an automatic transmission is fitted, disconnect the two fluid lines (9) from the radiator. Collect escaping transmission fluid in a suitable container and plug the open connecting pipe on the radiator with a suitable plug and the fluid lines with caps. Otherwise wrap sticky tape around the openings.
- Unscrew the combination bolt (13). This is located on the radiator on the R.H. side, seen in the direction of drive, i.e., shown in the upper, L.H. circle in Fig. 1.77.
- Remove the metal clip (7) on the L.H. side of the radiator.
- If an air conditioning system is fitted, detach the condenser (11) with the cover (10) from the guides at the radiator (1). Do not disconnect any of the hoses or pipes.
- Unplug the plug connector from the electrical fan, detach the fan shroud from the radiator (see below) and withdraw the radiator (1) upwards to take it out. Take care not to damage the air conditioning lines.

The installation is a reversal of the removal procedure. Tighten the bolts (3) for the reinforcement (Fig. 1.78) to 2.3 kgm (16 ft.lb.), the bolts (2) to 1.1 kgm (8 ft.lb.) at the door A-pillars and the union nuts for the fluid lines to 2.5 kgm (18 ft.lb.). Finally fill the cooling system and check the fluid level in the automatic transmission (if fitted), if you have noted some fluid loss.

1.7.4   WATER PUMP

The complete power unit together with the front axle carrier must be lowered to obtain access to the attachment of the water pump. The coolant pipe is either fitted with a support bracket to the water pump or no bracket is used. We would like to point out that removal and installation is a time-consuming operation, but described all the same. Fig. 1.80 shows the parts to be removed. Proceed as follows:

Fig. 1.80 – Details for the removal and installation of the coolant pump.
1 Coolant pipe
2 Torx-head bolt
3 Torx-head bolt
4 Sealing ring
5 Torx-head bolt
6 Sectional rubber seal
7 Coolant (water) pump
8 Tory-head bolt
9 Water pump pulley
10 Combination bolt

- Drain the cooling system at the radiator and the cylinder block as already described.
- Lower the front axle carrier together with the engine/transmission unit as described during the removal of the engine.
- Slacken the combination bolts (10) from the water pump pulley (9) as long as the Poly V-belt is fitted and then remove the V-belt as described near the end of the engine section. The pulley (9) can now be removed from the water pump (7). Remove the washers underneath the bolts (10).
- If the coolant pipe is supported with a mounting bracket on the water pump it must be removed. The instructions are given below. The coolant pipe is secured at the bottom with three Torx-head bolts. One is screwed into the cylinder block, one in the water pump and one into the oil filter housing. Pull the coolant pipe out of the cylinder block bore and push it to one side, with the coolant hoses attached. During installation tighten the bolt fitted to the cylinder block to 1.4 kgm, the other bolts are tightened to 0.8 kgm. Underneath the coolant pipe there is a sealing ring (4) which must always be replaced.
- Unscrew the water pump (7) from the crankcase.

The installation is carried out in reverse order. Clean the sealing faces of cylinder block and pump and fit together with a new sectional rubber sealing ring (6). Tighten the securing screws evenly to 0.8 kgm. Fit the water pump pulley, but only tighten them provisionally. The final torque (0.8 kgm) is applied after the V-belt has been refitted. Finally refit the front axle carrier and fill the cooling system.

1.7.5.   COOLANT PIPE – REMOVAL AND INSTALLATION

As already mentioned during the removal of the water pump the pipe is either attached with a support bracket or no bracket is used. Fig. 1.81 shows the version without bracket attachment, but with connections for the water-cooled alternator and heated crankcase ventilation. Fig. 1.82 shows the version without bracket and with connections for the water-cooled alternator and heated crankcase ventilation.
The following description assumed that the coolant pipe must be removed during the removal of the water pump. Remove the pipe as follows, with or without support bracket.

- Drain the cooling system as described earlier on.
- Lower the engine together with the front axle carrier.
- On engines with water-cooled alternator and heated crankcase ventilation disconnect hoses 6, 7, 8, 9,10 and 11 from the coolant pipe (1).

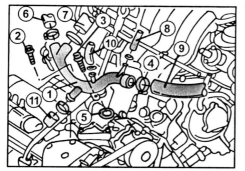

Fig. 1.81 – The coolant pipe without support bracket attachment to the water pump and connections to the water-cooled alternator and heated crankcase ventilation.

1 Coolant pipe
2 Torx-head bolt
3 Torx-head bolt
4 Torx-head bolt
5 Sealing ring
6 Coolant hose to thermostat
7 Coolant hose to heating system
8 Coolant hose to expansion tank
9 Coolant hose to radiator
10 Coolant hose to crankcase ventilation
11 Coolant hose to alternator

Fig. 1.82 – The coolant pipe with support bracket attachment to the water pump and without connections to the water-cooled alternator and heated crankcase ventilation.

1   Coolant pipe
2   Torx-head bolt
3   Torx-head bolt
4   Torx-head bolt
5   Sealing ring
6   Coolant hose to thermostat
7   Coolant hose to heating system
8   Coolant hose to expansion tank
9   Coolant hose to radiator

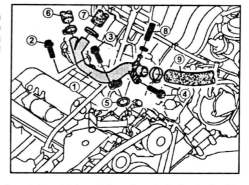

- Unscrew the Torx-head bolts 2, 3 and 4 and take off the pipe. Only the bolts (2) and (3) are used when the pipe is not fitted with a support bracket. Bolt (4) is fitted if the pipe is attached to the water pump.

The installation is a reversal of the removal procedure. Connect the hoses in accordance with the illustration. Replace the hoses and clamps if not in perfect condition. The sealing ring (5) must always be replaced. Tighten the Torx-head bolts and the water pump pulley bolts to 0.8 kgm. First screw in all bolts finger-tight before tightening them. The bolt attaching the pipe to the oil filter housing is tightened to 1.4 kgm.

1.7.6.   THERMOSTAT – REMOVAL AND INSTALLATION

The thermostat is located inside a housing, attached to the cylinder head, at the position shown in Fig. 1.83. The illustration also shows the parts to be removed. The thermostat is integrated in the housing, meaning that a faulty thermostat must be replaced together with the housing.. Remove the thermostat/housing as follows:

- Drain the cooling system as already described.
- Remove the coolant temperature sensor for the diesel fuel injection system as described below..

Fig. 1.83 – Details for the removal and installation of the thermostat.

1   Coolant thermostat
2   Torx-head bolt
3   Coolant hose
4   Hose clamp
5   Coolant hose
6   Hose clamp
7   Coolant hose
8   Hose clamp
9   Gasket

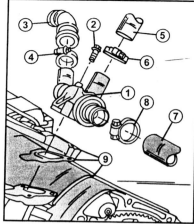

- Remove the coolant hoses (3), (5) and (7) after slackening the respective hose clamps (4), (5) and (8) respectively from the thermostat housing (1).

- Remove the bolts (2) and remove the housing (1) from the cylinder head. The bolts are of different length. Mark where you have removed them from

The installation is a reversal of the removal procedure. Make sure that the cylinder head surface and the thermostat housing sealing face are clean before fitting the gasket (9).. The bolts (2) are tightened evenly to 0.9 kgm. After completed installation of all parts removed, fill the cooling system , start the engine and check the operation of the thermostat. Hose clamps and/or coolant hoses must be replaced if no longer in perfect condition. You decide.

Fig. 1.84 – Checking a thermostat.

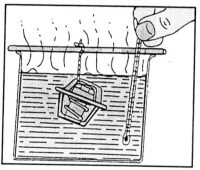

1.7.6.1   Checking a Thermostat

A thermostat cannot be repaired, but can be tested by immersing it in a container of cool water and gradually raising the temperature to check the opening temperature.
Suspend the thermostat on a piece of wire so that it does not touch the sides or the bottom of the container. Suspend a thermometer in a similar manner. Fig. 1.84 shows the arrangement, but it should be noted that the illustration shows a removable thermostat, .

- Gradually heat the water and observe the thermometer. The thermostat should begin to open at around 87° C and should be fully open at 105° C.
- Otherwise replace the thermostat together with the housing. The thermostat pin must emerge at least 7 mm from the thermostat. Allow the thermostat to cool down and check if it closes properly.

1.7.7. COOLANT TEMPERATURE SENSOR

The location of the coolant temperature sensor is shown in Fig. 1.85. The sensor (4) is secured by means of a retaining clip (2). To replace the sensor drain the cooling system. The clip (2) is removed with a screwdriver. After withdrawing the   plug connector (1) withdraw the sensor (4). Replace the sealing ring (3) if a new sensor is fitted.

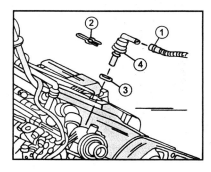

Fig. 1.85 – Coolant temperature sensor. The numbers are referred to in the text.
1   Plug connector
2   Retaining clip
3   Sealing ring
4   Coolant temperature sensor

1.7.8.   FAN SHROUD AND FAN

The installation of the fan shroud is shown in Fig. 1.86.

1.7.8.0.   Fan Shroud – Removal and installation

• Disconnect the battery earth cable.
• Remove the air intake module (described in the engine section).

Fig. 1.86 – View of the fan shroud. The arrows show the guides in the radiator (also on the other side).
1a Without A/C system,
1b With A/C system
2   Cooling fan
3   Torx-head bolt
4   Plug connector

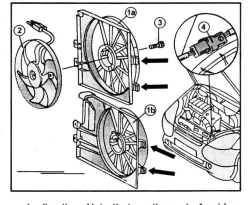

• Unplug the fan motor plug connector (4) located at the position shown on the L.H. side of the vehicle at the bottom of the shroud.
• Remove the fan shroud (1a) or (1b), depending on the version, out off the guides on the radiator (arrows) and remove together with the fan (2) in an upwards direction. Note that another set of guides are located on the other side.
• If the fan must be replaced refer to the description below.
The installation is a reversal of the removal procedure.

1.7.8.1.   Fan – Removal and installation

The fan can be replaced as follows. Fig. 1.87 shows the attachment of the fan to the fan shroud. The installation is identical for models with and without air conditioning system. The fan is secured by means of a retaining collar which must be rotated as shown by the arrow during removal and installation.

• Disconnect the battery earth cable and remove the fan shroud as described above.
• Unscrew the Torx-head bolts (2), followed by the Torx-head bolt (3). The latter bolt acts as an anti-twist lock for the retaining collar (4).

Fig. 1.87 – After removal of the fan shroud the fan can be removed. The arrows are referred to in the text.
1   Fan shroud
2   Torx-head bolt
3   Torx-head bolt
4   Anti-twist lock
5   Cooling fan

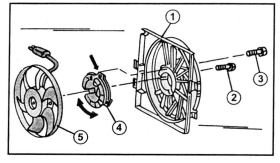

- Twist the retaining collar and pull and remove the fan (5) towards the front out of the fan shroud.

The installation is a reversal of the removal procedure. The threaded hole in the anti-twist lock, shown by the arrow, must be aligned with the bolt (3). Make sure that the fan motor cable is routed correctly.

1.7.9.   CHECKING THE COOLING SYSTEM

Various checks can be carried out on the cooling system before any major operations are carried out. Some of them are listed below. Some of the faults also concern parts which have been replaced or removed and re-fitted.

- Check the correct fitting of coolant hoses on radiator, water pump, thermostat and heater and make sure that all hose clamps are properly tightened.
- Coolant hoses must show no cuts or other damage. Hoses can split after a long service, mostly when no immediate help is available.
- Check the radiator for leaks. If small leaks seek the advice of a radiator specialist as it may be possible that it can be repaired.
- A leaking water pump can mostly be recognised by dripping of water below the pump. In this case replace the water pump.
- The cap of the expansion tank or the radiator could be defective. A defective vacuum valve inside the cap could be the reason for deformed radiator hoses.

1.8.   Diesel Fuel Injection System

1.8.0.   INTRODUCTION

Absolute cleanliness is essential during any repairs or work on the diesel fuel injection system, irrespective of the nature of the work in question. Thoroughly clean union nuts before unscrewing any of the injection pipes.

The high pressure injection pump, the injectors, the "Common Rail" fuel distributor and the injection pipes are the main components of the fuel injection system. Additionally an electric shut-off valve, the pre-delivery fuel pump a pressure sensor, a camshaft position sensor, the glow plugs and the fuel filter and, where fitted, the turbo charger, are component parts of the system. The turbo charger is covered together with the exhaust system.

In all cases we recommend to read the instructions in full before you commence with any removal work. In general there are no special tools required, but you will need some experience working on the engine. Many of the removal operations are only

70

mentioned and you will have to refer to the relevant chapter or section for a full description.

1.8.1. PRECAUTIONS WHEN WORKING ON DIESEL INJECTION SYSTEMS

Whenever repairs are carried out on a diesel fuel injection system, whatever the extent, observe the greatest cleanliness, apart from the following points:

- Only carry out work on diesel injection systems under the cleanest of conditions. Work in the open air should only be carried out when there is no wind, to prevent dust entering open connections.
- Before removal of any union nut clean all around it with a clean cloth.
- Removed parts must only be deposited on a clean bench or table and must be covered with a sheet of plastic or paper. Never use fluffy shop rags to clean parts.
- All open or partially dismantled parts of the injection system must be fully covered or kept in a cardboard box, if the repair is not carried out immediately.
- Check the parts for cleanliness before Installation.
- Never use an air line to clean the exterior of the engine when connections of the injection system are open. With the availability of air compressors which can be plugged into a cigar lighter socket, you may be tempted to use air for cleaning.
- Take care not to allow diesel fuel in contact with rubber hoses or other rubber parts. immediately clean such a hose if it should happen accidentally.
- Do not use naked lights anywhere near the engine. Although diesel fuel is less inflammable, there is always the risk of fire.

1.8.2. HIGH PRESSURE PUMP – REMOVAL AND INSTALLATION

As you will be in contact with diesel fuel during the following operations you will have to take the necessary precautions. Under no circumstances work with naked flames or smoke during any of the operations described. Fig. 1.88 shows where the pump is fitted to the end of the cylinder head. Remove as follows:

Fig. 1.88 – Removal and installation of the high pressure pump.
 1 Torx-head bolt
 2 Securing bracket
 3 Fuel feed pipe
 4 Fuel return pipe
 5 Retainer for pressure pipe
 6 Torx-head bolt
 7 Torx-head bolt, 1.4 kgm
 8 Sealing ring
 9 Driver
10 High pressure pump
11 Pressure line to high pressure pump

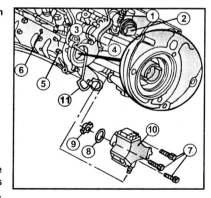

- Disconnect the battery earth cable.
- Unscrew the pressure line (11) from the high pressure pump (10). The pipe is connected by means of a union nut. During slackening or tightening of the union nut apply an open-ended spanner to the threaded connection of the pipe. Otherwise it may be possible for the connection to come out of the pump. Tighten the union nut to 2.3 kgm (16.5 ft.lb.) during installation, again counter-holding the hexagon with the spanner. The

torque must not be exceeded as it would be difficult to remove the union nut at a later stage.

- Remove the bracket (2) at the high pressure pump.
- Thoroughly clean the connecting areas of the two fuel pipes, i.e. the supply pipe (3) and the return pipe (4) and disconnect the two pipes from the pump. The seals of the fuel pipes must be replaced during installation.
- Remove the three Torx-head bolts (7) from the high pressure pump and pull out the pump. The driver (9) can, if required, taken off.

Attention: The high pressure pump must not be opened.

The installation is a reversal of the removal procedure. The sealing faces must be thoroughly cleaned before installation. The sealing ring (8) must always be replaced. If the driver has been removed make sure that it engages in the recess of the camshaft, shown in the illustration with the arrow. Tighten the pump securing bolts (7) to 1.4 kgm (10 ft.lb.).

1.8.3. INJECTION PIPES – REMOVAL AND INSTALLATION

The precautions given about the fuel must be observed. Remove the injection pipes as follows. Fig. 1.89 shows the pipes.

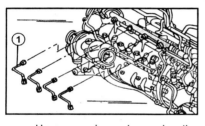

Fig. 1.89 – The high pressure injection pipes (1) are located at the positions shown. Tighten the union nuts to 2.3 kgm.

- Remove the intake module (inlet manifold) as described during the removal of the cylinder head.
- Remove the oil filler neck together with the crankcase ventilation as described earlier on.
- Unscrew union nut securing the pressure line (1). The pipe is connected by means of a union nut. During slackening or tightening of the union nut apply an open-ended spanner to the threaded connection of the pipe. Otherwise it may be possible for the connection to come out of the pump. Tighten the union nut to 2.3 kgm (16.5 ft.lb.) during installation, again counter-holding the hexagon with the spanner. The torque must not be exceeded as it would be difficult to remove the union nut at a later stage. To prevent that the injection pipes are fitted under tension it is advisable to slacken the "Common Rail" distributor and fit the pipes. The distributor can then be re-tightened.
- Remove the injection pipes without bending or kinking them. Close off the open ends of the pipes in a suitable manner. We must repeat again – do not fit the injection pipes under tension.

1.8.4. ELECTRIC SHUT-OFF VALVE – REMOVAL AND INSTALLATION

The shut-off valve is fitted above the pre-delivery pump to the cylinder head cover as shown in Fig. 1.90 (models to end of Feb. 2001) and is shown in the illustration with "Y75". As a fuel pipe must be disconnected, observe the precautions regard the fuel.

- Disconnect the fuel pipe (1) from the side of the valve. Some fuel may flow out which can be soaked up with a rag. The pipe is connected with a locking arm.

72

Fig. 1.90 – Details for the removal and installation of the electric shut-off valve Y75.

1   Fuel pipe
2   Sealing ring
3   Plug connector for shut-off valve
4   Torx-head bolts
5   Seal
6   Connecting piece
7   Securing bracket
8   Pre-delivery pump

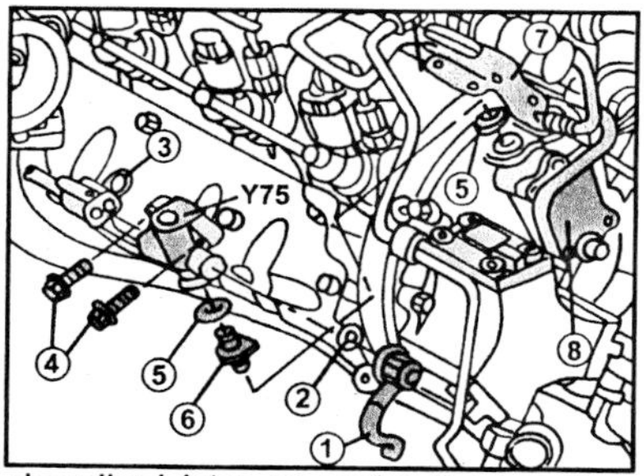

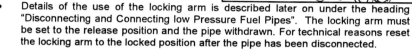

- Details of the use of the locking arm is described later on under the heading "Disconnecting and Connecting low Pressure Fuel Pipes". The locking arm must be set to the release position and the pipe withdrawn. For technical reasons reset the locking arm to the locked position after the pipe has been disconnected.
- Separate the plug connection (3) from the other side of the shut-off valve.
- Detach the shut-off valve from the bracket (7) after unscrewing the bolts (4) and pull it upwards out of the pre-delivery pump (8).
- Carefully detach the connecting piece (6) at the pre-delivery pump, replace the sealing ring (5) and refit the connecting piece again.

The installation is a reversal of the removal procedure. Tighten the bolts to the bracket and the cylinder head cover to 0.9 kgm. Refit the fuel pipe with a new sealing ring (2). Make sure that the pipe is locked in position.

1.8.5. INJECTORS – REMOVAL AND INSTALLATION

The injectors have a tight fit in the cylinder head. The workshop uses a puller to remove the injectors. The component parts to be removed are shown in Fig. 1.91. The injectors are identified by their electrical component identification "Y76". The precautions given already above must be observed at all times, as diesel fuel is involved during some of the operations.

Fig. 1.91 – Details for the removal and installation of the fuel injectors.

1   Heat shield
2   Torx-head bolt
3   Securing clamp
4   Clamping piece
5   Torx-head bolt
6   Two-arm puller
7   Impact extractor
8   Injection pipe
9   Plug connector, injector
10 Sealing ring, injector
11 Leak-off pipe

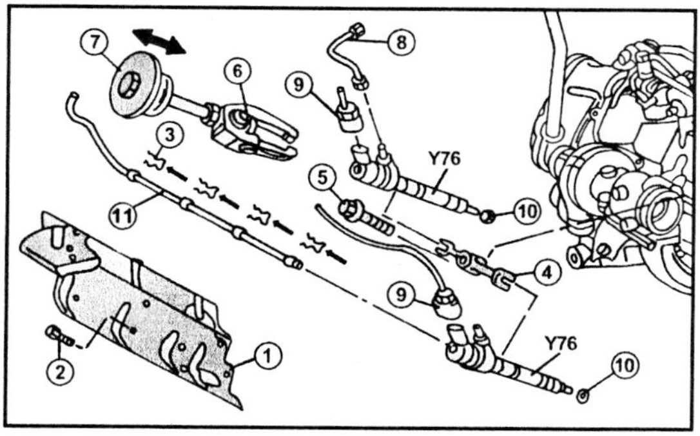

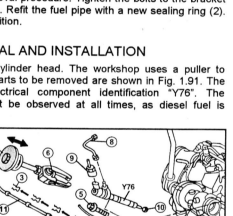

- Remove the induction module (inlet manifold) as described during the removal of the cylinder head.
- Remove the catalytic converter and the turbo charger as described under separate headings (section "Exhaust System").
- Withdraw the plug connector (9) from the four fuel injectors.
- Disconnect the fuel injection pipes at both ends. Union nuts securing the injection pipes are used. During slackening or tightening of the union nut apply an open-ended spanner to the threaded connection of the pipe. Otherwise it may be

possible for the connection to come out of the fuel distributor rail. Tighten the union nut to 2.3 kgm (16.5 ft.lb.) during installation, again counter-holding the hexagon with the spanner. The torque must not be exceeded as it would be difficult to remove the union nut at a later stage. Do not bend or kink the pipes during removal.

- Remove the bolts (2) and remove the heat shield (1).
- Remove the securing clamps (3) securing the leak-off line (11). To remove the clamps press them together at the leak-off line at the connections and remove them (arrows). The clamps remain on the fuel injectors. Note: A removed securing clamp must not be re-used. A new clamp must be fitted to ensure a secure fitting of the fuel injectors.
- Unscrew the Torx-head bolts (5) securing the clamping piece (4).
- Remove the fuel injector together with the clamping piece from the threaded adaptor using a suitable screwdriver blade. Tight injectors can only be removed with an impact extractor (7) and a two-armed puller (6). Maybe you are able to hire this equipment. The impact extractor has the number 602 589 00 33 00, the puller 668 589 00 34 00. In this case a new injector must be fitted.
- Clean the injector recesses and the fuel injectors with a wire brush before installation.

The installation is a reversal of the removal procedure. Note the following points:
- The sealing ring (10) must always be replaced. Fit a new Torx-head bolt (5). Make sure you obtain a bolt suitable for this engine (type 668).
- Slacken the fuel distributor ("common rail") and refit the injection pipe without tension.
- Fit the injection pipe with the union nut to the injector, without tightening the nut. The loose fuel distributor can now be tightened (0.9 kgm).
- Tighten the bolt (5) securing the clamping piece (4) to 0.7 kgm and from the final position tighten it a further one quarter of a turn.
- The union nut (8) is now tightened to 2.3 kgm. Again use the open-ended spanner on the hexagon of the injector. Do not exceed the torque setting.
- Fit the leak-off line (11) and secure with the securing clamp.
- All other operations are carried out in reverse order.

1.8.6. "COMMON RAIL" – REMOVAL AND INSTALLATION

The attachment of the fuel injector rail, fuel distributor rail or "Common Rail" is shown in Fig. 1.92. The precautions given earlier on must be strictly observed.
- Disconnect the battery earth cable.
- Remove the induction module.
- Separate the cable strap (8) from the fuel rail. The cable straps must be replaced.
- Separate the plug connector (1) from the rail pressure sensor and the connector (2) from the pressure control valve at the opposite end.
- Disconnect the injection pipes (11) as already described (see also Fig. 1.89). The union nuts are tightened to 2.3 kgm as explained during the removal/installation.
- Disconnect the high pressure pipes (7) from the high pressure pump and the rail (8) and detach the bracket (3) securing one of the pipes.
- Disconnect the fuel return flow line (10) between rail and high pressure pump from the rail. To do this open the locking arm and close it again as explained under the next heading. The sealing ring (6) must be replaced during installation.

74

Fig. 1.92 – Details for the removal and installation of the "Common Rail" fuel distributor,

1 Connector plug, rail pressure sensor
2 Plug, pressure control valve
3 Pressure line bracket
4 Torx-head bolt
5 Banjo bolt
6 Sealing ring
7 High pressure pipe
8 Common rail
9 Leak-off pipe
10 Fuel return flow line
11 Injection pipes
12 Fuel return line
13 Seals
14 Rail pressure sensor
15 Pressure regulating valve

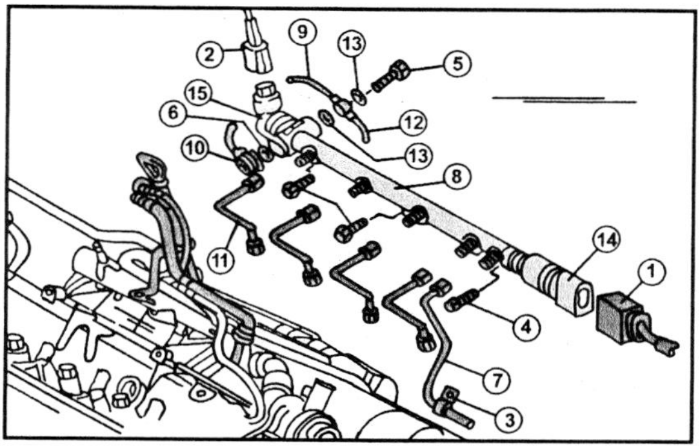

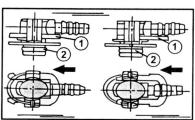

- Detach the fuel return flow line (12) and the leak-off line (9) after removal of the bolt (5) from the rail. The seal (13) must always be replaced. The bolt (5) is tightened to 2.0 kgm (14.5 ft.lb.).
- The rail (8) is now removed. If a new distributor rail is fitted it will come together with a pressure sensor (15). The bolts (4) securing the rail to the cylinder head cover are tightened to 0.9 kgm (7 ft.lb.) during installation.

The installation is a reversal of the removal procedure, noting the various points given above.

Disconnecting and Connecting low pressure fuel lines

These are the pipes which are not under pressure from the high pressure fuel injection system, leading to the fuel distributor rail and the fuel return lines. The pipes are fitted with a locking arm in place of a screw connection and are sealed off with a sealing ring. Fig. 1.93 shows details to disconnect and connect any of theses pipes in a schematic drawing. The disconnection and re-connection is difficult to describe if you have no experience.

Fig. 1.93 – Details for the disconnecting (view "A") and connecting (view "B") lower pressure fuel pipes.
1   Locking arm
2   Sealing ring

Disconnection

- Move the locking arm to its stop into the released position as shown by the arrow in view "A".
- Remove the connection from the low pressure line.
- Move the locking (1) back to the locked position as shown in view "A". The locking arm must not remain in the released position over an extended period as this could lead to leaks in the fuel line. *After disconnecting the fuel line make absolutely sure that the locking arm is back to the locked position, otherwise you will have to replace the fuel line.*

Connecting the Fuel Line

- Check that the locking lever (1) is in the fitting position as shown in view "B".

- Insert the fuel line connector. Check that the connection is free of fuel leaks after installation.

1.8.7.   PRESSURE SENSOR IN "COMMON RAIL"

The location of the pressure sensor is shown with (14) in Fig. 1.92. After disconnecting the connector plug (1) unscrew the sensor from the fuel distributor rail. The hexagon on the rail must be prevented from rotating by applying an open-ended spanner. Tighten the sensor to 3.5 kgm (25 ft.lb.) to production number 86512 or to 2.2 kgm (16 ft.lb.) after this number.

1.8.8.   PRE-DELIVERY PUMP – REMOVAL AND INSTALLATION

The fitted position of the pump is shown in Fig. 1.94. The pump must be removed for certain operations. Precautions given must be observed.

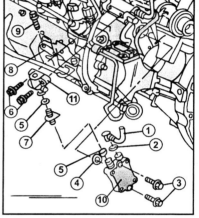

Fig. 1.94 – Details for the removal and installation of the pre-delivery pump.
1 Fuel feed line
2 Sealing ring
3 Torx-head bolt
4 Sealing ring
5 Seals
6 Torx-head bolts
7 Connecting piece
8 Bracket
9 Torx-head bolt
10 Pre-delivery pump
11 Electric shut-off valve

- Remove the electric shut-off valve as already described (to end of February 2001).
- Remove the bracket (8). The bracket must engage in the slot of the pre-delivery pump (10) during installation.
- Disconnect the fuel feed pipe (1) from the pump (10). This is a low pressure line, i.e. disconnect it as described above. Some fuel may flow out. Soak it up with a rag. The oil seal (2) must be replaced during installation.
- Remove the Torx-head bolts (3) securing the pump (10). The bolts are tightened to 0.9 kgm.
- Pull out the pre-delivery pump (10). The driver will come away from the camshaft.
- Carefully detach the connecting piece (7) from the pre-delivery pump (10), replace the seals (5) and refit the connecting piece.

The installation is a reversal of the removal procedure. The pump must not be opened. Clean the sealing surface and fit a new sealing ring (4). Fit the pump so that the driver engages with the camshaft end. If a new pump is fitted, fill it with diesel fuel and rotate it a few times. This will pre-lubricate the pump and ensures immediate delivery of fuel.

1.8.9.   CAMSHAFT POSITION SENSOR

The sensor is fitted in the cylinder head cover between the injectors for the cylinders No. 3 and 4 (cylinder No. 1 on the timing side). To remove the sensor, withdraw the plug connector and remove two Torx-head bolts. The installation is a reversal. Tighten the bolts to 1.4 kgm (10 ft.lb.).

1.8.10.   GLOW PLUGS – REMOVAL AND INSTALLATION

Fig. 1.95 shows where the glow plugs (5) can be found. To remove the plugs you will need a socket wrench as shown by (3) to reach the plugs. Also note that the glow plugs of cylinders Nos. 2 and 3 can only be reached through the recesses shown by the arrows in the exhaust manifold (4).

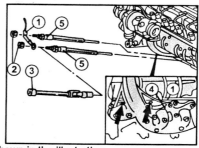

Fig. 1.95 – Details for the removal and installation of the glow plugs.

1   Busbars
2   Securing nuts
3   Special wrench
4   Exhaust manifold
5   Glow plug

• Switch off the ignition and remove the bottom section of the soundproofing capsule.

• Detach the busbars (1) from the glow plugs and unscrew the plug or the plugs with the wrench mentioned and shown in the illustration.

The installation is a reversal of the removal procedure. The plugs are tightened to 1.5 kgm (11 ft.lb.). When new plugs are purchased always quote the engine type and the model year as plugs are sometimes changed to improve the running of the engine.

1.8.11.   FUEL FILTER – REMOVAL AND INSTALLATION

The fuel filter should be replaced every 50 000 miles. Looking into the engine compartment you will find the filter at the position shown in Fig. 1.96. Replace the filter element as follows, noting all precautions given previously. Escaping fuel should be soaked up with a clean rag.

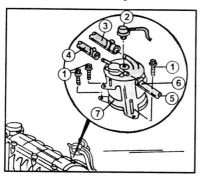

Fig. 1.96 – Fuel filter with the connected fuel lines and hoses.

1   Securing bolts, 0.9 kgm
2   Fuel outlet to high pressure pump
3   Fuel inlet hose
4   Fuel hose
5   Fuel hose
6   Hose clam (all hoses)
7   Fuel filter

• Disconnect the battery earth cable.

• Disconnect the fuel feed line (2) to the high pressure pump. This is a low pressure fuel line which must be connected and re-connected as explained earlier on. The instructions must be followed. Remember that the locking arm must be re-positioned to the locked position. See also Fig. 1.93.

• Disconnect the fuel feed hose (3) and the fuel hoses (4) and (5) after slackening of the hose clamps (6). The clamps should be replaced if no longer in perfect condition. If not sure where each hose is connected, mark them accordingly.

• Unscrew the fuel filter (7) from the induction module (inlet manifold) and lift it off. The filter is secured with the three bolts (1).

During installation fit the filter to the induction module, screw in the bolts and tighten them to 0.9 kgm. All other operations are carried out in reverse order. Make sure that the locking arm of the fuel line (2) is in the locked position as described earlier on. If this is not the case the fuel line must be replaced.

1.8.12. AIR CLEANER – REMOVAL AND INSTALLATION

You will know where the air cleaner is located. On one side of the filter housing you will see a cover with a handle in the centre, as shown in Fig. 1.97. Grip the handle and rotate the cover in an anti-clockwise direction, until a lug on the cover is in line with a notch in the filter housing. Lift off the filter housing cover and remove the filter element (2) out of the housing (3).

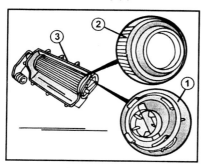

Fig. 1.97 – The component parts of the air cleaner. Shown is the version from June 2000 onwards.
1   Air cleaner housing cover
2   Air cleaner
3   Filter housing

The installation is a reversal of the removal procedure. Note that the air cleaner element and the filter housing have been changed from June 2000 onwards. Only the new filter element is available as replacement part. If the new element is fitted into an old filter housing (which may often be the case), you will have to use the new filter housing cover. Your parts supplied should be able and willing to advise you.

2   CLUTCH

2.0.   Introduction

The clutch is operated by means of a hydraulic system. Pressure is generated by the depressing of the clutch pedal and transmitted via the clutch master cylinder to a so-called central clutch operator inside the clutch bell housing which takes the place of the clutch slave cylinder but incorporates the clutch release bearing. The diameter of the clutch is not the same on all engines and we refer you to your MB parts department if the clutch must be replaced, quoting the engine type and engine number.

All diesel engines are fitted with a dual-mass flywheel. For the technically minded we will tell you how it operates. This flywheel consists of two opposing, rotable masses, i.e. the engine side primary part and the secondary part at the transmission end. The primary part is bolted directly to the crankshaft of the engine (located by means of a dowel pin). The clutch is bolted to the secondary part.

The torque is transferred between the primary and the secondary part by the torsional damper, which is a spring/damper system. The torsional damper reduces the torsional vibrations of the engine and thus the noises of the drive train. The characteristics of the dual-mass flywheel torsional damper depends on the engine and its properties and on the vehicle in which it is used. It may therefore be necessary to use a different flywheel with the same engine but in a different vehicle.

2.1.   Technical Data

Type:

Single plate, dry clutch with dia-phragm spring.

Clutch operation:
Pedal adjustment:
Clutch release bearing

By hydraulic system (see below)
Automatic take-up
Sealed ball-type bearing in constant contact with the clutch plate, incorporated in sealed clutch operator.

2.2   Clutch Unit

2.2.0.   CHECKING THE CLUTCH OPERATION

The clutch can be checked for proper operation when fitted to the vehicle. To do this, proceed as follows:

• Start the engine and allow to idle. Depress the clutch pedal and wait approx. 3 secs. Engage the reverse gear. If grating noises can be heard from the transmission, it can be assumed the clutch or driven plate needs replacement, as the driven plate no longer connects the clutch pressure plate with the flywheel.

• To check the clutch for signs of slipping, drive the vehicle until the clutch and transmission have reached operating temperature. Stop the vehicle, firmly apply the handbrake and engage the 3rd gear. Keep the clutch pedal fully depressed and accelerate the engine to approx. 3000 - 4000 rpm. Release the clutch pedal suddenly. The clutch operates satisfactorily if the engine stalls immediately.

2.2.1.   REMOVAL AND INSTALLATION

Important Note: pressure plate and diaphragm spring cannot be dismantled and must be replaced together. Clutches and driven plates are sometimes modified to improve their operation. If a new clutch or driven plate is purchased always quote the model and the engine type and number.

The clutch cannot be removed without removing the engine and the transmission or by removing the engine. Removal of the engine together with the transmission and the front axle carrier is described in the engine section. To remove the transmission on its own refer to section "Manual Transmission". The operation are the same on all models. After the clutch has been removed you will have the parts shown in Fig. 2.1.

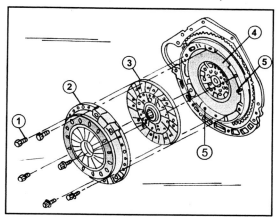

Fig. 2.1 – The component parts of the clutch.
1   Clutch securing bolts
2   Clutch pressure plate
3   Clutch driven plate
4   Flywheel
5   Dowel pins

• Remove the engine and transmission or the transmission (Section 3.1).

• Mark the clutch in its fitted position on the flywheel if there is a possibility that the clutch unit is re-used. To remove the clutch, unscrew the six bolts (1) in Fig. 2.1, securing the pressure plate (2) to the flywheel (4) and lift off the clutch unit and then the driven plate (3), now free. Before removing the driven plate, note the position of the longer part of the driven plate hub, as the driven plate must be refitted in the same way. Note that the clutch plate is located in position by means of the dowel pins (5).

- Immediately check the friction face of the flywheel, as it is possible that the rivets of the driven plate have left their mark on the flywheel face if the linings have worn excessively.

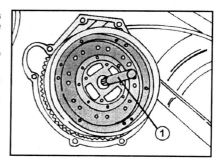

Fig. 2.2 – The clutch centring mandrel (1) is inserted into the driven plate and the flywheel before the clutch is fitted.

Install in the reverse sequence to removal, noting the following points:

- If the old clutch unit is fitted, align the marks made before removal. A new clutch can be fitted in any position.

- Coat the splines of the clutch drive shaft with a little Molykote BR2 grease, *but not if a dual-masse flywheel is fitted.*

- A centring mandrel is required to centre the clutch driven plate inside the flywheel. Tool hire companies normally have sets of mandrels for this purpose. An old transmission (clutch) shaft for the transmission in question, which you may be able to obtain from a Mercedes workshop, can also be used. Experienced D.I.Y. mechanics will also be able to align the clutch plate without the help of a mandrel. Insert the mandrel as shown in Fig. 2.2. Fit the clutch pressure plate (2) over the dowel pins (5) in Fig. 2.1.

- Fit and tighten the six clutch to flywheel bolts (1) to a torque reading of 2.5 kgm (18 ft.lb.), but again note the difference when a dual-mass flywheel is fitted as the torque value is only 1.0 kgm (7.5 ft.lb.).. The flywheel must be locked against rotation when the clutch bolts are e tightened.

- Refit the engine and transmission or the transmission and operate the clutch pedal at least 5 times before the engine is started.

Fig. 2.3. – To check the driven plate for run-out, clamp it between the centres of a lathe and check with a dial gauge.

2.3. Servicing

The cover assembly – pressure plate and diaphragm spring – must not be dismantled. Replace, if necessary with a complete assembly from your dealer or distributor.

Inspect the driven plate and the linings, replacing the complete plate if the linings are worn down close to the rivets. A driven plate with the linings contaminated with grease or oil cannot be cleaned successfully and should also be replaced.

All rivets should be tight and the torsion springs should be sound and unbroken. Check the condition of the driven plate splines. Clamp the driven plate between the centres of a lathe and apply a dial gauge to the outside of the plate as shown in Fig. 2.3, at a diameter of approx. 175.0 mm (6.4 in.). The max. run/out of the driven plate should be no more than 0.5 mm (0.02 in.).

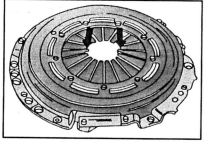

Fig. 2.4 – The "fingers" of the diaphragm spring can wear at the positions shown. All must be at the same height.

Check the rivet fastening of the clutch pressure plate and replace the plate, if loose rivets can be detected.

Check the inner ends of the clutch plate at the position shown in Fig. 2.4. If wear is detected (more than 0.3 mm) replace the clutch unit. The fingers of the diaphragm spring must all be at the same height. It may be possible to bend them slightly with a pair of pliers, but renewal is always the best remedy.

Place a straight edge (steel ruler) over the friction face of the pressure plate and insert feeler gauges between the ruler and the surface. If the gap at the innermost spot of the friction face is no more than 0.03 mm (0.012 in.), the plate can be re-used. Fig. 2.5 shows this check.

A190 Model only: If the old clutch unit is to be re-used but a new driven plate is fitted it will be necessary to re-adjust the adjusting ring of the self-adjusting clutch, fitted up to a certain production number. It will, however, be possible to fit a new clutch and driven plate to these models.

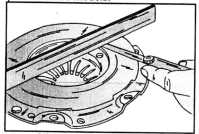

Fig. 2.5 – Checking the clutch pressure plate for distortion. The gap should not be more than given below.

2.4.   Clutch Release Mechanism

Engagement and disengagement of the clutch is by means of the central clutch operator inside the transmission housing with incorporated clutch release bearing. The system is free of clearance and any wear of the driven plate is automatically compensated by the system.

2.4.0.   HYDRAULIC CLUTCH OPERATOR – REMOVAL AND INSTALLATION

Precautions when working with Brake Fluid

As the hydraulic system is filled with brake fluid read the notes below before any operations are carried out on the hydraulic clutch system.

- Only store brake fluid in a closed container, tin, etc. which must be marked accordingly. Brake fluid can damage your health if swallowed.
- Protect your hand with gloves and if possible your eyes with goggles. If your hands come into contact with brake fluid immediately wash them with water and soap.
- Take care not to drip brake fluid onto painted areas of the vehicle. Brake fluid will damage the paint. If it happens, wipe it off immediately.

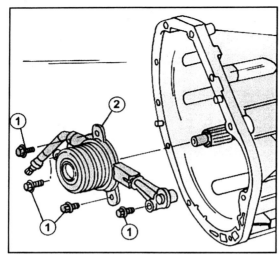

Fig. 2.6 – Attachment of the central clutch operator inside the gearbox housing. The numbers are referred to during the removal instructions.

- Brake fluid is able to absorb moisture from the air. This is the reason that it must be kept in a closed container.
- Even the smallest quantity of oil in the brake fluid can damage the rubber parts of the hydraulic system.
- Brake fluid released from the system, as is the case during the bleeding operation, must not be re-used to top-up the fluid reservoir.

The transmission must be removed to gain access to the hydraulic clutch operator. Fig. 2.6 shows the attachment of the parts in question. With the transmission removed unscrew the four bolts (1) and take off the central clutch operator (2) from the gearbox (3).

The installation is carried out in reverse order. Use new micro-encapsulated bolts (1). Tighten the bolts to 1.0 kgm (7 ft.lb.). Mercedes-Benz recommends to use a suitable thread cutter to re-cut the bolt threads inside the gearbox housing before the clutch operator is fitted. After installation of the gearbox bleed the clutch system as described further on in the text.

2.4.1. CLUTCH MASTER CYLINDER – REMOVAL AND INSTALLATION

Fig. 2.7 shows the attachment of the clutch master cylinder near the clutch pedal. There is no need to remove the cylinder unless a malfunction has developed. The cylinder can, however, be removed as follows:

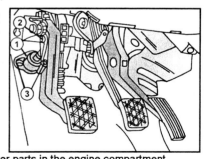

Fig. 2.7 – Work to be carried out near the clutch pedal during removal of the clutch master cylinder. The cylinder (1) can be removed after removal of the retaining pin (2) and unscrewing the nuts (3).

Remove the container for the windscreen washer fluid and place it to one side or lift it out.

- Extract the brake fluid out of the fluid reservoir until the fluid level is below the fluid hose. Fluid can be withdrawn as shown in Fig. 2.8, using a suction tool. Take care not to drip brake fluid over parts in the engine compartment.
- In the engine compartment disconnect the connecting hose from the master cylinder and plug the open hose end in suitable manner. We would like to point

out that the hose has been modified. If a new hose is purchased you will find that it is made of a different material.

• Remove the hydraulic hose at the bottom of the master cylinder. Again plug the open hose end. To remove the hose, pull out a retaining clip at the connection on the cylinder. Both ends of the hose are sealed with a sealing ring which must be replaced when the connecting hose is refitted.

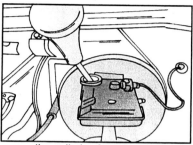

Fig. 2.8 – Brake fluid can be removed from the fluid reservoir in the manner shown.

Note: The hoses must be disconnected. Do not try to "pinch" the hoses together with a clamp to prevent loss of brake fluid.

• Remove the retaining pin (2) in Fig. 2.7 from the clutch pedal. The pin must be slightly greased before installation.

• Remove the collar nuts (3) and remove the cylinder from its locating bore. The nuts are tightened to 0.8 kgm during installation.

The installation is a reversal of the removal procedure. After installation bleed the clutch system as described below.

2.5. Bleeding the Clutch System

A pressure bleeder is used by Mercedes workshops. The following description involves the brake system and is therefore to be treated with caution.

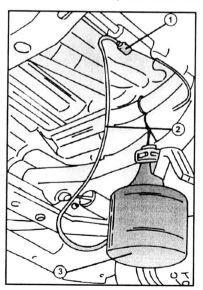

Fig. 2.9 – The bleeding screw (1) is located on the side of the gearbox. The attached bleeder hose (2) is inserted into a glass jar (3).

Make absolutely sure that the brakes have correct operating pressure after the clutch has been bled. The instructions do not apply to vehicles with an automatic clutch operating system. These vehicles must perhaps be bled in a workshop if the following operations are not successful. A transparent hose of approx. 1 metre (3 ft.) in length is required. Proceed as follows:

• Fill the brake/clutch fluid reservoir.

• Remove the dust cap of the bleeder screw in the side opening of the gearbox, shown in Fig. 2.9 and push the hose over the bleeder screw and place the hose end into a glass container filled with some brake fluid. Open the bleeder screw.

• Ask a second person to operate the brake pedal until the hose is completely filled with brake fluid and no more air bubbles can be seen in the glass container. Place a finger over the hose end to prevent fluid from running out.

- Tighten the bleed screw and remove the hose from the end of the screw.
- Check the fluid level in the reservoir and, If necessary, top it up to the "Max." mark. Do not overfill. If necessary extract some fluid in the manner shown in Fig. 2.8. Start the engine, depress the clutch pedal and engage reverse. No grating noises should be heard.

2.6. Automatic Clutch Operating System

The hydraulic central clutch operator with the clutch release bearing, the driven plate and the clutch pressure plate (self-adjusting as mentioned earlier on) operate in the same manner as described above. Additional a separate clutch control unit, an adjusting motor, a clutch master cylinder specially designed for this system and certain sensor are fitted. The sensor are necessary to monitor the position of the gearchange linkages.

When a gear is engaged, the sensor(s) transmit the movement to the clutch control unit. The remaining clutch operation is controlled is controlled by the unit, i.e. the electrically operated adjusting motor transmits the necessary information to the central clutch operator to operate the clutch. The complete system is supplied as in the case of the normal clutch release mechanism from the fluid reservoir with the necessary fluid.

As you can see from the short description you will have to leave all repairs on this type of release mechanism to the experts, i.e. a Mercedes-Benz dealer, mainly as the system is also connected to a fault storage system which can only be read with diagnostic equipment.

2.7. Clutch Faults

Below we list some faults which may occur in connection with the clutch. The faults are not directed specifically to the models covered in this manual.

A Slipping Clutch

1 Clutch plate slipping	Replace driven plate
2 Clutch pressure to low	Replace clutch unit
3 Clutch plate linings full of oil	Replace driven plate, find oil leak
4 Clutch overheated	Replace driven plate, maybe clutch plate
5 Hydraulic operator leaking	Replace central clutch operator

B Clutch will not release

1 Air in the system	Bleed clutch system
2 Master cylinder or operator leaks	Replace cylinder in question
3 Distorted clutch driven plate	Replace driven plate
4 Driven plate linings broken	Replace driven plate
5 Driven plate jammed on shaft	Investigate and rectify
6 Clutch plate lining sticking on flywheel (after long lay off)	Engage 1st gear and depress clutch pedal. Have the vehicle towed a short distance, with ignition switched off

C Clutch jerky

1 Refer to point A3	
2 Wrong driven plate (after repair)	Check and rectify

3 Release bearing defect   Replace central clutch operator
4 Pressure plate has uneven pressure   Replace pressure plate
5 Engine/gearbox mountings defect   Check and if necessary replace
D Clutch does not release and slips
1 Clutch pressure plate damaged   Replace pressure plate

---

3   Manual Transmission

All models covered in the manual are fitted with a five-speed transmission of the type "716", but different gearboxes are fitted depending on the model version. The following list specifies the different transmissions fitted to petrol and diesel models:

A140 in model 168.031:	716.501/503/506/507
A140 L in model 168.131:	716.501/503/506/507
A160 in model 168.033:	716.501/503/506/507/511/512
A160 L in model 168.133:	716.501/503/506/507
A190 in model 168.032:	716.501/503/506/507/511/512
A190 L in model 168.132:	716.506/507
A160 CDI, model 168.006:	716.500/502/504/505
A160 CDI, model 168.007:	716.004/505/
A170 CDI, model 168.008:	716.500/502
A170 CDI, model 168.009:	716.500/502
A170 L CDI, model 168.109:	716.500/502

The overhaul of the transmission is not described in this manual. The description in the overhaul section is limited to some minor repair operations, not involving the gear train or the gear shafts. If the transmission appears to be damaged or faulty, try to obtain an exchange unit. Transmission overhaul is now limited to specialised workshops which are equipped with the necessary special tools.

3.0.   Technical Data

Fitted transmission: .... See above

Transmission Ratios:	A140, A160, A190	A160 CDI, A170 CDI
- First gear	3.27 : 1	3.27 : 1
- Second gear:	1.92 : 1	1.92 : 1
- Third gear:	1,26 : 1 (or 1.34 : 1, A190)	1.26 : 1
- Fourth gear:	0.88 : 1 (or 1.03 : 1, A190)	0.88 : 1
- Fifth gear:	0.70 : 1 (or 0.83 : 1, A190)	0.70 : 1
- Reverse rear:	3.29 : 1	3.29 : 1
- Final drive:	4,06 : 1 (or 3.72 : 1, A190)	3.05 : 1

Transmission Ratios:	Vaneo 1.6, 1.9	Vaneo 1.7 CDI
- First gear	3.27 : 1	3.27 : 1
- Second gear:	1.92 : 1	1.92 : 1
- Third gear:	1,34 : 1	1.26 : 1
- Fourth gear:	1.03 : 1	0.88 : 1
- Fifth gear:	0.82 : 1	0.70 : 1
- Reverse rear:	3.29 : 1	3.29 : 1
- Final drive:	3,76 : 1 (or 4.06 : 1, 1.9)	4.06 : 1

Oil capacity: ....2.0 litres

3.1. Transmission – Removal and Installation

The following text also describes vehicles fitted with petrol models. The removal of the transmission is, however, not the same on all models, as it is possible to remove the transmission on some vehicles built up to the end of June 2000 without removal of the complete front axle carrier together with the engine/transmission assembly. A160 CDI, A170 CDI and A190 (petrol) are amongst them. The necessary operations are described in the following text and can be carried out as desired. Only by reading the text before starting the work will you be able to decide which method is followed.

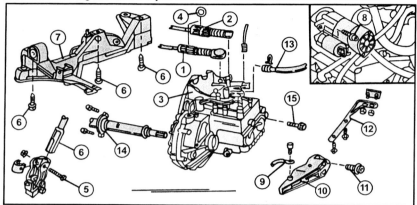

Fig. 3.1 – Details for the removal and installation of the transmission in the case of vehicles built before July 2000.

1 Gear shift cable	6 Torx-head bolt, 12 kgm	11 Torx-head bolt, 5.5 kgm
2 Gear selector cable	7 Front axle carrier	12 Exhaust bracket
3 Shift module	8 Starter motor bolts, 2.0 kgm	13 Hydraulic hose and clip
4 Spacer ring	9 Earth cable	14 Intermediate bearing
5 Bolt, 2.0 kgm	10 Engine support	15 Torx-head bolt, 2.0 kgm

If the vehicle has been built after June 2000 the engine/transmission must be removed together with the front axle carrier as described during the removal of the engine. After separating the engine and transmission from the axle carrier remove the bolts securing the transmission to the engine and withdraw the transmission. The transmission is located on the engine by means of two dowel pins which must be refitted to the cylinder block before the transmission is fitted to the engine.

Before the transmission is fitted check the condition of the clutch. How many miles has the vehicle completed, is the clutch working properly, etc. Maybe it is a good idea to replace the clutch and driven plate.

The installation of the transmission is a reversal of the removal procedure, but note the following points:

- Coat the splines of the clutch drive shaft with a little Molykote grease (except engines with two-mass flywheel, for example diesel engines).

- Lift the transmission and engage the clutch drive shaft with the splines of the clutch driven plate. Rotate the crankshaft on the pulley/vibration damper to facilitate the engagement. Push the transmission against the engine, engaging the dowel pins.

- Fit the bolts into the clutch housing and tighten them evenly all round to 2.0 kgm (14.5 ft.lb.). All other tightening torque have already been specified during the removal and installation of the engine.

- Re-connect the plug connector to the reversing light switch.

- Fill the transmission with transmission oil. If the oil has not been drained, check the oil level all the same.
- Re-connect the battery and do the necessary operations to reset the radio code, electric clock, etc.

Removal and Installation of Transmission (before July 2000)
A160 CDI, 170 CDI and A190

Fig. 3.1 on the previous page shows the parts to be disconnected or removed. In this case only the L.H. front axle carrier must be removed and the engine must be lowered. A suitable lifting tackle and suitable chains must be available to lift the engine. Proceed as follows:
- Disconnect the battery earth cable.
- Remove the fluid container for the windscreen washer.
- Remove the air cleaner as described in the respective section.

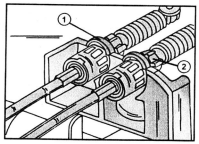

Fig. 3.2 – Refitting the gearchange cables. Fit the spacer ring (1) as described and tighten the nut (2) anti-clockwise until the ring can be inserted fully.

- Disconnect the gearchange cables (1) and (2) from the transmission (3). The ball joints are carefully separated with a screwdriver blade. During installation refer to Fig. 3.2 to make sure you re-connect the cables properly. Open the spacer ring (1) and turn the nut (2) in an anti-clockwise direction until the spacer ring can be inserted fully. The spacer ring must not project beyond the outer diameter of the housing. The gearchange cable is now inserted into the recess of the shift model. Press the cable down until you can feel that it has locked in position. After the gearchange cables have been fitted, do not press down the spacer ring.

Fig. 3.3 – The engine and transmission is suspended with chains attached at the positions shown.

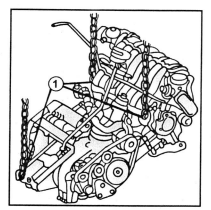

- In the case of a vehicle with automatic clutch operating system disconnect the electrical connections for the shift and selector sensor on the shift module.
- Disconnect the connector plug from the reversing light switch. The arrow in Fig. 3.1 shows where the plug is connected.
- Unscrew the bolt (5) and separate the steering shaft (6) from the steering universal joint (7). Fig. 1.3 shows a large view of the connection. Do not remove the steering coupling.
- Attach the engine to a suitable lifting device and use chains, attached as shown in Fig. 3.3 and lift the engine.
- Use a suitable screwdriver and press the L.H. front drive shaft out of the transmission. Further details are given during the removal of the drive shaft in the

relevant chapter. During installation push the L.H. drive shaft carefully into the longitudinal splines in the transmission until the circlip in the end of the shaft locks the shaft securely.

- Remove the L.H. front axle carrier as described in the section covering the front suspension.
- Slacken the bolts (6) from the R.H. front axle carrier (7). The bolts must not be fully removed. The bolts are tightened to 12.0 kgm (86.5 ft.lb.).
- Lower the engine with the lifting device but not by more than 80 mm. In the case of a vehicle with air conditioning system the bracket for the A/C line on the rear right front axle carrier must be detached. Pay attention to coolant hoses, A/C hoses, fuel lines and electrical cables when the engine is lowered.
- Remove the bolts (8) securing the starter motor. Tighten the bolts to 2.0 kgm (14.5 ft.lb.) during installation.
- Unscrew the earth cable (9) and remove the carrier (10) after removal of the bolts (11). The installation position is determined by means of a dowel pin. Tighten the bolts to 5.5 kgm (40 ft.lb.) when the carrier is installed.
- Remove the exhaust bracket (12).
- Disconnect the fluid hose for the clutch operation (13) after the small securing clip has been removed from the connection. Some brake fluid may run out – take care.
- Remove the intermediate bearing (14) for the R.H. drive shaft after removal of the two bolts. Tighten the bolts to 2.0 kgm (14.5 ft.lb.) during installation to the crankcase.
- Support the transmission from below on a jack and one after the other remove the bolts (15) securing the transmission to the engine. The engine and transmission must be lowered at an angle in order to reach all bolts. Take care that the exhaust pipe does not make contact with the front axle carrier when the engine/transmission is lowered. Before installation check that the fitted sleeves are positioned in the crankcase. If not transfer the two sleeves to the crankcase.

The installation is a reversal of the removal procedure, noting the points given above. After installation check and if necessary correct the oil level in the transmission.

3.2.   Transmission Repairs

As many operations can be carried without completed dismantling of the transmission, we will describe some of the more simple operation which in general require no special tools or pullers. For a complete dismantling of the transmission a complete set of special tools is required. If the transmission has developed an internal fault we highly recommend to obtain an exchange transmission from a local source.

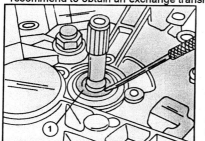

Fig. 3.4 – The oil seal (1) for the clutch drive shaft can be removed in the manner shown.

Removal and Installation of radial Oil Seal in Clutch Housing

The transmission must be removed from the vehicle to replace the oil seal inside clutch bell housing. The hydraulic clutch operator must also be removed, as described in section "Clutch".

Remove the oil seal, using a screwdriver as shown in Fig. 3.4 and fit a new seal. Fill the space between the sealing lips with M.P. grease. A suitable drift must be available to drive in the oil seal, until the outer face is flush with the bore in the housing. Refit the hydraulic clutch operator.

Removal and Installation of rear Transmission Cover

The cover is shown in the L.H. view of Fig. 3.5. Sometimes oil leaks can be detected around this area. The transmission must be removed to rectify a leak. After removal of the bolts (1) take off the cover (2) from the transmission housing (3). Clean the sealing surface of the transmission and the cover and coat the surfaces with "Loctite 5970" sealing compound. Fit the cover and the bolts and tighten the bolts to 1.0 kgm (7.2 ft.lb.).

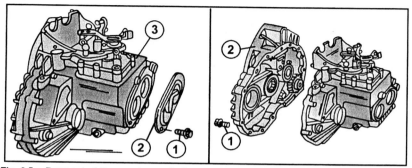

Fig. 3.5 – Removal of the rear transmission cover (left) and the clutch housing (right). The numbers are explained in the text.

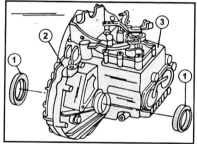

Fig. 3.6 – The two oil seals (1) for the drive shafts are fitted to the clutch housing (2) and the transmission housing (3).

Removal and Installation of Clutch Housing

The transmission must be removed, the transmission oil drained. The removed clutch housing can be seen in Fig. 3.5 on the R.H. side. After removal of the bolts (1) remove the clutch housing (2) from the transmission housing. Before installation clean the jointing surfaces of clutch housing and transmission housing thoroughly of old sealing compound, using a wooden wedge and coat the clutch housing face with "Loctite 5970" sealing compound. Fit the housing, screw in the bolts and tighten them evenly to 2.5 kgm (18 ft.lb.). Finally fill the transmission with 1.8 litres of gearbox oil.

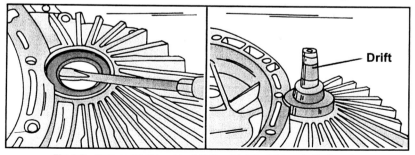

Fig. 3.7 – Removal (left) and installation (right) of drive shaft oil seals.

Replacing the Drive Shaft Oil Seals

The two oil seals are shown in Fig. 3.6. One oil seal is fitted to the transmission housing (1) and the other one in the clutch housing (2). The removal of the oil seals is carried out as shown in Fig. 3.7 in the L.H. view, using a screwdriver. Before installation coat the sealing lip of the oil seal or oil seals with gearbox oil and drive them in position as shown in the R.H. view of Fig. 3.7 until the outside of the seal is flush with the housing.

3.3.   Oil Level Check and Oil Change

The gearbox is filled with 1.8 litres of gearbox oil. There is no need to change the transmission oil as transmissions fitted to vehicles covered in this manual are filled for live.

Fluid or oil can only be lost if a leak has developed. To check the oil level, remove the oil filler plug from the side of the transmission and check that the fluid/oil is up to the lower edge of the plug bore. If the oil cannot be seen, insert the forefinger to check whether you can reach it. If necessary top-up with the specified gearbox oil. A grease gun (thoroughly cleaned) can be used to fill in the required fluid/oil.

If necessary drain the transmission fluid/oil in the usual manner, i.e. remove the drain plug at the bottom of the transmission. Allow the vehicle to stand for a while until all old oil has been drained. Then fill the transmission with the specified amount of oil.

---

4   Drive Shafts

Two drive shafts with CV joints are used to transmit the drive from the transmission to the front wheels. The L.H. and R.H. drive shafts are not the same as one the R.H. drive shaft is connected with an intermediate shaft, the bearing of which is bolted to the cylinder block. Figs. 4.1 and 4.2 show the attachment of the two shafts.

4.1.   Removal and Installation of Drive Shafts

Irrespective of the differences of the attachment of the two shafts the following text summarises the operations. Notes for the installation are immediately given when applicable. Before commencing with the removal obtain some Teflon spray from your dealer as this will be required during installation. Proceed as follows:

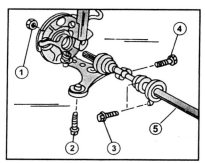

Fig. 4.1 – Attachment of the R.H. drive shaft with the intermediate bearing.
1 Drive shaft nut
2 Bolt, suspension arm to knuckle, front
3 Bolts, intermediate bearing to cylinder block
4 Bolt, suspension arm to knuckle, rear
5 R.H. drive shaft

•   Mark the wheels in relation to the wheel hubs with a spot of paint to ensure installation in the same position and slacken the wheel bolts and the two axle shaft nuts (1). The front end of the vehicle can now be placed on chassis stands.

•   Unscrew the Torx-head bolts (2) and (4) in Fig. 4.1 or (2) and (3) in Fig. 4.2 and separate the lower suspension arm from the front subframe. To gain access to the rear bolts (2) you will have to remove the cover from the front subframe. Note that the bolts (2) and (4) in the R.H. suspension arm and the bolts (2) and (3) in the L.H. arm are of different length. Mark where they are fitted.

Fig. 4.2 – Attachment of the L.H. drive shaft.
1 Drive shaft nut
2 Bolt, suspension arm to knuckle, front
3 Bolt, suspension arm to knuckle, rear
4 L.H, drive shaft

• Extract the front axle shaft with a suitable puller from the end of the wheel hub flange, using an extractor. The extractor must work on the principle shown in Fig. 4.3. The extractor is attached with bolts (3) to the wheel hub flange (4). By tightening the centre spindle (2) the shaft will come out of the flange towards the inside.

• To remove the R.H. drive shaft and the intermediate shaft (5) in Fig. 4.1 unscrew the bearing from the crankcase. Bolts (3) secure the bearing. Tighten the bolts to 2.0 kgm (14.5 ft.lb.) during installation. New bolts must always be used.

Fig. 4.3 – Removal of a drive shaft with the extractor.
1 Extraction tool
2 Centre spindle
3 Securing bolts
4 Hub flange

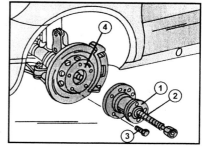

• Use a suitable screwdriver and pry the intermediate shaft together with the drive shaft (5) out of the transmission. **Attention:** Never pull the shaft out of the transmission by pulling on the shaft itself, as irreparable damage would take place. Only remove in the manner described. The shaft can now be fully removed. During installation insert the shaft with the long end into the splines of the transmission and push it fully in. After removal immediately check the condition of the rubber boot and replace it if necessary as described later on.

• Use a suitable screwdriver and pry the L.H. shaft out of the transmission. The same applies to this shaft – never pull on the shaft to remove it. On this shaft check that the circlip in the end of the shaft has a tight seat. During installation rotate the circlip until the gap is facing downwards and insert the shaft splines into the splines inside the transmission gear. Push the shaft fully in until you can feel that the circlip has snapped into place.

• The L.H. shaft can now be removed. Again check the rubber boot for damage.

The installation is a reversal of the removal procedure. In addition to the points already mentioned note the following:

• Insert the intermediate shaft and the R.H. drive shaft as described above into the gearbox and bolt the intermediate shaft bearing to the cylinder block. Tighten the bolts to 2.0 kgm (14.5 ft.lb.). Mercedes-Benz warns that the threads in the cylinder block must sometimes be re-cut.

- Thoroughly clean the splines (arrow in Fig. 4.4) and the contact area of the front axle shaft flange and spray them with Teflon spray. The spraying must be carried out in stages to allow the faces to air in between stages.
- Push the drive shaft into the wheel bearing as far as it will go.

Fig. 4.4 – Spray the area indicated by the arrow with the Teflon spray.

- Fit the lower suspension arm with new nuts to the front axle subframe. Remember the difference of the bolt length. Tighten the nuts to 10.5 kgm (75 ft.lb.). Section "Front Suspension" will give further details about the suspension arms.
- Fit new drive shaft nuts and tighten tem fairly tight. Refit the wheel in accordance with the marks made before removal and lower the vehicle onto its wheels. The vehicle must be jacked up later on, i.e. do not tighten the wheel bolts at this stage.

The drive shaft nuts are now tightened in four stages as follows:
- Tighten the nut(s) with a torque setting of 8.0 kgm (58 ft.lb.).
- Slacken the nut(s) completely.
- Tighten the nut(s) with a torque of 8.0 kgm (58 ft.lb.).
- Without using the torque wrench, i.e. with the socket and the tommy bar only, tighten the nut(s) by a further 45°. This is half of a quarter of a turn.
- Jack-up the front end of the vehicle, remove the wheel or wheels and refit the hub grease cap carefully, using a soft-faced mallet.
- Refit the wheel or wheels in accordance with the marks made before removal and fit the wheel bolts. After the wheels are back on the ground tighten the wheel bolts to 11.0 kgm (79 ft.lb.).

4.2.   Replacing the Drive Shaft Rubber Boots

Fig. 4.5 shows the attachment of a rubber boot (bellows) to one of the shafts. The boots are replaced in the same manner on both shafts. When fitting a rubber boot a certain dimension must be observed which will be referred to during installation. The drive shaft must be removed as described above to replace a rubber boot. Do not replace the vehicle on its wheels if a drive shaft has been removed.

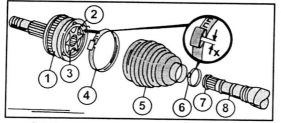

Fig. 4.5 – Dismantled drive shaft.
1 Drive shaft CV joint
2 Joint cage
3 inside star
4 Large boot clamp
5 Rubber boot (bellows)
6 Small boot clamp
7 retaining circlip
8 Drive shaft

- Cut the boot clamps (4) and (6) with a side cutter (must always be replaced). **Note:** A special pair of pliers is used to tighten the clamps. Refer to Fig. 4.7 before a rubber boot is replaced.
- Clamp the drive shaft into a vice and remove the rubber boot (5). Detach the relevant joint (1) from the drive shat (8). A suitable drift must be used to drive the

CV joint from the shaft. The drift is applied to the point shown by the arrow at the inside star (3). Take care not to damage the contact surface of the radial shaft seal.

- Thoroughly clean the joint. If water or dirt has entered the joint, the outside joint must be disassembled. To do this, mark the position of the joint (1), the inside star (3) and the cage (2) inn relation to each other. The inside joint cannot be dismantled. If contaminated. The complete drive shaft must be replaced.

The assembly of the drive shaft is carried out as follows:

- Fit the small boot clamp (6) onto the drive shaft (8) and slide the rubber boot (5) onto the shaft.

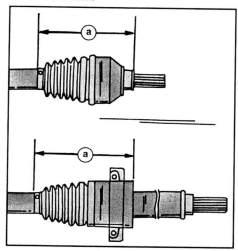

Fig. 4.6 – measure the length "a" of the rubber boot between the arrows. The upper view shows the L.H. shaft, the lower view the R.H. shaft.

- Fill the joint to the upper edge with grease, noting the different amounts required. In the case of the wheel side joint (outer joint) an amount of 100 grams is used, in the case of the gearbox side joint (inner joint) an amount of 120 grams is used. This is the total amount required. Some grease will not be used at this stage. The recommended grease must be obtained from a dealer.

- Slide the joint (1) onto the drive shaft. On the other joint install a new circlip (7) into the groove of the shaft.

Fig. 4.7 – Tightening the boot clamps with the pair of pliers mentioned in the text. The pliers grip the clamp ends at (B). The bolt (A) is tightened with the torque wrench.

- Fill the rubber boot (5) and the joint (1) with the remaining grease, in each case the grease left for each joint.

- The rubber boot is now fitted to the drive shaft and stretched to obtain a dimension of 159 mm, as shown by dimension "a" in Fig. 4.6. Note the points where you measure from in the case of a shaft with and without intermediate bearing.

- Fit boot clamp and tighten it with a suitable pair of pliers. The workshop uses a special pair of pliers as shown in Fig. 4.7. The pliers grips the ends of the clamp at the positions shown and the bolt (A) is tightened (approx. 3.0 kgm). The gap "X" in Fig. 4.5 must be at least 2.5 mm (or less). Without this tool it may be difficult to fit the boot clamp properly, however, the same pair of pliers is used by other car manufacturers, not only in Mercedes workshops and may be available from a tool hire shop.

- Thoroughly clean the assembled drive shat, mainly to remove any grease or oil on the outside of the shaft and the rubber boots to prevent the accumulation of road once the vehicle is back on the road.

5   Front Suspension

5.0.   Technical Data

Type	Independent suspension with McPherson spring struts, lower suspension arms, integral shock absorbers, coil springs. With stabiliser bar. Stabiliser bar mounting: Mounting clamps and rubber bushes, bolted to vehicle floor and connected to spring struts with links.
Front springs	Colour coded. Only fit springs with original colour code.
Front Wheel Bearings	
Type	Wheel hub with wheel bearing, pressed into steering knuckle

5.1.   Regular Maintenance Operations

The suspension ball joints between the suspension arms and the wheel bearing housings, also known as steering knuckles, require no maintenance. Rubber dust caps prevent the entry of dirt or moisture. Entry of dust has a grinding effect, entry of moisture leads eventually to rust formation. During regular maintenance work, you can check the ball joints as follows:

- Place the front of the vehicle on chassis stands and turn the steering wheel into full lock.
- Check the rubber dust caps on both sides for cuts or other damage. A damaged dust cap must be replaced by fitting a new ball joint. Apart from the fact that the dust caps cannot be replaced individually, there is the possibility that dirt has already entered the joint, thereby leading to wear.

5.2.   Front Spring Struts

5.2.0.   REMOVAL

The following text describes the removal of the complete spring strut together with the lower suspension arm and the drive shaft. In general the individual parts of the suspension can, however, be removed without removal of the complete assembly. Fig. 5.1 shows the front suspension on one side with the location of the various component parts. If a new spring strut is to be fitted have the front wheel alignment checked at a dealer of specialist workshop.

- Apply the handbrake, engage 1st gear and slacken the wheel bolts and the drive shaft nut. Remember that the drive shaft nut torque is very high. Ask a helper to apply the brake pedal. A good socket is necessary, with a piece of tube over the tommy bar.

94

- Place the front end of the vehicle on chassis stands and remove the front wheel on the side in question. Mark the wheel in relation to the wheel hub flange to make sure it is refitted to the same position.
- If ABS is fitted, disconnect the cable connection to the wheel speed sensor (12) and the sensor for the brake pad wear indicator in the wheel housing. Free the cables from the retainers.

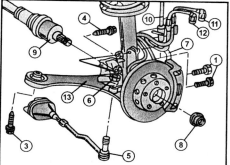

Fig. 5.1 – Removal and installation of a spring strut.
1 Bolts, strut to steering knuckle
2 Self-locking nut, 10 kgm
3 Torx-head bolt, suspension arm front
4 Torx-head bolt, suspension arm, rear
5 Track rod ball joint
6 Track rod ball joint nut, 3.0 kgm+90°
7 Brake hose
8 Drive shaft nut
9 Drive shaft
10 Plug, brake pad wear sensor
11 Plug, wheel speed sensor

- Separate the stabiliser bar connecting rod from the spring strut. The ball joint at the end of the connecting rod must be prevented from rotating by applying an open-ended spanner. The other end at the bottom can be removed in the same manner.
- Unscrew the brake caliper and suspend it with a piece of wire to some part of the body. Never allow the caliper to hang down on the brake hose. It is also possible to disconnect the brake hose (7) from the brake pipe (10). Close the open end of the brake pipe to prevent entry of foreign matter. In this case the brake system must be bled of air after installation. During installation make sure that the brake hose is not twisted when the connection to the brake pipe is tightened.
- Remove the track rod ball joint nut (6) and disconnect the track rod ball joint (5) from the steering lever on the steering knuckle. A puller is required to detach the ball joint connection.
- Remove the drive shaft as described in section "Drive Shafts" earlier on.
- Remove the bolts securing the suspension arm as described during the removal of the drive shafts. Note the different length of the bolts. These are boths (3) and (4) in the illustration.
- The spring strut is secured with its centre inside the engine compartment to the wing inner panels. Two bolts secure the strut and you will see also two clips which must be pressed together. If the L.H. strut is removed remove the container for the windscreen washer fluid to gain access.
- Remove the complete spring strut from the vehicle.

5.2.1. INSTALLATION

Install the spring strut as follows:
- Insert the spring strut into its upper bearing and engage the clips. Screw in the bolts and tighten them to 4.0 kgm (30 ft.lb.).
- Insert the suspension arm into its mounting on the inside and fit the rear bolt (4) from the outside on one side of the suspension arm and the lower bolt (3) from below. Make sure that the correct bolt is used (different length). The nuts must be replaced. Tighten the bolts to 10.5 kgm (79 ft.lb.).

- Fit the stabiliser bar connecting rods. Again a new nut must be used. Place the washer in position, screw on the nut and tighten the nut to 4.5 kgm (32.5 ft.lb.). Counterhold the ball joint with an open-ended spanner when the nut is tightened. If removed, connect the lower end of the rod in the same manner. The torque value above is valid for vehicles manufactured before the 25.8.2002. After this date the torque value has been increased to 6.0 kgm (43 ft.lb.).
- Refit the drive shaft to the transmission and insert it into the steering knuckle. The drive shaft nut is only tightened provisionally at this stage.
- Re-connect the track rod ball joint and tighten the nut to 3.0 kgm (22 ft.lb.). From the final position tighten the nut a further 1/8 of a turn.
- Refit the wheels in accordance with the marks made before removal, lower the vehicle to the ground and tighten the axle shaft nut as described in Chapter 4, it is has bee slackened during removal. Also tighten the wheel bolts (11 kgm).
- If necessary bleed the brake system (if the brake hose has been disconnected). Otherwise refit the brake caliper.

5.3.   Front Spring Struts without Suspension Arm
5.3.1.   REMOVAL AND INSTALLATION

The operations are carried out in the manner described in the last section with the difference that the suspension arm and the drive shaft remain in the vehicle. Fig. 5.1 will help during the removal and installation procedure.

After the connecting rod has been disconnected from the spring strut as described above, mark the exact seat of the spring strut on the steering knuckle with paint and remove the nuts (2). Drive out the bolts (1) carefully, remembering on which side the bolt heads are located.

Separate the spring strut at the upper end as described and remove the strut towards the bottom.

Installation is carried out as follows:
- Insert the upper end of the spring strut into its mounting and engage the clips. Screw in the bolts and tighten them to 4.0 kgm (30 ft.lb.).
- Align the spring strut with the marks made before removal, with the bolt holes in line and insert the bolts (1) into the steering knuckle. When aligned drive the bolts carefully in position. The bolt heads must be on the side shown in Fig. 5.1. Fit and tighten the nuts (2). Both nuts are now hand-tightened, but first the lower nut and then the upper nut. Now tighten the lower nut to 10.0 kgm (72 ft.lb.) and then the upper nut to the same torque.
- Re-connect the stabiliser bar connecting rod. Place the washer in position and fit a new nut. Tighten the nut to 4.5 kgm (32.5 ft.lb.). This torque value is valid for vehicles manufactured before the 25.8.2002. After this date the torque value has been increased to 6.0 kgm (43 ft.lb.). The ball joint must be counter-held with an open-ended spanner when the nut is tightened. Attach the lower end of the rod (if removed) in the same manner.
- Refit the wheels in accordance with their markings, lower the vehicle to the ground and tighten the wheel bolts (11 kgm).

If a new spring strut has been fitted have the front wheel alignment checked in a workshop.

5.4.   Front Spring Struts - Dismantling

The following instructions will enable you to replace the coil spring or the spring strut after it has been removed as described earlier on.

- Using a spring compressor, for example of the type shown in Fig. 5.2, compress the coil spring until all tension has been removed from the upper and lower spring seats. The strut should be clamped into a vice. Make sure that the spring compressor cannot slip off. Never dismantle a spring strut without compressing the spring.

- Remove the nut securing the piston rod in the centre of the upper strut bearing. To prevent the piston rod from rotating insert a suitable Allen key into the end of the rod. A cranked ring spanner can be used to undo the nut. The workshop uses, of course, a special wrench. Remove the washer and the spring strut bearing from the end of the piston rod and remove the spring strut. The spring can remain compressed if only the shock absorber requires replacing. Otherwise remove the compressor. Mercedes-Benz advises to replace a shock absorber together with the coil spring.

Fig. 5.2 – Compressing a coil spring.

- The remaining parts, incl. the coil spring can be removed from the upper end of the strut.

The strut/shock absorber assembly should be checked as follows:

- Coil springs are selected for a specific model. If a spring is replaced make sure to fit one which is correct for the model in question. Coil springs are marked with a spot of paint on one of the coils for identification purposes.

- The shock absorber can be checked for correct operation by clamping the spring strut in upright position into a vice. Screw the nut back onto the piston rod and grip the nut with a pair of pliers. Move the piston rod up and down. The piston rod should move with even resistance. Any "dead play" indicates a faulty shock absorber. If the same shock absorber is fitted store it in a vertical position.

The assembly of the spring strut is carried out as follows, noting the following points.

- If a coil spring or a shock absorber is replaced it is of advantage to replace the parts on the other side as well.

- Insert the rebound buffer and the rubber plug into the upper spring plate and compress the new coil spring with the spring compressor as explained and shown earlier on. Otherwise place the original spring with the compressor attached over the spring strut.

- Fit the upper spring seat and the other removed parts to the coil spring and fit the shock absorber.

- Fit the washer and the spring strut bearing and screw a NEW piston rod nut over the piston rod end. Prevent the piston rod from rotating by inserting an Allen key (7 mm A/F) and tighten the nut to 6.0 kgm (43.5 ft.lb.). As the torque cannot be obtained in the manner described tighten the nut as described, until it is tight enough to rotate. Now use the torque wrench and a socket so obtain the torque value.

- Slowly release the spring compressor, at the same time checking that the spring is located correctly at its upper and lower ends. Remove the spring compressor.

- The spring strut can now be refitted to the vehicle in the manner described.

5.5. Suspension Arms – Removal and Installation

Note: If the connection between suspension arm and front axle carrier has been separated you must always replace the nut. The necessary operations are described later on during the removal of the front axle carrier.

Fig. 5.3 shows the component parts to be removed on one side of the vehicle. We must point out again that the suspension arm bolts are not of the same length.

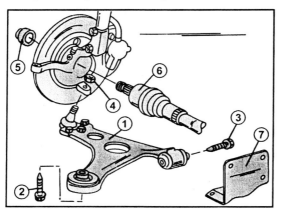

Fig. 5.3 – Details for the removal and installation of a lower suspension arm (wishbone).

1 Lower suspension arm
2 Torx-head bolt, front
3 Torx-head bolt, rear
4 Self-locking nut
5 Collar nut
6 Drive shaft
7 Cover

• Slacken the wheel bolts with the wheels on the ground. Also slacken the collar nut (5) from the end of the drive shaft, without removing it. The drive shaft end must be extracted from the hub flange.

• Jack up the front end of the vehicle and place chassis stands in position. Mark the wheel with a spot of paint in relation to the wheel hub flange and remove it. The nut (5) can also be removed.

• Detach the cover (7) from the front axle carrier.

• Remove the two Torx-head bolts (3) and (4) at the front and rear of the suspension arm (1). The bolts must be marked accordingly (different length).

• Withdraw the axle shaft out of the wheel hub flange as described during the removal of the drive shafts. The section must be referred to, as it will tell you about the use of Teflon spray during installation and the use of the extractor.

• Remove the nut (4) securing the suspension ball joint at the bottom of the steering knuckle and separate the joint stud with a suitable puller from the knuckle.

• Remove the suspension arm.

The installation is a reversal of the removal procedure. The following points must be noted:

• Check the suspension ball joint for wear. The joint can be replaced as described later on.

• If the front or the rear rubber bearings in the suspension arm are worn (after many miles) it is possible to have them replaced in a workshop. A complete special tool set is required to replace the bushes.

• Refit the drive shaft to the wheel hub flange as described during the installation of the drive shaft. The nut (5) is tightened hand-tight at this stage.

• Fit the suspension arm as shown in Fig. 5.3 and insert the bolts (2) and (3), noting their length. Tighten the bolts to 10.5 kgm (79 ft.lb.).

• Fit a new self-locking nut (4) to the inserted ball joint of the suspension ball joint and tighten the nut to 3.0 kgm (22 ft.lb.). From the final position tighten the nut a further 120°, i.e. a quarter of a turn (90°) and one flat of the hexagon (30°).

• Fit the wheel in accordance with the marks you made before removal, tighten the wheel bolts hand-tight and lower the vehicle to the ground. The drive shaft nut is tightened as during the installation of the drive shaft. Finally tighten the wheel bolts to 11.0 kgm (79 ft.lb.).

Replacing the Suspension Ball Joint

The suspension ball joint is fitted as a complete assembly to the bottom of the steering knuckle, as can be seen in Fig. 5.4. To replace the ball joint you have to remove the suspension arm (wishbone) as described above.

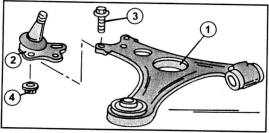

Fig. 5.4 – Removal and installation of a suspension ball joint.
1 Suspension arm
2 Ball joint
3 Securing bolts
4 Self-locking nut

A ball joint can be checked by clamping the suspension arm into a vice (soft-metal jaws), gripping the ball joint stud and moving it up and down. Excessive clearance will indicate a new assembly.

Unscrew the nuts (4) from the three bolts (3) and remove the joint (2). The installation is a reversal of the removal procedure. The nuts (4) must always be replaced. Tighten the nuts first to 2.0 kgm (14.5 ft.lb.) and from the end position half of a quarter of a turn.

5.6.   Stabiliser Bar – Removal and Installation

The removal and installation is not an easy operation as the engine must be lifted out of its mountings. You will need a lifting device and chains to attach the engine as shown in Fig. 3.3 on page 88. Provided that this equipment is available and you are confident enough, proceed as follows. The parts to be removed are shown in Fig. 5.5. The description is valid for petrol and diesel models.

*   Slacken the wheel bolts, jack up the front end of the vehicle, place chassis stands in position and remove the front wheels after marking the relationship between wheels and wheel hub flanges.

*   **In the case of a diesel model** remove the bottom section of the sound-proofing panelling as described earlier on. The front engine compartment lining and the left and right engine compartment lining must be removed.

*   **In the case of a petrol model** remove the lower engine compartment sound-proofing panelling as described. The R.H. front engine compartment lining must be removed.

*   Unscrew the nuts (9) securing the front engine mounts (8) to the front axle carrier from below. Tighten the nuts during installation to 4.0 kgm (29 ft.lb.).

*   Disconnect the plug connections of the engine and vehicle harness on the engine control unit. In the case of a petrol engine unlock and separate the plug the plug connections. During installation insert the plug into the guides, establish the connections and lock.

Disconnect the stabiliser bar (2) from the connecting rods (6). The connecting rods are attached by means of ball joints and held in position by the nuts (7). If one of the ball joint studs rotates when the nuts are slackened, apply an open-ended spanner at the inside to prevent the ball stud from rotating. Take care not to damage the rubber boots. The ball joint stud nuts are tightened to 4.5 kgm of the vehicle has been manufactured before the 25.8.2002 or to 6.0 kgm after this date.

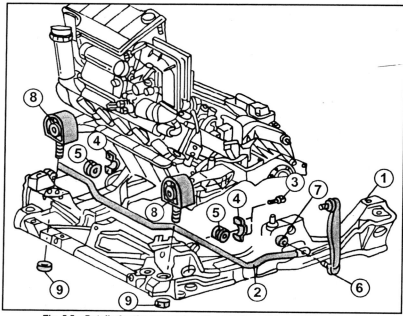

Fig. 5.5 – Details for the removal and installation of the stabiliser bar.

1 Rack and pinion steering	4 Bracket	7 Self-locking collar nut
2 Stabiliser (anti-roll) bar	5 Rubber bushing	8 Front engine mount
3 Bolt, mounting clamps, 2.8 kgm	6 Connecting rods	9 Nuts, 4.0 kgm

- Remove the air cleaner as described in the fuel section.
- The engine is now lifted as far as it will go, taking care not to damage any hoses, cables, etc.

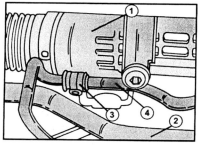

Fig. 5.5 – The fluid line (4) near the steering box (1) and the stabiliser bar (2) must be detached after unscrewing the retaining clamp (3).

-
- Remove the bolts (3), take off the mounting clamps (4) and free the stabiliser bar (2) from the front axle carrier (1) . Immediately check the rubber bushings (5) and fit new ones if the old ones show signs of wear. Fit the bushes without grease or other lubricants during installation. The mounting clamps are tightened to 2.8 kgm (20 ft.lb.).
- The next operation s carried out by referring to Fig. 5.6. Near the steering (1) and above the stabiliser bar (2) you will find the fluid line (4) for the power-assisted steering. Remove the retaining clamp (3) and free the fluid line.
- Turn the steering into the R.H. lock and remove the stabiliser bar towards the left hand side. During the last parts of the removal turn the steering towards the left (helper) until the bar can be removed.

The installation is a reversal of the removal procedure, noting the point already given during removal. Check the exact position of the stabiliser bar before tightening the mounting clamps.

5.7. Steering Knuckle – Removal and Installation

The removal and installation of the steering knuckle is carried out in a similar manner as described for the removal of the spring strut.

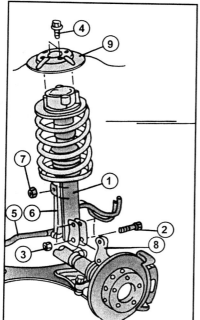

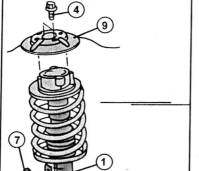

Fig. 5.7 – View of a spring strut with steering knuckle.

1 Spring strut
2 Bolt, spring strut to steering knuckle
3 Nut, spring strut to steering knuckle
4 Bolt, spring strut bearing to body
5 Stabiliser bar
6 Connecting rods, stabiliser
7 Nut, connecting rod nut
8 Steering knuckle
9 Upper spring strut bearing

There is no need to remove the spring strut and the drive shaft, but the drive shaft must be separated from the front wheel hub as described in the section covering the drive shafts (axle shafts). Fig. 5.7 shows the spring strut with the fitted steering knuckle.

Follow the instructions in section 5.2.0 until the track rod ball joint has been separated from the steering lever.

To separate the steering knuckle (8) from the spring strut (1) remove the two nuts (3) from both bolts (2) and drive out the bolts. The bolts must be knocked out carefully in order not to damage the bolt threads. Insert a strong screwdriver behind the steering knuckle and pry it away from the spring strut. The nuts (3) must always be replaced.

During installation follow the instructions follow the instructions in section 5.2.1. Mainly note the tightening sequence for the steering knuckle to spring strut bolts.

5.7. Wheel Bearings – Replacement

If only the wheel bearing requires replacement you can remove the steering knuckle as described above or replace the bearing as described below. In the latter case you will need, however, a puller and it may therefore be better to remove the steering knuckle.

Fig. 5.8 shows how the wheel bearing is fitted to the steering knuckle. *You must replace the double-row angular wheel bearing if the wheel hub flange is withdrawn.* Also remember that you will need Teflon spray when the axle shaft flange is refitted to the end of the shaft (refer to section "Drive Shafts").

- Slacken the wheel bolts and the drive shaft nut (7) with the wheels resting on the ground, mark the position of the wheel in relation to the wheel hub flange and place the front end of the vehicle on chassis stands. Remove the wheel and fully unscrew the drive shaft nut.

Fig. 5.8 – Removal and installation of the front hub flange and the wheel bearing.
1 Spring strut
2 Lower suspension arm
3 Bolt, suspension ball joint plate
4 Self-locking nut
5 Steering knuckle
6 Front wheel hub flange
7 Drive shaft nut
8 Double-row angular wheel bearing
9 Drive shaft

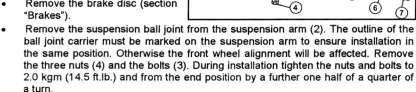

- Remove the brake disc (section "Brakes").

- Remove the suspension ball joint from the suspension arm (2). The outline of the ball joint carrier must be marked on the suspension arm to ensure installation in the same position. Otherwise the front wheel alignment will be affected. Remove the three nuts (4) and the bolts (3). During installation tighten the nuts and bolts to 2.0 kgm (14.5 ft.lb.) and from the end position by a further one half of a quarter of a turn.

- Extract the drive shaft (9) out of the wheel hub flange (6). The operations are described during the removal of the drive shaft (see also Fig. 4.3). The installation is described in the same section.

- The hub wheel flange must now be removed. The workshop uses a special puller for this operation, but you should be able to use a suitable two- or three-arm puller, with the puller claws gripping the edges of the flange to remove it.

- The wheel bearing is now removed with the puller shown in Fig. 5.9 and the additional parts. First remove the bearing retaining ring (1). Then fit the illustrated parts to withdraw the bearing (7) out of the steering knuckle (2).

Note – Removal of bearing with the steering knuckle removed

If the special tools mentioned above cannot be obtain, remove the steering knuckle as described earlier on. Then place the steering knuckle under a hydraulic press and press the wheel hub flange out of the steering knuckle. The wheel bearing can be removed in the same manner after the bearing retaining ring (1) in Fig. 5.9 has been removed.

Fig. 5.9 – Special tool set (168 589 01 43 00) to remove a front wheel bearing.
1 Bearing retaining ring
2 Steering knuckle
3 Thrust piece
4 Centre spindle
5 Nut on rear of steering knuckle
6 Washer, placed over bearing
7 Double-row angular wheel bearing

The installation is carried out as follows, with and without the special tool set:

With the tool set shown in Fig. 5.9:

- Insert the new bearing from the outside into the steering knuckle and fit the items shown in Fig. 5.9 to the steering knuckle. Fit the nut (5) to the inserted centre spindle and tighten it as tight as possible. Prevent the nut from rotating (ring spanner) and tighten the spindle on the outside until the wheel bearing has reached its stop. Finally fit the bearing retaining ring (1).

102

Without the tool set shown in Fig. 5.9:

- Place the steering knuckle onto the bed of a press, insert the bearing from the outside and using a piece of tube of suitable diameter press the bearing into the steering knuckle. The pressure must be applied to the outer bearing race only. Engage the bearing retaining ring.
- Fit the wheel hub flange into the steering knuckle in a similar manner.

5.8. Front Axle Carrier – Removal and Installation

As already mentioned throughout the manual you will find the removal and installation of the front axle carrier a comprehensive and complicated operation which must, however, be carried out in many circumstances to reach other parts located at the front end of the vehicle. Fig. 5.10 shows the parts to be removed.

During the following description any tightening values and other points to be observed are immediately given after each operation and must be referred back during installation. All self-locking bolts and nuts must be replaced where indicated. The instructions are valid for petrol and diesel models.

- Remove the washer fluid reservoir for the windscreen washer.
- Mark the position of the front wheels on the wheel hub flanges and remove the front wheels.
- **In the case of a diesel model** remove the bottom section of the sound-proofing panelling as described earlier on. The front engine compartment lining and the left and right engine compartment lining must be removed.
- **In the case of a petrol model** remove the lower engine compartment sound-proofing panelling as described. The R.H. front engine compartment panelling and the centre underbody panelling must be removed.
- Disconnect the plug connections of the engine and vehicle harness on the engine control unit. In the case of a petrol engine unlock and separate the plug the plug connections. During installation insert the plug into the guides, establish the connections and lock.
- Lift the engine with a suitable lifting tackle and chains or by means of a jack and suitable wooden planks until the engine mounts are no longer under tension.
- Remove the wheelhouse panelling at the rear on both sides and fold them down.
- Detach the support strut (23) from the front axle carrier (1). The bolt (24) is tightened to 6.0 kgm (43.5 ft.lb.) during installation of the strut. An Allen-key is required.
- Detach the panelling on the side of the suspension arm (2). Not shown in the illustration. Must be removed to gain access to the suspension arm bolt.
- Disconnect the stabiliser bar (9) after removal of the mounting clamps (10) from the front axle carrier (1). Tighten the bolt to 2.8 kgm (20 ft.lb.) during installation.
- Unscrew the suspension arm (6) from the plate for the suspension arm ball joint (11). Before removal mark the outline of the support plate on the suspension arm with a scriber and refit it accordingly. Otherwise the front wheel alignment will be affected. Take care not to damage the ball joint rubber boots. The three bolts are tightened to 2.0 kgm (14.5 ft.lb.) during installation and then one half of a turn of a quarter of a turn (45°).
- Remove the steering pump (14) from the front axle carrier (1).
- Detach the rack and pinion steering (3) from the front axle carrier. The bolts securing the steering are inserted from the front and are tightened to 4.5 kgm (32.5 ft.lb.) and then a further 60°.

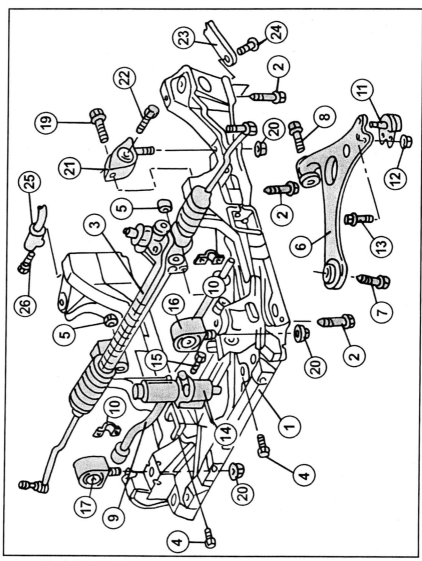

Fig. 5.10 – Details for the removal and installation of the front axle carrier.

- In the case of a diesel engine remove the charge air cooler as described in the relevant section (Diesel Fuel Injection).
- Place a jack with suitable supports underneath the transmission and carefully lift the transmission until just under tension.
- Remove the engine mounts (16) and (17) at the front from the axle carrier. Tighten the nut with a washer to 5.5 kgm (40 ft.lb.) during installation.

104

Legend – Fig. 5.10

1 Front axle carrier	10 Clip	19 Bolt, rear engine mount
2 Torx-head bolt in front axle carrier	11 Support joint	20 Nut, engine mount
3 Rack and pinion steering	12 Self-locking nut	21 L.H. rear engine mount
4 Bolt	13 Bolt to arm	22 Bolt, engine mount
5 Nut	14 Power steering pump	23 Support strut
6 Lower suspension arm (wishbone)	15 Bolt, steering pump	24 Allen-head bolt
7 Front Torx-head bolt, wishbone	16 R.H. front engine mount	25 Bracket, A/C line
8 Rear Torx-head bolt, wishbone	17 L.H. front engine mount	26 Bolt
9 Stabiliser (anti-roll) bar		

- Remove the engine mounts (18) and (21) at the rear from the front axle carrier (1). During installation tighten the bolts (19) and (22) to 5.5 kgm (40 ft.lb.).
- Remove the bracket of the climate cable (25) at the R.H. rear from the axle carrier (1), if an A/C system is fitted. To free the cable unscrew bolt (16).
- Remove the front axle carrier (1) from the body and lower it carefully to the ground. During installation ensure that the guide pins on the front axle carrier engage with the centering holes in the body. The M12 bolts (2) are tightened to 12.0 kgm (86.5 ft.lb.).
- Disconnect the suspension arm (6) from the front axle carrier. Once more, note that the mounting bolts are of different length. Mark the accordingly. The securing nuts must be replaced.

Note: In accordance with advise by Mercedes-Benz we have to point it out:: The nuts securing the suspension arms to the front axle carrier must be replaced as follows each time the bolted connection has been separated. Fig. 5.11 shows details:

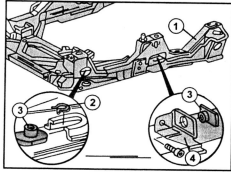

Fig. 5.11 – details for the replacement of the nuts securing the front suspension arms in the front axle carrier.
1 Front axle carrier
2 Retaining clip
3 Nut in guide
4 Bracket (rear suspension arm)

Nut, suspension arm, front to front axle carrier

- Remove the retaining clip (2) for the front nut. To remove the clip press the front end of the clip together and pull it out towards the front.
- Remove the nut (3) from the guide.
- Install in the reverse order.

Nut, suspension arm, rear to front axle carrier

- Remove the bolt from the bracket (4), take off the bracket and remove the nut (3).
- Install the new nut in reverse order.

5.9.   Front Suspension – Tightening Torques

Suspension arm to front axle carrier:...10.5 kgm (75.5 ft.lb.)
Suspension ball joint plate to steering knuckle: ....2.0 kgm (14.5 ft.lb.) + 45°

Spring strut to body: ....4.0 kgm (29 ft.lb.)
Piston rod nut (spring strut): ....6.0 kgm (43.5 ft.lb.)
Stabiliser bar connecting linkage:
- to 25.8. 2002 (nut): ....4.5 kgm (32.5 ft.lb.)
- after 25.8. 2002 (nut): ....6.0 kgm (43 ft.lb.)
Stabiliser bar to crossmember: ....2.8 kgm (20 ft.lb.)
Support strut to front axle carrier: ....6.0 kgm (43.5 ft.lb.)
Drive shaft nuts: ....20.0 kgm + 90° (144 ft.lb.) + 90°
Wheel speed sensor to steering knuckle: ....0.8 kgm (6.5 ft.lb.)
Track rod ball joint nut to steering lever: ....3.0 kgm + 90° (22 ft.lb.) + 90°
Spring strut to steering knuckle, top and bottom: ....10.0 kgm (72 ft.lb.)
Front axle carrier to body: ....12.0 kgm (86.5 ft.lb.)
Wheel bolts: ....11.0 kgm (80 ft.lb.)
Steering mounting bolts: .... 4.5 kgm + 60° (32.5 ft.lb. + 90°)

---

6   Rear Axle and Rear Suspension

6.0.   Short Description

The rear suspension consists of a steel axle tube with welded longitudinal control arms, coil springs and gas-filled shock absorbers. A stabiliser bar is fitted in front of the axle tube. The shock absorbers are fitted separately in front of the coil springs, but the spring must be removed in order to remove a shock absorber.

The rear suspension and the rear axle is maintenance-free. Brake drums are fitted to most models. Only Vaneo models and the A190 petrol version is fitted with disc brakes at the front and rear.

We would like to point out that a modified rear axle is fitted after the 19. Of February 2001 which will, however, not affect most of the operations described.

Note: The wheel bolts are tightened to 11.0 kgm (80 ft.lb.). This is not always mentioned during the following instructions.

The following operations cover the work most likely to be necessary. Although the complete axle can be removed on its own, it will not be considered as one of the major tasks.

6.1.   Rear Coil Springs – Removal and Installation

Fig. 6.1 shows details of the fitted coil spring and the associated parts on one side. The following operations should be carried out by referring to this illustration. The removal of a spring requires, as for the front springs, a spring compressor or suitable compressor hooks. Proceed as follows:

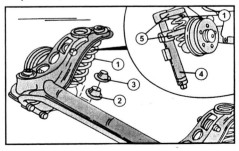

Fig. 6.1 – Details for the removal and installation of a rear spring. Shown is the special spring compressor as used in a workshop. A compressor as shown in Fig. 5.2 can also be used.

1   Rear spring
2   Rubber boot
3   Buffer stop
4   Spring compressor
5   Compressor claws

• Place the rear end of the vehicle on chassis stands and remove the wheel to have better access to the individual parts (not absolutely necessary).

- Attach the spring compressor (4) as shown in the illustration to the spring. There must be at least 3 coils between the claws (5) of the spring compressor. Make sure they are securely fastened. Keep the fingers away from this area. Also make sure that the compressor is strong enough to take the pressure.
- Slowly compress the spring (1) until it is free of the upper and lower spring seats and can be removed together with the compressor. If necessary remove the buffer stop (3) and the rubber boot (2) from the longitudinal control arm. Immediately check the two parts for wear or damage and replace as necessary. Note that the parts are not fitted to all models.

The installation is a reversal of the removal procedure. If a new spring is fitted, compress it with the spring compressor until it will fit between the upper and lower spring seats. Again make sure that at least 3 coils are gripped with the compressor. Insert the spring, make sure it is correctly located and slowly release the compressor, continuously checking the spring is in its seats. Refit the wheel if it has been removed and lower the vehicle to the ground.

6.2.   Shock Absorbers – Removal and Installation

The attachment of a shock absorber can be seen in Fig. 6.2. The shock absorber is attached at its upper end with a bolt and a nut, but bolt and nut have been changed in line with the modified rear axle mentioned in the introduction, as a flanged bolts and a flanged nut are now used. This also involved the alteration of the tightening torque as given during the installation. The lower shock absorber mounting, also with a nut and bolt has remained unchanged. To make things more complicated it is also possible that some vehicles after the specified date of manufacture are still fitted with the earlier nut and bolt. A shock absorber (damper) is removed as follows:

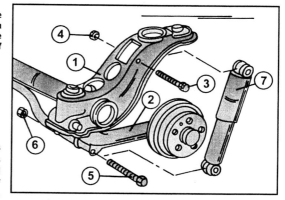

Fig. 6.2 – Details for the removal and installation of a rear shock absorber. Note the different tightening torques of bolt (3) and nut (4).

1   Rear axle carrier
2   Trailing arm
3   Upper damper bolt
4   Nut
5   Lower damper bolt
6   Nut
7   Shock absorber

- Slacken the wheel bolts as long as the wheels are on the ground and jack up the rear end of the vehicle. Mark the wheel position on the wheel hub flange with paint and remove the wheel.
- Remove part of the rear wing lining without removing it fully. Fig. 6.3 shows details of the removal. Remove the three clips (3), undo the two collar nuts (2) and remove the wing liner (1)
- Remove the rear spring as described earlier on..
- Detach the shock absorber (5) in Fig. 6.2 from its lower attachment on the longitudinal control arm, i.e. the trailing arm (2) and from its upper attachment from the rear axle carrier (1). To slacken the upper nut prevent the bolt from

rotating by applying an open-ended spanner to the bolt head on the other side. Note that the bolt head size of the upper and lower bolt is not the same.
- Remove the shock absorber.

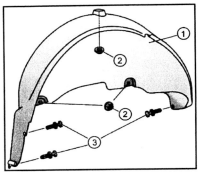

Fig. 6.3 – Attachment of the rear wing liner inside the wing.
1   Liner
2   Collar nuts
3   Securing clips

- Check the shock absorber for re-use as described for the front dampers.

The installation is a reversal of the removal procedure, but the following points must be noted when the mounting bolts and nuts are tightened:

- The bolt head of the upper mounting bolt (or the nut) must again be prevented from rotating with the open-ended spanner. In the case of vehicles before the 18. February 2001 tighten the nut to 4.0 kgm (29 ft.lb.) and from the final position a further 90° (quarter of a turn). After this date (with flanged nut and bolt) tighten the nut t 4.5 kgm (32.5 ft.lb.) and again by a further 90°.
- In the case of all models tighten the lower nut and bolt to 8.0 kgm (58 ft.lb.) and from the final torque setting a further 90°.
- Fit the wing liner in Fig. 6.3. Finally fit the rear wheel (if removed), lower the vehicle to the ground and tighten the wheel bolts.

6.3.   Trailing Arms – Removal and Installation

Fig. 6.4 shows the attachment of a trailing arm to the rear axle carrier. Removal and installation is carried out by following the numbers in the illustration. All self-locking nuts and bolts must be replaced as indicated. Differences must be noted when disc brakes are fitted. The illustration shows the version with drum brakes.

- Remove the centre and the rear underbody panelling as described earlier on in the manual.
- Remove the rear spring as described earlier on, i.e. the rear of the vehicle will be on chassis stands.
- Release the handbrake cable as described in section "Brake System".
- Disconnect the R.H. rear handbrake cable (11) from the brake adjuster (18) or the L.H. rear handbrake cable (12) at the front handbrake cable (12), depending on the side of the vehicle.
- Remove the inner wing panel liner in the lower area of the rear wing as described during the removal of the shock absorber (see also Fig. 6.3). Push the liner to one side until the bracket (13) can be reached.
- Detach the R.H. rear handbrake cable (11) or the L.H. rear cable (12) from the brackets (13) on the frame floor.
- Unscrew the bolt (17) and detach the L.H. rear wheel speed sensor (20) from the rear axle carrier (1). Tighten the bolt (17) during installation to 0.8 kgm. The electrical lead (19) must be detached from the tensioner (18). The cable straps must be replaced during installation.

108

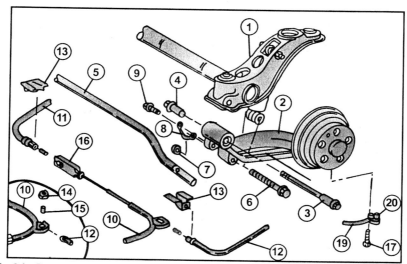

Fig. 6.4 – Removal and installation of a trailing arm together with the brake drum or with the brake disc in the case of the A190 and Vaneo models.

1 Rear axle carrier
2 Trailing arm
3 Bolt, trailing arm mounting, 14 kgm
4 Threaded bush, trailing arm mounting
5 Rear stabiliser bar
6 Bolt, stabiliser bar mounting
7 Nut, 7.0 kgm
8 Spacer plate
9 Bolt
10 Front handbrake cable

11 Rear, R.H. handbrake cable
12 Rear, L.H. handbrake cable
13 Bracket, handbrake cables
14 Securing clip
15 Securing pin
16 Handbrake adjuster
17 Bolt, wheel speed sensor
18 Tensioner
19 Electric lead
20 Wheel speed sensor

- Detach the L.H. rear handbrake cable (11) or the L.H. rear handbrake cable (12) from the trailing arm (2) and the tensioner (18). Again the securing straps must be replaced during installation.
- Remove the cap above the brake line, detach the brake line from the brake hose and unclip the connection from the bracket.
- Remove the rear torsion bar (5), i.e. the stabiliser bar, from the trailing arm (2).
- Detach the rear shock absorber from the trailing arm (2) and remove the trailing arm together with the drum brake or the disc brake.

The installation is a reversal of the removal procedure. Before installation check the mountings in the trailing arm. The trailing arms are mounted with two angular ball bearings which can be replaced without using many special tools.

Fit the stabiliser bar with the spacer plate (8) and the nut (7) and tighten the nut to 7.0 kgm (50.5 ft.lb.). From the final position tighten the nut a further quarter of a turn. The trailing arm is secured with the bolt (3) and the threaded bush (4). The threaded bush (4) is tightened to 14.0 kgm (101 ft.lb.) and then angle-tightened by a quarter of a turn. Tighten the brake pipe-to-brake hose connection to 1.4 kgm (10 ft.lb.) and the lower shock absorber mounting to 8.0 kgm (58 ft.lb.) and a quarter of a turn.

6.4.   Trailing Arm Bearings – Replacement

Fig. 6.5 shows the details of the trailing arm mountings, but it must be noted that the sealing of the trailing arm bearing has been changed from serial number 515390. In the new version a sealing ring is integrated in the bearing shell, providing additional sealing. Only the new version is available as spare part. Fig. 6.6 shows the difference between the old type (view A) and the new type (view B). To replace the bearing remove the trailing arm with the fitted brake assembly (drum brake or disc brake) and proceed as described. The instructions refer to Fig. 6.5:

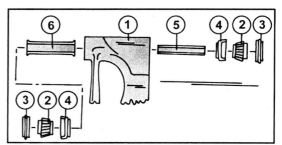

Fig. 6.5 – Details for the replacement of the taper roller bearings in a trailing arm. Seal (3) and (4) have been modified – Attention.
1   Trailing arm
2   Taper roller bearings
3   Seal, old type
4   Outer bearing race
5   Spacer sleeve
6   Plastic sleeve

• Remove the spacer sleeve (5). Immediately clean it and check it for damage. Replace the sleeve if worn or damaged.

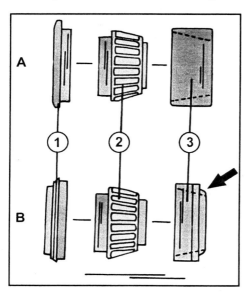

Fig. 6.6 – View of the outer seal (1) for the taper roller bearing (2) and the integrated seal (3) before the modification. In view "A" and after the modification in view "B".

• Remove the angular roller bearing (2) together with the sealing ring (3). A two-arm puller is required to withdraw the bearing, the claws of which are placed underneath the bearing race as can be seen in the L.H. view of Fig. 6.7. After removal of the bearing withdraw the plastic sleeve. Clean the sleeve thoroughly and replace if damaged. The opposite bearing (2) is removed in the same manner.

Install the new parts (view B, Fig. 6.6) as follows:

• Coat the two bearings (2) with 5 grams of bearing grease per bearing and using a suitable drift drive the bearing to its stop into the trailing arm. Fit the spacer sleeve (5). Fit the bearing on the other side in the same manner.

• Install the sealing rings (3) in the same manner with a suitable drift as can be seen in the R.H. view of Fig. 6.7 until it contacts the trailing arm. Make sure the sealing ring is driven in straight.

110

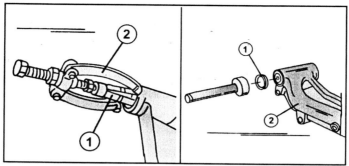

Fig. 6.7 – The L.H. view shows the removal of a taper roller bearing from the trailing arm. The centre piece (1) grips the bearing, the claws (2) rest against the trailing arm. The R.H. view shows the installation of the oil seal (1) into the trailing arm (2).

6.5. Rear Axle Flange and Wheel Bearing

6.5.1. REMOVAL AND INSTALLATION

Fig. 6.8 shows details of the removal and installation.

Fig. 6.8 – Details for the removal and installation of the rear wheel hub flange and the wheel bearing. The dimension "X is referred to during installation.

1   Rear axle spigot
2   Rear hub flange
3   12-point nut, 17 kgm
4   Bearing retaining ring
5   Grease cap
6   Taper roller bearing
7   Washer
8   Impact puller, No. 116 589 22 22 00

• Slacken the wheel bolts, place the rear of the vehicle on chassis stands and remove the wheel after marking its position.

• Remove the brake drum or the brake disc as described in section "Brake System".

• Remove the hub grease cap. In the workshop the extractor (8) is used. Otherwise use a suitable impact hammer and adapter. Be careful when removing the cap by inserting a strong screwdriver on opposite sides to pry off the cap. It may have to be replaced.

• Remove the staking from the 12-point nut (3). The nut is tightened to a very high torque. Therefore make sure that the vehicle is securely resting on the chassis stands before the nut is slackened. The nut is tightened to 17.0 kgm (122,5 ft.lb.) and then staked to lock it in position.

- Remove the rear hub flange (2) and the washer (7). If necessary you can use a two-arm puller the claws of which are hooked under the flange with the centre spindle pressing on the axle stump.
- Remove the bearing retaining circlip (4) and remove the angular ball bearing, but only if required.

The installation is a reversal of the removal procedure. If necessary replace the wheel bearing and secure it with a new circlip (4).

Before fitting the wheel hub flange a measurement is necessary. The measurement takes place on the wheel hub spigot (1) and the length "X" is measured from the front face of the contact surface on the spigot. If the length is 62,5 mm, fit a shim (7) of 4 mm in thickness.

The wheel hub flange (2) is fitted together with the washer (7) over the spigot. Fit the nut (3) as described above and stake the nut into the groove of the spigot.

Finally fit the hub grease cap (5) carefully. As already mentioned, replace it if a good fit can no longer be obtained.

6.6.　Rear Wheel Alignment

The alignment of the rear wheels can only be checked in a workshop with electronic equipment. The toe-in setting of the wheels cannot be adjusted. For information only, the setting is 0° 18'. Vaneo models have a different setting (0° 55'), but this has been changed from the original setting of 0° 18' before March 2002.

7　Steering

7.0.　Technical Data

Type	Rack and pinion steering with electric-hydraulic servo assistance, fitted in front of drive shafts to the front axle carrier. Steering ID: All models use the same steering.
Type of fluid used	As in automatic transmissions
Fluid used	MB steering fluid
Fluid capacity:	0.8 litres

The rack and pinion steering cannot be repaired and must be replaced if defect. Otherwise try to obtain an exchange steering unit.

The power-assisted steering is fitted with an electrically operated steering pump at the side of the fluid reservoir and delivers the fluid under high pressure to a control valve in the steering box. The control valve is connected mechanically to the steering spindle and directs the fluid either to the L.H. or R.H. operating cylinder inside the rack and pinion steering housing, depending on the steering lock. The fluid in the steering system is the same as used in automatic transmission.

7.1.　Steering – Removal and Installation

The following must be observed before any operations are carried out on the steering gear or the associated parts:

- All work must be carried out under clean conditions.
- Before disconnecting any of the hoses or pipes clean around the connection and the immediate area.
- All removed parts must be placed on a clean surface, if possible on a clean sheet of paper or cloth and well covered until installation
- Never use fluffy rags to clean parts of the steering system.
- New parts, always original parts, must be removed from their packing just before installation.
- Never used fluid drain from the system to top-up or to fill the reservoir.

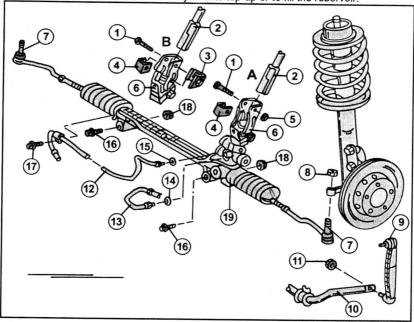

Fig. 7.1 – Details for the removal and installation of the power-assisted steering.

1 Bolt, steering coupling, 2.0 kgm	8 Nut, 3.0 + 90°	15 Sealing ring
2 Steering shaft	9 Stabiliser connecting rod	16 Steering bolt, 4.5 kgm
3 Cage nut	10 Stabiliser bar	17 Bolt
4 Thrust piece	11 Nut	18 Steering mounting nut
5 Coupling clamp nut	12 High pressure pipe	19 Steering gear
6 Steering coupling	13 Low pressure pipe	
7 Track rod ball joint	14 Sealing ring	

Fig. 7.1 shows the attachment of the steering gear together with the parts to be removed. As in the case of many operations near the front axle carrier the engine must be lifted out of its mountings in order to remove the steering. In addition some secondary operations must be carried out, many of which have already been covered or are described on the pages that follow. The operations are valid for petrol and diesel models. Proceed as follows:

- Set the bonnet in vertical position and tie it up.
- Remove the windscreen washer fluid reservoir.

- Place the front wheels and the steering lock in the straight ahead position and turn the ignition key to position "locked".
- Slacken the wheel bolts and place the front end of the vehicle on chassis stands. Mark the positions of both wheels in relation to the front wheel hub flange and remove the wheels. Make sure that the vehicle is well supported on the chassis stands. After the wheels have been removed place one of them in front of the rear wheels – just in case.
- Release and disconnect the engine and vehicle cable harness from the engine control unit. In the case of a petrol engine the plug must be unlocked. During installation insert the plug into the guides, establish the connection and lock.
- Remove the air cleaner as described in the relevant section (Fuel Injection System).
- Raise the engine with suitable lifting equipment until the engine mountings are no longer under tension.
- Detach the power steering pump from the front axle carrier as described later on without disconnecting the hydraulic lines from the pump.
- Remove the bolt (3) in Fig. 7.2 and remove the front engine mount (1). The bolt is tightened to 5.5 kgm (40 ft.lb.).

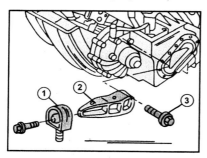

Fig. 7.2 – Parts to be removed during removal of the steering. The numbers are referred to in the text.

- Lower the engine with the lifting equipment until the bolts of the engine support can be reached from the left-hand side of the wheel housing. The engine mount (2) in Fig. 7.2 can now be removed. Tighten the bolt (3) to 5.5 kgm (40 ft.lb.). After installation raise the engine once more to its upper stop without damaging any of the hoses or pipes.

- Remove the bolt (1) securing the steering universal joint (6) to the steering shaft (2) after removal of the nut (5) in the case of the earlier version, indicated by "A" or in the case of the later version, shown by "B", remove the captive nut (3) from the thrust piece (4). In the case of all types observe the installation position of the thrust piece must always be replaced. Tighten the nuts to 2.0 kgm (14.5 ft.lb.).
- Tilt down the universal joint (6) from the steering shaft (2) to separate the parts. During installation the steering must be set to the centre position. The modified universal joint (from June 2000) is detailed near the end of this section.
- Separate the two track rod ball joints from the steering levers as described later on. Take care not to damage the rubber boots. The operation must be carried out on both sides of the vehicle. When re-connecting the ball joints during installation clean the taper of the ball joint studs thoroughly. The nuts (8) are tightened to 3.0 kgm (22 ft.lb.) and from the end position a further quarter of a turn.
- Detach the connecting rods (9) on both sides from the stabiliser bar (10) as described during the removal of the stabiliser bar. The nuts (11) are tightened to 4.5 kgm or 6.0 kgm, depending on the date of manufacture (see section "Front Suspension", "Removal and Installation of Stabiliser Bar).
- To prevent loss of hydraulic fluid during the following operations extract some fluid with a suitable suction tool out of the steering fluid reservoir. Escaping fluid must be collected in a container or wiped off with a suitable cloth.

114

• Remove the retaining bracket for the high pressure line (12) from the steering gear (1) and disconnect the high pressure line and the low pressure line (13) from the steering box. Close the pipe ends in suitable manner to prevent entry of foreign matter and escaping of fluid. The two sealing rings (14) and (15) must be replaced during installation. Tighten the pipe union nuts to 4.0 kgm (29 ft.lb.).

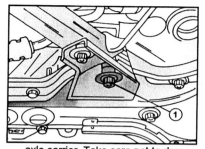

Fig. 7.3 – Remove the bolt (1) at the position shown from the front axle carrier.

• Remove the bolt (1) in Fig. 7.3 at the position shown out of the front axle carrier. The bolt connects the L.H. side of the front axle carrier with the R.H. side of the carrier. This M12 bolts must be tightened to 12.0 kgm (86.5 ft.lb.).

• Remove the bolts (16) securing the steering box (19) after removal of the nuts (18) and lift off the steering from the front axle carrier. Take care not to damage the rubber mounts during removal.

• Remove the rack and pinion steering towards the left. The stabiliser bar must be moved upwards the steering wheel turned into the left-hand lock to facilitate the removal. Take care not to damage the rubber bellows. The steering mounting bolts are tightened to 4.5 kgm (32.5 ft.lb.) and from the final setting must be tightened by a further 60°.

The installation is a reversal of the removal procedure, noting the points already mentioned during the removal instructions. Finally fill the system with fluid and bleed the steering as described later on.

After the vehicle is back on its wheels, start the engine and turn the steering wheel from one lock to the other. Any leaks will be noticed by drops of fluid on the ground immediately underneath the steering area.

7.2. Track Road Ball Joints and Rubber Bellows

Replacing a Track Rod Ball Joint
The front of the vehicle must be resting on chassis stands and the front wheel must be removed. The steering gaiter (rubber bellows) can only be removed after removal of the track rod ball joint.

Fig. 7.4 – Removal and installation of a track rod.

1	Rack and pinion steering
2	Inner track rod
3	Locknut, 5.0 kgm
4	Track rod and with ball joint
5	Self-locking nut, 3.0 kgm + 90°

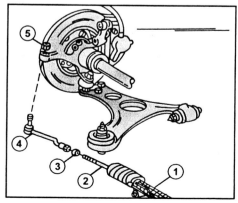

The removal of a track rod ball joints is carried out by referring to Fig. 7.4. Make sure that the vehicle is securely supported.

• Slacken the locknut (3) on the track rod (2).

• Unscrew the self-locking nut (5) and separate the track rod ball joint with a suitable puller as the one shown in Fig. 7.5. Any suitable ball joint puller can, however, be used. The operations must be carried out on both sides of the vehicle if both track rod ball joints/steering rubber gaiters must be replaced. Tighten a new self-locking nut (5) during installation to 3.0 kgm and then a further quarter of a turn.

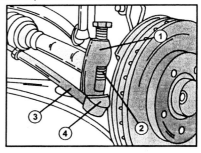

Fig. 7.5 – Separating a track rod ball joint. The puller (1) presses with the spindle (2) against the track rod ball joint. Take care not to damage the rubber dust boot (4) of the track rod (3).

• Unscrew the track rod end (4) from the end of the track rod. Count the exact number of turns (also half turns) until the ball joint end is free. If the track rod end is screwed on by the same number of turns there should be no need to adjust the toe-in setting. It is also possible to mark the track rod end (still fitted) and inner track rod (2) with paint to ensure correct installation. In this case allow the paint to dry.

Replacing a Rubber Gaiter

The replacement of a rubber gaiter is carried out by referring to Fig. 7.6. As already mentioned the track rod must be removed as described above.

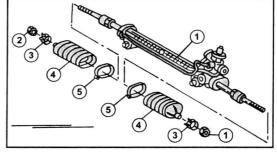

Fig. 7.6 – Removal and installation of the steering rubber gaiters (bellows).
1 Steering unit
2 Outer locknuts
3 Outer clamp (small)
4 Bellows
5 Inner clamp (large)

• Remove the gaiter clamp (4) at the inside of the steering rack (1) and push the clamp as far as possible. On the outside of the track rod remove the small clamp (3) and slide off the gaiter. The clamps should be replaced to ensure proper fitting of the gaiter.

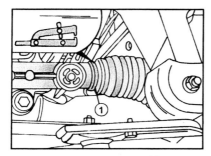

Fig. 7.7 – The steering rubber gaiter (1) at the inner end as shown. A suitable pair of pliers (inset) must be used to tighten the clamp.

• Slide the new gaiter over the track rod and attach it at the inside with the large clamp (5). Make sure the gaiter is not twisted. Fig. 7.7 shows the attachment of the gaiter on the inside. Spring-type clamps must be tightened with a suitable pair of special pliers.
• Screw the track rod end onto the track rod, counting the number of rotations as described above. If a new track rod end is fitted screw it to the approximate position.

116

- Clean the ball joint taper from grease and oil and insert it into the taper bore of the steering lever. Fit a new self-locking nut and tighten it to 3.0 kgm (29 ft.lb.). From the final position tighten the nut a further quarter of a turn. The track rod locknut (3) in Fig. 7.4 is tightened to 5.0 kgm (36 ft.lb.).
- Refit the wheel (observe the markings), lower the vehicle to the ground and tighten the wheel bolts to 11.0 kgm (80 ft.lb.). Check the toe-in setting as described later on or have the setting checked.

7.3.   Track Roads – Removal and Installation

As it is very difficult to reach the track rods, the steering must be removed if the replacement of a track rod is required. The front end of the vehicle on chassis stands, the wheels taken off and the steering removed as already described. Further removal takes place by referring to Fig. 7.8.

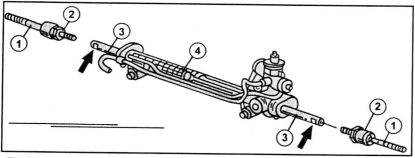

Fig. 7.8 – Removal and installation of a track rod together with the inner ball joint. An open-ended spanner is applied to the flat (arrow) when the ball joint is slackened or tightened.
1 Track rod   2 Inner ball joint, 9-0 kgm   3 Steering rack   4 Steering unit

- Remove the steering bellows as described above on the side in question. Immediately check the ball joint (2) at the inside of the track rod. If corrosion has taken place or the steering is leaking a new steering must be fitted. The following description can therefore be ignored.
- Counterhold the steering rack (3) at the position shown with the arrow with an open-ended spanner and unscrew the inner ball joint with a suitable spanner. Remove the complete track rod.
- Fit the new track rod with the ball joint to the steering rack and tighten it. The workshop uses a special 41 mm wrench, allowing the use of a torque wrench. Otherwise you will have to estimate a torque of 9.0 kgm (65 ft.lb.).
- All other operations are carried out in reverse order. The toe-in setting must be checked, or have it checked, after the work is completed.

7.4.   Checking the Steering Mechanism

The following information will help you to check some parts of the steering system. With the results of the check you will be able to decide to take the necessary measures to correct the fault(s).

Fig. 7.9 – Play in the steering can be checked by moving the steering wheel as shown. If the dimension "a" exceeds 30 mm, you can assume that the steering gear is worn.

Checking the free play of the steering: Start the engine and set the front wheels to the straight-ahead position. Grip the steering wheel on the rim and move it to and fro

117

as shown in Fig. 7.9. If the free play is more than 30 mm (approx. 1 inch), you can check the moving parts of the steering for wear or excessive play. If the play is in the actual steering, you will have to fit a new steering, as steering are no longer repaired.

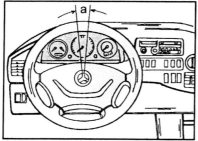

Fig. 7.9 – Play in the steering can be checked by moving the steering wheel as shown. If the dimension "a" exceeds 30 mm, you can assume that the steering gear is worn.

Checking the track rod ball joints and the steering rubber gaiters: With the wheel fitted and from underneath the vehicle grip the ball joint (1) in Fig. 7.10 and move it up and down. A worn ball joint can be detected by an up and down movement of more than 2.0 mm. The rubber dust caps must have no cuts. Dust caps cannot be replaced individually, i.e. a new ball joint is due.

Fig. 7.10 – View of a fitted track rod. The track rod ball joint (1) and the steering gaiter (2) must be checked.

Check the steering gaiters (2) in Fig. 7.10 over their entire length and circumference for cuts or other damage. Mainly the underside of the gaiters can get damaged. Make sure that the gaiter is securely attached to the track rod ball joint and the steering box. Gaiters can be replaced as already described during the replacement of the ball joints.

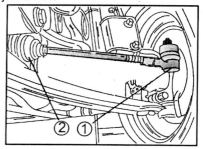

7.5. Operations on the hydraulic System
7.5.0. FILLING THE HYDRAULIC SYSTEM

After the installation of the steering or after draining the system, it must be filled with the fluid recommended by Mercedes-Benz (0.8. litre) and bled in accordance with the instructions below. Fluid drained during removal operations must not be re-used.

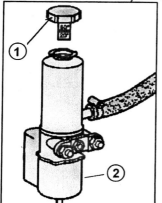

Fig. 7.11 – The steering pump together with the fluid reservoir. The cap (1) has a dipstick with the temperature marking.

Remove the filler cap (1) in Fig. 7.11 from the fluid reservoir. The reservoir is correctly filled, i.e. the fluid level is correct, when the fluid level is approx. 10 mm below the upper edge of the reservoir. The cap has a dipstick with a temperature marking and the exact fluid level will be shown in cold and hot condition.

Check the filler cap seal before refitting it. The fluid level in the reservoir should be checked during each engine oil change. Take care that no foreign matter can enter the fluid reservoir.

7.5.1.   BLEEDING THE HYDRAULIC SYSTEM

After the fluid level in the reservoir remains steady after the engine has been started, turn the steering wheel several times from one lock to the other to expel the air. Ask a helper to observe the fluid level during this operation. If necessary correct the fluid level to keep it on the "Max" mark. No air bubbles must be visible when the steering wheel is turned as described above.

7.5.2.   CHECKING THE STEERING SYSTEM FOR LEAKS

Sometimes fluid can drain from the steering system which may be difficult to trace. Check as follows:

- Ask a helper to turn the steering wheel from one lock to the other until its stop and keep it there for a short moment. This will develop the maximum pressure and any fluid can escape, if leak has developed.
- From underneath the vehicle check the area around the steering pinion, slacken the steering gaiters at the track rod ends and the ends of the gaiters near the rack and pinion housing. Also check all hose connections. Moist areas point to leaks.

7.6.   Steering Pump – Removal and Installation

Fig. 7.12 shows the attachment of the steering pump. The pump can be removed without lowering or removing the front axle carrier. The air pump of a petrol engine must be removed to remove the steering pump. The following operations include petrol engines. Ignore the instructions if a diesel engine is fitted.

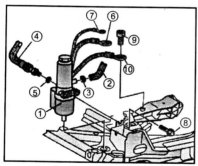

Fig. 7.12 – Removal and installation of the steering pump.

1	Steering pump
2	Return hose
3	Hose clamp
4	High pressure pipe
5	Sealing ring
6	Cable to terminal 30
7	Cable to terminal 61
8	Bolt
9	Hexagonal had bolt
10	Earth cable to terminal 31

Removal and Installation of the Air Injection Pump (petrol engine)
The pump is fitted at the front of the engine compartment behind the headlamp, seen in the direction of drive. Remove as follows:

- In the case of a vehicle with heated reservoir for the windscreen washer system drain the cooling system, in the case of all models remove the reservoir for the washer system.
- Disconnect a hose from the pump and remove a plug connector at the rear.
- Slacken two collar nuts by approx. 2 turns and remove the pump in an upwards direction.

The installation is a reversal of the removal procedure.
The steering pump can now be removed irrespective of the engine:

- Remove the reservoir cap (1) in Fig. 7.11 and extract the fluid with a suitable suction tool. Take care not to drip fluid onto painted surfaces. Fig. 2.8 shows a suitable suction tool. Press together the rubber ball, insert the end into the fluid, and release the rubber ball. Empty the fluid in the suction tool into a container and remove any remaining fluid.

- Remove the return hose (2) from the pump (1). The hose clamp (3) must be replaced.
- Disconnect the high pressure pipe (4) from the pump. Close the end of the pipe in suitable manner (sticky tape) to prevent entry of dirt. The sealing (5) must be replaced during installation. The hose end is tightened to 3.5 kgm (25 ft.lb.).
- Disconnect the earth cable (10) after removal of the bolt (9) from the engine mount.

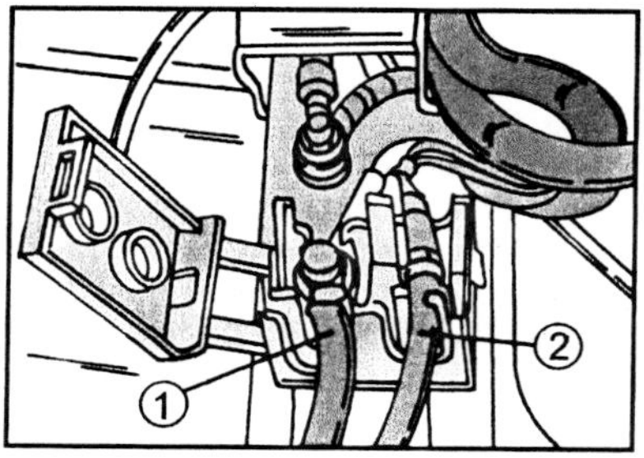

Fig. 7.13 – Disconnect the cables (1) and (2) at the positions shown. In Fig. 7.12 the cables are identified with (6) and (7) respectively.

- On the L.H. side member disconnect the two pipes shown. These are a positive power cable to terminal 30 (1) and a control cable (2) in Fig. 7.13. The cover must be opened as shown.
- Unscrew the power steering pump (1) from the front axle carrier. Immediately check the condition of the rubber mounting and replace if necessary. During installation make sure that the mounting spigot of the pump engages properly into the rubber mounting in the front axle carrier.

The installation is a reversal of the removal procedure, noting the points given above. After installation fill and bleed the steering system as described.

7.7.   Steering Universal Joint – Removal and Installation

Two different steering universal joints, also known as steering coupling, have been used during production. The earlier type fitted to the end of May 2000 is shown in Fig. 7.14 and is more difficult to remove.

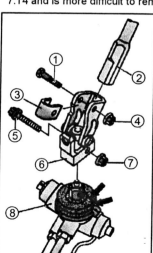

Fig. 7.14 – Details of the steering universal joint as fitted to end of May 2000.

1   Bolt
2   Steering shaft
3   Thrust piece
4   Nut, 2.0 kgm
5   Bolt
6   Steering coupling
7   Nut. 2.0 kgm
8   Rack and pinion steering

The later version is mentioned below. To remove the joint proceed as follows. Note that the self-locking nuts shown in the illustration must be replaced during installation:

- Set the front wheels and the steering wheel into the straight-ahead position and engage the steering lock. The markings on the cover cap and the rack and pinion steering shown by the two arrows must be in line. Also see Fig. 7.17 which shows an enlarged view.
- Unscrew the bolt (1) from the steering coupling

(6) on the steering shaft (2) and remove the thrust piece (3). During installation the thrust piece (3) must lie on the flattened area on the steering shaft.

- Swing the steering coupling downwards and separate it from the steering shaft.
- Undo the steering coupling (5) from the steering (8). During installation position the steering coupling (8) so that the bolt (5) can be inserted without force.

Fig. 7.15 – View of the steering with the modified steering coupling fitted from June 2000. The arrows shows the locking device mentioned below.

Modified Steering Coupling

The modified steering coupling has been fitted from approximately from June 2000 onwards. The major difference is that the joint can be fitted directly onto the teeth of the steering shaft at the bottom of the rack and pinion steering. The clamping bush on the steering shaft is no longer needed as the cover on the control valve housing is provided with a locking device, as shown in Fig. 7.15 with the arrow.

7.8.   Front Wheel Alignment

The front wheel alignment can only be measured with optical equipment. We therefore must recommend to have the alignment checked at a dealer or in a workshop dealing with Mercedes-Benz vehicles, if there is a possibility that something is not right with the setting.

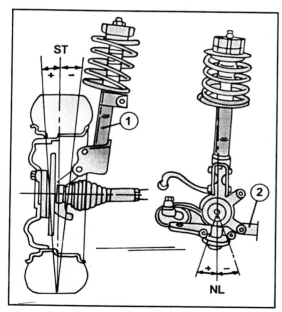

Fig. 7.17 – Diagram of the camber adjustment in the L.H. view and the castor adjustment in the R.H. view.
1   Spring strut
2   Lower suspension arm

Caster setting

The castor is adjusted at the support plate for the lower suspension ball joint. For this reason it has been pointed out several times in section "Front Suspension" that the outline of the plate must be marked on the steering knuckle if it is removed for any reason. After removal of the plate you will see that the outer holes can be set to two positions. By using one or the other hole the workshop will adjust the castor setting after the alignment has been checked. The castor angle is given in degrees (°) and minutes ('). The castor angle is set top 2° 11' plug or minus 20' in the case of all models. The R.H. view of Fig. 7.16 shows a diagram of the castor angle.

Camber Setting

The camber is determined by the attachment of the steering knuckle to the spring strut. As already mentioned during the removal of a spring strut in section "Front Suspension" the bolts securing the spring strut to the steering knuckle must be marked in their fitted position before they are removed. The workshop will move the spring strut sideways to obtain the necessary camber angle. The camber angle is negative and is set to –0° 59' (near 1°) plus or minus 30'. The L.H. view of Fig. 7.16 shows a diagram of the camber angle.

Toe-in

Toe-in is the difference in the distance between the front of the front wheels and the rear of the front wheels, measured at the wheel rims and in the height of the wheel hubs, when the front wheels are in the straight-ahead position. The toe-in is measured in degrees, but the following instructions will enable you to adjust the wheels correctly, if measured in millimetres. The dimension should be 0.5 mm with a tolerance of plus or minus 1 mm.

Excessive toe-in of the front wheels can be recognised on wear on the outside of the tyres. Wear on the inside of the tyres points to excessive toe-out, also called negative toe-in.

The toe-in can only be checked properly with the correct equipment, i.e. a good tracking gauge must be available. The adjustments is carried out by rotating the track rod (2) in Fig. 7.17 after slackening the locknut (1).

Fig. 7.17 – The locknut (1) on the track rod ball joint must be slackened before the track rod tube can be rotated. Take care not to twist the steering gaiter.

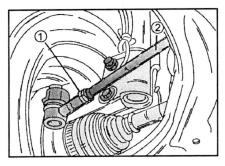

- Turn the steering into the centre position. To do this, set the front wheels to the straight-ahead position and check underneath the steering universal joint (coupling) that the marks in the cap underneath the coupling (1) and the control housing (2) are in line as shown in Fig. 7.18.

Fig. 7.18 – When the steering is in the centre position, the marks on the steering coupling (1) and the steering (2) must be aligned at the points shown by the arrows.

- Place the tracking gauge against the front of the wheel rims, in height with the wheel hubs and set the gauge to zero. Mark the points where the gauge is applied with chalk.
- Push the vehicle forward by half a turn of the wheels until the two points marked with chalk are at the rear of the wheels, again at the same height as the hubs. Apply the tracking gauge to the rear of the wheel rims and read off the value. This should be within the values given above. If this is the case, there is no need to carry out any adjustments.

122

- If the setting is outside the value given, adjust the toe-in by altering the length of the track rods after slackening of the track rod clamps. Before tightening of the track rods, push both track rod ball joints against their stops. After tightening the clamps check that both track rod ball joints can be moved to and fro.
- Re-check the toe-in setting as described above and tighten the clamps. We suggest, however, that you have the toe-in checked professionally at an early opportunity.

7.9. Steering – Tightening Torques

Bolt for universal joint to steering and steering shaft: ....2.0 kgm (24 - 25 ft.lb.)
High pressure hose to steering box: ....4.0 kgm (29 ft.lb.)
Low pressure hose to steering box: ....4.0 kgm (29 ft.lb.)
Steering mounting bolts to front axle carrier:.........................4.5 kgm (32.5 ft.lb.) + 60°
L.H. front axle carrier bolt to R.H. front axle carrier:.....................12.0 kgm (86.5 ft.lb.)
Engine mounts/engine supports: ....5.5 kgm (40 ft.lb.)
Front engine support to transmission: ....5.5 kgm (40 ft.lb.)
Engine carrier to engine mount:..5.5 kgm (40 ft.lb.)
Nuts, connecting rod to stabiliser bar:
- Up to 28.8. 2002:..4.5 kgm (32.5 ft.lb.)
- From 1.3 2002:...6.0 kgm (43 ft.lb.)
Track rod ball joints to steering knuckle: ....3.0 kgm (22 ft.lb.) + 90°
Track rod locknuts: ....5.0 kgm (36 ft.lb.)
Inner track rod ball joint to steering rack:...9.0 kgm (65 ft.lb.)
Wheel bolts: ....11 kgm (80 ft.lb.)

8 Brake System

8.1. Technical Data

Type of system: ....See description below
Caliper type, front and rear: ....Sliding caliper, one piston
Piston diameter of front calipers: ....54 or 57 mm
Thickness of brake pads (without metal plate):
- Models A140, A160 CDI: .... 10.0 mm
- Models A160, A170 CDI, A140 L, A160 L:... 10.0 mm
- Models A190, A190 L:.. 10.0 mm
- Vaneo models: .... 14.0 mm
Min. thickness of brake pad linings:
- Except Vaneo: ....2.0 mm
- Vaneo: ....3.0 mm

Diameter of Brake Discs:
- Models A140, A160 CDI: .... 260.0 mm (solid material)
- Models A170 CDI, A140 L, A160, A160 L:................................ 260.0 mm (ventilated)
- Models A190, A190 L:.. 276.0 mm (ventilated)

Thickness of Brake Discs:
- Models A140, A160 CDI: .... 12.0 mm
- Models A170 CDI, A140 L, A160, A160 L:.. 22.0 mm
- Models A190, A190 L:... 22.0 mm

- Vaneo models: .... 22.0 mm

Min. permissible thickness of brake discs:
- Models A140, A160 CDI: .... 10.0 mm
- Models A170 CDI, A140 L, A160, A160 L: .... 19.4 mm
- Models A190, A190 L: .... 19.4 mm
- Vaneo models: .... 19.4 mm
Max. run-out of brake discs: .... 0.10 mm
Wear limit of brake discs, per side: .... max.0.05 mm

Rear Drum Brakes
Inner diameter of brake drums: .... 180.0 – 180.2 mm
Max. Diameter of brake drums: .... 181.2 mm
Thickness of brake linings, new: .... 4.5 mm
Min. thickness of brake linings: .... 1.5 mm

Rear Disc Brakes (A190, A190 L, A 160 L, Vaneo)
Diameter of brake caliper piston:
- Models A190, A190 L, A160 L: .... 28.0 mm
- Vaneo models: .... 30.0 mm
Brake disc diameter, all models: .... 258.0 mm
Brake disc thickness: .... 8.0 mm
Min. brake disc thickness: .... 7.0 mm
Brake pad material thickness without metal plate, new: .... 9.0 mm
Min. permissible brake pad material thickness without metal plate: .... 2.0 mm

8.1.   Short Description

The following description covers petrol and diesel models and the Vaneo version. All models covered in this manual are fitted with a hydraulic dual-circuit brake with vacuum-operated brake servo unit. The brake servo unit is supplied with vacuum from a separate exhauster pump in the case of a diesel model or from the inlet manifold in the case of a petrol model.

Sliding brake calipers with one piston are used for the front wheels. The brake discs are either made of solid material, for example A140 and A160 CDI models or are ventilated, all other A-Class and Vaneo models. A190 and A190 L models and Vaneo models have disc brakes with sliding calipers on the rear wheels. The brake discs on the rear wheels are made of solid material.

The brake system is diagonally split, i.e. one circuit serves one of the front brake calipers and the diagonally opposed rear brake caliper. The other circuit operates the other two brake assemblies accordingly. If one brake circuits fails, the brakes will operate as normal, but more brake force will be required.

Depending on the model, ABS, an anti-slip mechanism (ASR) or an electronic stability program (ESP) can be fitted to your vehicle. Some models are also fitted with a so-called brake assist system (BAS). It is not the purpose of this manual to refer to the function of each system mentioned, as you will be able to read about it in your Owners Manual or any sales brochures you may have received with the car or van.

8.2   Front Disc Brakes

As already mentioned, sliding brake calipers with one piston are fitted to the front wheels. The assemblies consist of a caliper mounting bracket bolted rigidly to the front axle steering knuckle and a separate caliper cylinder. When the brake is operated, the piston pressed first with its brake pad against the brake disc. The caliper cylinder then slides on glide bolts and moves against the direction of the pressure, until the other brake pad is pressed against the brake disc on the other side. Only the caliper cylinder must be removed to replace the brake pads, the mounting bracket remains on the steering knuckle.

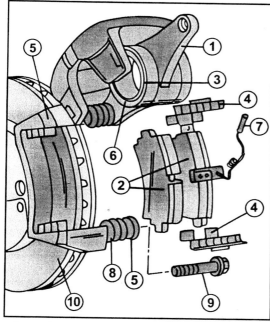

Fig. 8.1 – Details for the removal and installation of a front brake caliper.
1 Brake caliper
2 Brake pads
3 Piston
4 Retaining spring
5 Guide bolt
6 Rubber dust boot
7 Front brake pad wear sensor
8 Rubber dust boot
9 Bolt, 3.0 kgm

8.3.0. BRAKE PAD REPLACEMENT

If the remaining brake pad material thickness is less then 2.5 mm, a warning light will light up in the dashboard, indicating that the brake pads must be replaced. The thickness of the brake pad linings can also be checked through the openings in the brake caliper after the wheels have been removed. Fig. 8.1 shows the parts belonging to the brake pads. Refer to the illustration during the following instructions, if you are not familiar with this type of arrangement. If the brake pads are to be refitted mark their position before removal, including if they have been removed from the left-hand or right-hand side. Proceed as follows:

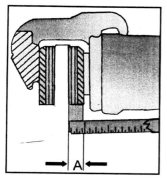

Fig. 8.2 – The thickness of brake pads can be measured with a ruler as shown. In this case the pad thickness is measured together with the metal backing plate.

• Operate the brake pedal a few times to clear the system of vacuum.

• Remove the fluid reservoir cap.

• Slacken the wheel bolts and place the front end of the vehicle on chassis stands. Mark the fitted position of the wheels in relation to the front hub flange and remove the two wheels.

• The thickness of the brake pad material can now be measured. This can best be carrier out with a caliper or with a ruler as shown in Fig. 8.2. If less than 2.0 mm replace the brake pads as a set.

Fig. 8.3 – Disconnecting the plug connector from the brake pad wear sensor (1) on one of the brake pads.

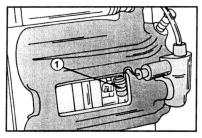

- Remove the electrical cable from the front brake sensor (7), i.e. the plug connector is pushed away as shown in Fig. 8.3. and then remove it from the connection. Under no circumstances pull just on the cable.

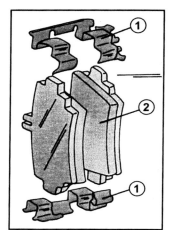

Fig. 8.4 – Brake pad set (2) together with the retaining springs (1).

- Unscrew the bolt (9) from the lower guide pin (5) and carefully tilt the brake caliper (1) slowly upwards. If the caliper is very tight, slacken the upper bolt (5) The caliper is not removed completely. Use a piece of wire and tie up the caliper in the raised position to prevent it from dropping down.

- Remove the two brake pads with the retaining springs (4) from the side of the brake caliper. The second brake pad may remain on the brake caliper mounting bracket and must be removed from the side of the disc. The removed brake pads and the two retaining springs, as removed, are shown in Fig. 8.4. Immediately check the condition of the retaining springs (1) and replace them if necessary.

Fig. 8.5 – Measuring the thickness of brake discs.

If the brake pad material has worn to a thickness of 2.5 mm, fit a new set of pads. Although the min. permissible material thickness is considered to be 2.0 mm, you will find that the brake pad wear indicator warning light will light up, when the thickness has been reduced to 2.5 mm. Never replace one brake pad only, even though if the other one appears to be in good condition.

If brake pads have worn more than expected, there is a possibility that the piston(s) have seized inside the bores. In this case it may be necessary to have the brake calipers overhauled, as we do not recommend the overhaul of the brake calipers for reasons of safety.. The same applies if the rubber dust boots on the cylinder housing are damaged.

Check the brake disc faces and clean them thoroughly before new pads are fitted. If possible have measure the brake disc thickness as shown in Fig. 8.5 and compare the result with the dimensions given below. The minimum thickness for solid brake discs must still be 10.0 mm or for ventilated discs 19.4 mm. If the min. thickness has been reached, replace the disc(s). Disc with uneven faces can perhaps be re-faced. Check with a MB workshop.

126

Fig. 8.6 – Piston reset pliers fitted to the caliper cylinder. Push the piston to the bottom of the bore. A piece of wood can also be used.

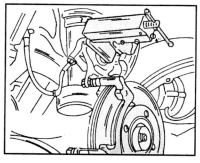

Refit the brake pads as follows:

- Clean the contact areas for the brake pads inside the caliper housing.

- Remove some brake fluid from the fluid reservoir, if it is fairly full, to prevent fluid overflow during the next operation. You will have the push the piston into the caliper bore, to fit the new brake pads. Normally a special pair of pliers is used, which is employed in the manner shown in Fig. 8.6.

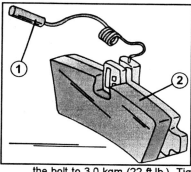

Fig. 8.7 – The cable for the brake pad wear indicator (1) is inserted into the brake pad (2) as shown.

- Fit the brake pad with the retaining spring (1) in Fig. 8.4 into the caliper.

- On the other brake pad withdraw the sensor for the brake pad wear out of the groove in the pad, shown in Fig. 8.7 and insert it into the new pad. Then insert the pad into the caliper.

- Place the cylinder caliper (1) carefully over the brake pads and lower it until the bolt (9) can be screwed into the slide bolt. Tighten the bolt to 3.0 kgm (22 ft.lb.). Tighten the upper bolt to the same torque if it has been slackened.

- Roll the brake pad wear indicator cable (7) to a spiral and connect to the connector spade terminal of the brake pad.

- Operate the brake pedal a few times to set the brake pads against the brake disc.

- Check the fluid level in the fluid reservoir and correct if necessary. Finally fit the wheels and tighten the wheel bolts to the correct torque setting.

- Treat the new brake pads with care during the first 100 miles or so, remember that the new material must "bed in" before they reach their full performance. To speed up the process, brake the vehicle several times from a speed of approx. 50 mph to 25 mph. Allow the brakes to cool between each braking operation.

8.3.1   BRAKE CALIPER – REMOVAL AND INSTALLATION

Fig. 8.8 shows the attachment details of a brake caliper. The brake pedal must be operated a few times to expel the vacuum in the system and the front of the vehicle must be on chassis stands, wheel(s) removed.

- Push a bleeder hose over one of the bleed screws in the brake calipers and insert the other end of the hose into a jar. Open the bleed screw and operate the brake pedal until the brake fluid has been drained.

- Slacken the brake hose connection (7) on the brake caliper so it can be unscrewed later on. It is also possible to disconnect the brake hose connection to the brake pipe (9). In this case unscrew the union nut from the brake pipe connection, remove the retaining clamp (8) from the hose/pipe connection and withdraw the hose. The hose connection on the caliper must, however, also be slackened. Close the open connections in suitable manner to prevent entry of foreign matter.

Fig. 8.8 – Details for the removal and installation of a brake caliper.

1   Brake caliper
2   Mounting bolt, 11.5 kgm
3   Bolt, 1.0 kgm
4   Caliper mounting bracket
5   Pad wear indicator sensor
6   Brake disc
7   Brake hose
8   Retaining clamp
9   Brake pipe

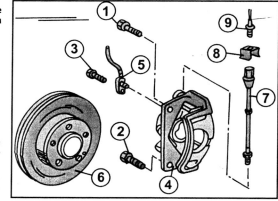

- Remove the brake pads as previously described.
- Remove the bolt (3) securing the brake pad wear indicator (5) and remove the sensor together with the cable. The self-locking bolt (3) must always be replaced.
- Remove the two bolts (2) securing the brake caliper (1) from the brake caliper mounting bracket (4) and lift off the caliper. The brake hose can be unscrewed from the caliper, if required.

The installation is carried out in reverse order, noting the following points:

- Use new, self-locking bolts for the mounting bracket. These are specially designed for the mounting bracket. Tighten the bolts to 11.5 kgm (83 ft.lb.).
- Screw the brake caliper onto the brake hose until nearly tight. The final tightening takes place when the cylinder is in position.
- Refit the brake pads and the cylinder as described above.
- Tighten the brake hose connection to 1.8 kgm (13 ft.lb.). Make sure that the hose cannot twist during this operation. If this is the case, you can slacken the connection between hose and pipe and reset the hose accordingly. The union nut connecting the brake hose to the brake pipe is tightened to 1.4 kgm (10 ft.lb.). Fit the retaining clamp securely. Move the steering from lock to lock and check that the hose cannot tub against other parts of the front suspension. The brake system must be bled of air after installation.

8.3.2   BRAKE CALIPERS – OVERHAUL

We do not recommend the dismantling and/or overhaul of the brake calipers. Either fit a new caliper or have the cylinder overhauled in a workshop dealing with brake cylinder units.

8.3.3   BRAKE DISCS

Brake discs cannot be re-ground and must be replaced if they are worn. The wear must not exceed 0.5 mm on each side. Measure the thickness of the discs at three positions with a micrometer or calipers as already shown in Fig. 8.5, noting the min. permissible thickness of 10.0 mm (solid discs) or 19.4 mm (ventilated discs). Brake discs should also be checked for run-out. To do this, attach a dial gauge so that the stylus is resting

128

against the edge of the disc approx. 5 mm from the edge. Rotate the disc. The dial gauge needle should not indicate more than 0.07 mm.

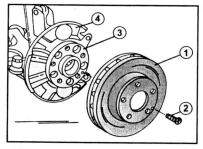

Fig. 8.9 – Attachment of front brake discs.
1 Brake disc
2 Securing screw, 1.0 kgm
3 Wheel hub flange
4 Splash shield

The brake pads must be removed to remove the brake disc. Then remove the caliper mounting bracket bolts from the steering knuckle and lift off the bracket. Do not unscrew the brake hose from the caliper. Suspend the brake caliper with a piece of wire to the front suspension. Do not allow the caliper to hang down on its hose.

The brake disc is secured by a single bolt to the wheel hub as can be seen in Fig. 8.9. Use a plastic or rubber mallet to remove a tight disc.

Note: Brake discs should always be replaced in pairs. If one of the discs is no longer re-useable, replace the other one without checking it.

The installation is a reversal of the removal procedure. Coat the seat of the brake disc with a little long-term grease before it is fitted in position. Tighten the disc securing bolt to 1.0 kgm (7 ft.lb.), the caliper mounting bolts to 11.5 kgm (83 ft.lb.). Finally refit the brake caliper mounting brackets, the calipers and the brake pads as already described. Take the vehicle out on a road test, but with care.

8.4.   Rear Drum Brakes
8.4.0.   REMOVAL AND INSTALLATION

The brake drums are secured to the rear hub flange with a single bolt (tightened to 1.0 kgm). The drum can, however, not be removed in a straight-forward operation, as the adjusting mechanism of the brake shoes inside the drum must be reset. To do this, use a screwdriver and insert it into one of the bolt holes in the brake drum, as shown in the L.H. view of Fig. 8.10 and push the handbrake operating lever inside the drum towards the centre of the vehicle as shown in the R.H. view. A small pin in the brake shoe will release from the lever. The lever can now be pushed towards the rear to release the automatic adjusting mechanism. The brake drum can now be removed. The brake drum must be rotated to align the threaded bore exactly.

The handbrake adjusted must be checked and if necessary corrected after the drum has been refitted.

Note: The drum diameter must not exceed 181.2 mm. New: 180.0 – 180.2 mm.

8.4.1.   BRAKE SHOES – REMOVAL AND INSTALLATION

After the removal of the brake drum it is best to draw a sketch with the location of the individual parts. This is mainly important for the anchorage points of the return springs. We suggest to remove the brake shoes first on one side and then on the other side. During installation you will then be able to check the correct location of the various parts at a glance.

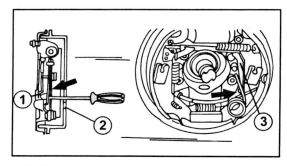

Fig. 8.10 – Removal of a brake drum. Insert a screwdriver into the drum (2) as shown in the L.H. view to push against the handbrake lever (1) and push it the lever (3) back and over the stop (arrow) in the R.H. view.

Note: We would like to point out that brake shoes must be replaced in sets. Only brake shoes released by Mercedes-Benz should be fitted.

The thickness of the brake shoe linings can be checked when the brake shoes and the drums are fitted, provided you have a torch. Measure the lining thickness of the front brake shoe. If the minimum thickness of 2.0 mm is reached, fit new brake shoes. The standard thickness of the brake shoe linings on the leading brake shoe is 4.5 mm, of the trailing shoe 3.5 mm.

Fig. 8.11 – After removal of the plug (1) in the brake back plate you can check the thickness of the brake lining on the leading shoe. A torch is required.

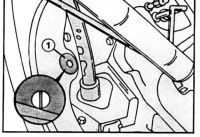

To check the lining thickness with the brake shoes and drums fitted, jack up the rear end of the vehicle and remove the plug (1) in Fig. 8.11. With the torch shine through the inspection hole and judge the thickness of the lining (shown in the circle). If not sure, remove the brake drum and check again.

After the removal of the brake drum as described earlier on you will see the construction of the brake assembly on the R.H. side of Fig. 8.12. The removal is carried out as follows, but we would like to point out that MB recommend to remove the rear hub flange to improve the access to the brake shoes. The necessary operations have been described in section "Rear Axle and Rear Suspension". After the removal of the brake shoes you will have the parts shown in Fig. 8.12.

- Unhook the lower shoe return spring (1) with a pair of pliers from the brake shoe. If a special pair of pliers, available for this purpose, is not used, care not to slip – Danger of injury.

- Release the brake shoes from the hold-down pins. This operation is shown in Fig. 8.13. Although the workshop uses a special pair of pliers it will be possible to remove the attachment with a pair of water pump pliers. From the rear of the brake back plate push against the hold-down pin (3) and from the front rotate the spring seat (2) as shown with the pliers until the end of the pin can be disengages from the slot in the spring seat. Release the pliers and remove the spring seat and the spring (1). The operation must be carried out on both brake shoes.

- Disengage the upper return spring (3).

- At the lower end lift the two brake shoes (4) and (5) out of the abutment. The return spring will be freed and can be removed.

- Push the two brake shoes together at the bottom and lift the upper ends out of engagement with the wheel cylinder. Immediately sling an elastic band around the wheel cylinder to keep the piston in position. Fig. 8.13 shows a special spring clip, which can be used, if available.

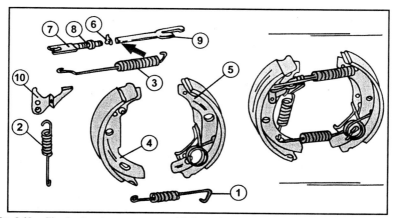

Fig. 8.12 – The brake shoes are assembled as shown on the right. On the L.H. side the component parts of the brake shoe assembly is shown on one side.

1 Lower shoe return spring
2 Adjusting lever return spring
3 Upper shoe return spring
4 Leading brake shoe
5 Trailing brake shoe
6 Thermoclip
7 Threaded push rod
8 Star wheel adjuster
9 Thrust sleeve
10 Adjusting lever

Fig. 8.13 – Removal of the brake shoes. Remove the show hold-down springs as shown.

1 Spring
2 Brake back plate
3 Hold-down pin
4 Water pump pliers
5 Clip for wheel brake cylinder
6 Brake shoe
7 Brake shoe
8 Brake shoe abutment bracket

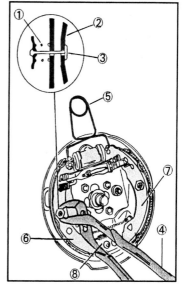

- The brake shoes can now be lifted off. Compress the spring of the handbrake cable and disconnect the cable end from the operating lever.

- Separate the adjusting lever (10) from the leading brake shoe (4) and disengage the spring (2) from the lever.

- Separate the adjusting lever (10) from the leading brake shoe (4) and disengage the spring (2) from the lever.

Thoroughly clean all parts, including the brake back plate. If petrol is used to clean the parts make sure not to allow it on the rubber dust caps of the wheel brake cylinder. If the thickness of the linings is down to 2.0 mm or the rivet heads are near the surface of the linings, fit new brake shoes. Check the wheel brake cylinders for signs of leakage.

The assembly and the installation is carried out as follows. Brake shoes and adjuster are fitted on a bench.

- If the shoes have been replaced, remove the adjusting lever from the old brake shoe. Place the lever over the lower roll pin of the leading shoe (4). The adjusting lever (10) must touch between the threaded push rod (7) and the brake shoe (4) and the lever (10) must engage in the star wheel (8).
- During assembly of the automatic adjuster turn the star wheel (8) all the way back and engage the locking lug on the thermo clip at the position shown by the arrow into the recess in the thrust sleeve (9).
- Fit the shoe return spring (2) to the adjusting lever (10) and the brake shoe and the lower return spring (1) between the two brake shoes.
- The brake shoes can now be fitted to the brake back plate. First engage the handbrake cable.
- Push the lower ends of the two shoes together and carefully engage the upper end with the wheel brake cylinder without damaging the rubber caps. The elastic band or the special clips must, of course, be removed before the shoes are fitted.
- Lift the lower ends into the abutment and secure the shoes to the brake back plate. To do this insert the shoe hold-down spring from the rear and fit the spring seat. Press with a finger from the rear of the back plate against the pin and guide the spring seat with a pair of pliers over the pin end. After the pin end appears in the opening, grip the spring seat with the pliers and rotate it until the pin is locked in position.
- Fit the adjuster assembly at the upper end of the brake shoes with the adjustable fork engaged with the leading shoe. The shoes may have to be expanded to insert the adjuster assembly. The flat side of the thermo clip (6) must be facing towards the brake back plate. As already mentioned, the lug of the thermo clip must engage with the groove of ten push rod (arrow).
- Engage the hook of the upper shoe return spring (3) with the rear brake shoe (trailing shoe) and hook the longer end of the spring into the other shoe, using a pair of pliers. The spring is engaged with the spring hooks from the outside towards the inside.
- Adjust the diameter of the fitted brake shoes to the diameter of the brake drum by rotating the star wheel (8) with a screwdriver. This will set the adjusting mechanism into the basic position. Thos operation must be carried out on both sides of the vehicle.
- Fit the brake drums.
- Have the brake pedal operated about 20 times. At the same time listen with an ear on one of the brake drums. A "clocking" sound should be heart, indicating the proper operation of the self-adjusting mechanism. It is of advantage if a helper checks the other brake assembly in the same manner.
- All other operations are carried out in reverse order.

8.4.2. WHEEL BRAKE CYLINDERS

Wheel brake cylinders cannot be repaired or overhauled. To remove a wheel brake cylinder remove the brake shoes as described above, disconnect the brake pipe at the rear of the brake back plate (union nut) and unscrew the cylinder. We would like to mention that the cylinder can also be replaced without removing the brake shoes completely. In this case disconnect the upper return spring and after disconnecting the brake pipe and unscrewing the bolts, move the upper ends of the brake shoes apart until the cylinder can be withdrawn. In this case take care not to damage the rubber caps of the cylinder on the sharp edges of the brake shoes when the cylinder is refitted.

The installation is a reversal of the removal procedure. Tighten the cylinder securing bolts to 1.4 kgm (10 ft.lb.), the pipe union nut to 1.5 kgm (11 ft.lb.). Bleed the brake system after installation.

8.5.   Rear Disc Brakes

8.5.0.   BRAKE PADS – REMOVAL AND INSTALLATION

The brake pads must be replaced if the thickness of the brake pad linings is worn down to 2.0 mm. The thickness can be checked with the brake caliper fitted after the wheel has been removed.

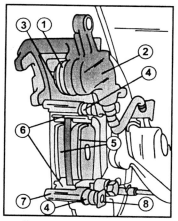

Fig. 8.14 – Details for the removal and installation of the rear brake pads.

1	Rubber dust boot
2	Floating caliper
3	Piston
4	Rubber dust sleeve
5	Brake pads
6	Retaining spring
7	Caliper mounting bracket
8	Guide pin

Fig. 8.14 shows details of a rear brake caliper and the brake pads in fitted position and can be referred to during the following description. The following operations describe the necessary work on one caliper, but the same work must be carried out on the other side of the vehicle if new brake pads must be fitted. As in the case of the front brake pads only a complete set of brake pads must be fitted. The rear end of the vehicle must be resting on secure chassis stands and the wheels removed.

- Carry out the operations described for the front brake pads until the thickness of the brake pads material has been measured.

- If removal is necessary remove the bolt from the lower guide pin (8) and slowly swing the caliper (2) upwards. If the caliper is very tight slacken the upper bolt as well. The brake caliper is not removed, but use a piece of wire and tie it to the rear axle. Do not allow it to hang down on the brake hose.

Fig. 8.15 – Brake pad set (1) and retaining springs (2).

- Remove the two brake pads (5) together with the retaining springs from the side of the caliper. The second brake pad remains normally in the caliper and must be removed from the side of the brake disc. The parts thus removed are shown in Fig. 8.15. Immediately check the condition of the retaining springs and replace them if necessary.

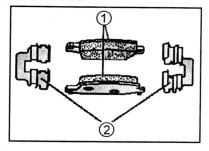

All points mentioned for the front disc brakes also apply to the rear brakes. This includes the brake discs. The standard thickness of the disc is 8.0 mm, with a minimum thickness of 7.0 mm.

The installation of the brake pads is also a copy of the instructions for the front brake pads. The bolts securing the slide pins are tightened to 3.0 kgm (22 ft.lb.). After installation operate the brake pedal a few time to set the brake pads against the discs. Check and if necessary correct the fluid level in the reservoir, fit the wheels, lower the vehicle to the ground and tighten the wheel bolts. Drive the vehicle carefully during the first few miles as brakes need a while to "bed" in.

8.5.1.   BRAKE CALIPERS – REMOVAL AND INSTALLATION

The removal and installation of the brake calipers is carried out in a similar manner as described for the front brake calipers. The tightening torques for the brake hose and the connection brake hose/brake pipe are also the same. Different is the attachment of the brake caliper to the caliper mounting bracket. The bolts are only tightened to 5.5 kgm (40 ft.lb.).

8.5.2   BRAKE CALIPERS – OVERHAUL

We do not recommend the dismantling and/or overhaul of the brake calipers. Either fit a new caliper or have the cylinder overhauled in a workshop dealing with brake cylinder units.

8.5.3   BRAKE DISCS – REMOVAL AND INSTALLATION

- Remove rear axle brake caliper bolts and remove the caliper. Do not disconnect the brake hose, but use a piece of wire and suspend the caliper from some part of the rear suspension. It must not hang down on the brake hose. During installation take care that the hose is not twisted or can touch other parts of the suspension.

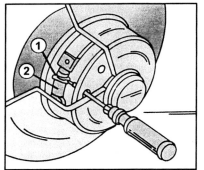

Fig. 8.16 – Releasing the handbrake mechanism inside the brake disc/drum. The screwdriver must engage with the adjuster wheel (1) of the adjusting mechanism (2).

- Remove the bolt securing the brake disc. The handbrake should be applied to unscrew the bolt. After removal re-apply the handbrake.
- Before the removal of the disc release the handbrake (parking brake). To do this insert a screwdriver as shown in Fig. 8.16 through a hole in the brake disc and turn back the adjuster wheel (1) of the adjusting mechanism. This will prevent that the parking brake shoes are too tight against the brake drum. On the right-hand side move the screwdriver from the rear towards the front, on the left-hand side move the screwdriver from the front towards the rear. The drum/disc assembly can now be removed. Use a plastic or wooden mallet to help the removal.

Before installation of the disc read the instructions below as the parking brake must be adjusted. The brake disc securing bolt must be tightened to 1.0 kgm (7 ft.lb.). After the completed installation check the brake hose as mentioned above.

The parking brake must now be re-set to the basic position:

- Insert the screwdriver as shown in Fig. 8.16 into the brake disc and "feel" for the adjuster wheel.
- Rotate the adjuster wheel until the brake disc can no longer be rotated. On the R.H. side rotate the adjuster wheel from the front towards the rear, on the L.H. side rotate the adjuster wheel from the rear towards the front.

134

- From the final position, i.e. the brake disc is locked, release the adjuster wheel by 8 notches (both sides of the vehicle).

8.5.   Master Brake Cylinder

All models are fitted with a tandem master cylinder with a double reservoir (although the cylinder only has one filler opening), supplying both circuits of the dual circuit with brake fluid. The brake lines are diagonally split.

The brake fluid level is indicated by means of a warning light in the dashboard, when it is below the "Min" mark.

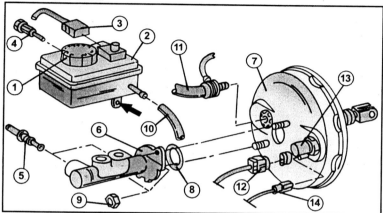

Fig. 8.17 – Details for the removal and installation of the master cylinder.

1 Filler cap (reservoir)	6 Master brake cylinder	11 Vacuum line
2 Brake fluid reservoir	7 Brake servo unit (booster)	12 BAS release switch
3 Connector plug, warning switch	8 Sealing ring	13 BAS travel sensor
4 Bolt	9 Securing nut, 2.0 kgm	14 Plug connector
5 Brake pipe to cylinder	10 Brake fluid hose	

8.5.0.   REMOVAL AND INSTALLATION

The master cylinder is fitted to the front face of the brake servo unit and is removed from the engine compartment. Fig. 8.17 shows the parts of the cylinder together with the brake servo unit. As the illustration shows various plug connectors and sensors are connected to the brake servo unit which, however, do not interfere with the removal of the cylinder. The plugs/sensors are part of the brake assist system (BAS). The cylinder can be removed as follows:

- Remove the cap (1) from the reservoir (2).
- Disconnect the plug from the from the brake fluid level switch connector (7) from the side of the cylinder (3).
- Remove the rubber cap from the bleeding screw of one of the front brake calipers, push a bleeding hose over the screw, guide the other end of the hose into a suitable container, open the screw and have the brake pedal operated until the system is empty. Otherwise empty the fluid reservoir as shown in Fig. 8.18.. Hold a rag underneath the reservoir to avoid brake fluid dripping on painted parts.

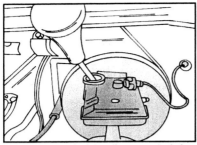

Fig. 8.18 – Brake fluid can be removed with a suction tool as shown.

• Disconnect the brake hose (10) from the reservoir.

• Remove the bolt (4) and lift off the reservoir (2). The bolt must be engage in the pin underneath the reservoir at the position shown by the arrow when the reservoir is refitted.

• Disconnect the brake pipe (5) leading to the master brake cylinder (6). Protect the open end of the disconnected. Again take care not to allow brake fluid to drip onto painted parts.

• Unscrew the master brake cylinder (6) from the brake servo unit (7) and lift it out. The sealing ring (8) must always be replaced. The nuts (9) are tightened to 2.0 kgm (14.5 ft.lb.) during installation.

The installation is a reversal of the removal procedure, noting the points already given above. Finally refit the reservoir, fill the system with brake fluid and bleed it as described later on.

8.5.1 MASTER CYLINDER – OVERHAUL

Master brake cylinders are no longer overhauled. A new cylinder must be fitted if the old one fails. Always quote the model and the chassis number when ordering a new cylinder, as cylinders are sometimes changed and a different cylinder may have been allocated to your particular vehicle.

8.6. The Handbrake (Parking Brake)

The handbrake is known as duo-servo-brake. "Duo" indicates that the braking effect is the same in both rotating directions of the brake disc. "Servo" indicates that the operation of one brake shoe is transmitted to the other brake shoe. The brake shoes for the handbrake are located inside the rear brake discs. The remaining component parts of the handbrake system are a normal handbrake lever, a compensating lever assembly underneath the vehicle, the necessary handbrake cables and the operating levers on the two rear brake calipers.

8.6.0. BRAKE SHOES – REMOVAL AND INSTALLATION

A special tool is required to remove the brake shoes in order to remove the shoe return springs. Otherwise you will have to remove the rear wheel hub to expose the brake shoes. Fig. 8.19 shows the component parts of the handbrake brake shoes on one side. The upper brake shoe is connected to the lower brake shoe with two springs. The following description assumes that the latter recommendation is followed, as it will not be possible to reach the springs. The operations are described for one side, but shoes must always be replaced as a set. The rear of the vehicle must be on chassis stands, with the wheels removed.

• Remove the rear brake disc as already described. If the disc cannot be removed immediately, slacken the nut at the end of the handbrake cable compensating lever. If still not possible, reset the brake shoes as described during the removal of the brake shoes (see also Fig. 8.16). The brake caliper will have to be removed during the operation.

Fig. 8.19 – Exploded view of the handbrake brake shoes on one side.

1 Upper brake shoe
2 Upper return spring
3 Vertical return spring
4 Adjusting mechanism
5 Vertical return spring
6 Pin for (7)
7 Spreader lock
8 Lower return spring
9 Lower brake shoe

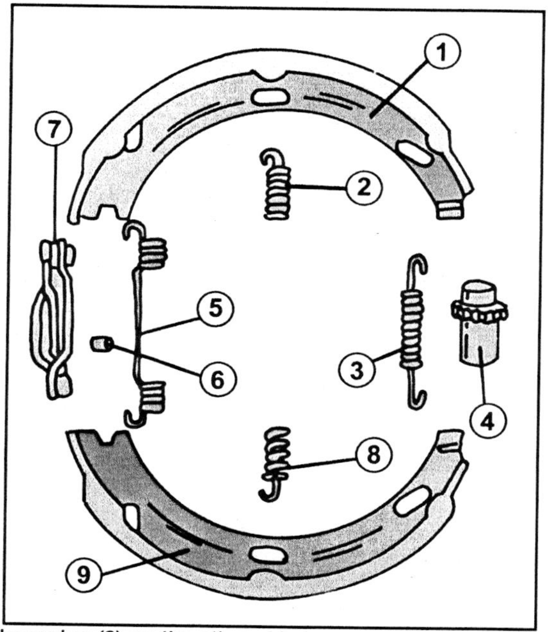

- Remove the vertically fitted spring (2). The workshop uses the special tool 116 589 01 62 00 for this operation, which is inserted from above. The tool has a hook, which is inserted between drive flange and brake shoes and engaged with the spring. By studying Fig. 8.20 you will be able to disengage the spring without the tool. The spring (3) on the other side is removed in the same manner.

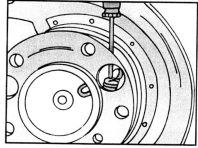

Fig. 8.20 – Removal of one of the vertically fitted spring, using a tool with a hook on the end.

- Remove the lower return spring (8) . Insert the tool shown in Fig. 8.21 (special tool 112 589 09 061 00, see next page) in the manner shown through the drive wheel flange, push the spring towards the inside and rotate it by 90°, unhook the spring from the rear cover and take it out. The spring must be rotated until the spring hook can be disengaged.
- The spring in the other side is removed in the same manner.

- If the rear hub flange is fitted you will have to rotate it until one of the threaded bores in line with the spring (torch required). The tool can perhaps be made-up by referring to the illustration. As you can see a small groove is cut into the end (approx. 2.5 mm in width), which can be placed over the spring.
- Expand the two brake shoes at the lower end until they are free to be removed over the rear hub flange. The adjuster (4) on one side will drop down or can be removed during the removal of the brake shoes.

The installation of the brake shoes is carried out as follows:

- New brake shoes are always fitted with new return springs.
- Connect the handbrake cable with the pin to the spreader lock (expanding lock) and push the spreader lock into the brake back plate.

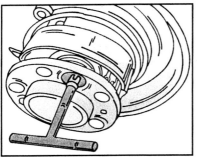

Fig. 8.21 – Removal of the lower return spring wit the special tool. A similar tool can be made-up as described on the previous page.

- Coat the thread of the adjuster push rod and the cylindrical part with long-term-grease and turn back the adjuster (4) into the body.
- Fit the adjuster mechanism into the brake shoes with the adjuster wheel at the upper end as shown in Fig. 8.19, i.e. the little adjuster wheel must be uppermost.
- Fit the upper return spring from the front into the brake shoe.

- Expand the brake shoes at the lower end and place them over the rear wheel hub until one shoe can be engaged with the spreader lock. Make sure that the spring is seated correctly.
- Fit the spring from the side into the brake shoe.
- Insert the tool mentioned above and shown in Fig.8.21 through one of the threaded holes in the rear hub flange, compress the spring from the front and turn it by 90° to secure it to the back plate.
- Fit the remaining spring between the brake shoes. Use a wire hook (or the special tool mentioned above and shown in Fig. 8.20 into the large hook of the spring and then fir the return spring to the other brake shoe.
- Refit the brake disc and the brake caliper assembly and adjust the handbrake as described below.

8.6.1. HANDBRAKE ADJUSTMENT

The handbrake must be adjusted if the handbrake lever can be pulled with medium force by more than 3 "clicks" before the braking effect takes place. The handbrake is adjusted inside the brake discs, but it may also be necessary to adjust the handbrake cables (see following section). Proceed as follows to adjust the brake shoes if disc brakes are fitted. Both petrol and diesel models are covered:

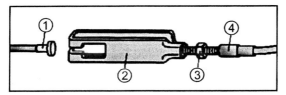

Fig. 8.22 – View of the handbrake adjuster underneath the vehicle.
1   R.H. rear handbrake cable
2   Adjuster
3   Locknut
4   Front handbrake cable

- Place the rear end of the vehicle on chassis stands. Steel rear wheels can remain on the rear axle flanges, light-alloy wheels must be removed.
- In the case of a petrol model (A190 and Vaneo) remove the lower engine compartment panelling as described earlier on, in the case of a diesel model remove the bottom section of the sound-proofing capsule.
- Refer to Fig. 8.22 slacken the locknut (3) on the handbrake cable and turn back the adjuster (2) until the handbrake cable is slack.
- Turn the wheel into the position shown in Fig. 8.23 and remove the wheel bolt. *If light alloy wheels are fitted the wheels must be removed.* Insert a screwdriver into the hole and engage it by "feeling" with the teeth of the adjuster wheel. Fig. 8.24 shows a cut-away view of the brake disc to show the brake adjuster with more

138

details. Turn the adjuster wheel on the adjusting mechanism until the brake shoes are applied and the rear wheel (or the disc in the case of light alloy wheels) can no longer be turned. The screwdriver must be moved as follows during the adjustment:

- **On the L.H.** side from the rear towards the front
- **On the R.H.** side from the front towards the rear

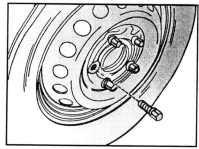

Fig. 8.23 – Turn the wheel into the position shown, remove the wheel bolt and insert a screwdriver into the hole to rotate the brake shoe adjuster inside the brake disc.

- Turn the adjusting wheel by approximately 8 teeth (both wheels must be turned by the same number of teeth) until the rear wheel (or the disc in the case of light alloy wheels) can be rotated freely.
- Refer to Fig. 8.22 and unscrew the adjuster (2) until both rear wheels can be rotated freely and then tighten the tighten

the locknut (3) against the adjuster.

Fig. 8.24 – Adjusting the small adjusting wheel inside the brake drum. The screwdriver must engage with the teeth on the adjuster wheel.

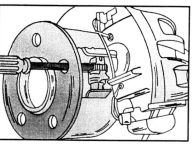

- Operate the handbrake lever a few times. After adjustment check that the brake shoes release the brake disc/drum. Otherwise re-adjust.
- Fit the removed wheel bolt (11 kgm) or refit the light-alloy wheel, depending on the version, and tighten it to the correct torque.
- Adjust the handbrake cables as described below.

8.7. Front Handbrake Cable

The handbrake cable is fitted between the handbrake operating lever and the cable adjuster, shown earlier on. The replacement of the cable requires a special tool to remove a retaining ring. It is also necessary to remove the rear console in the inside of the vehicle, which additionally has been changed after February 2001. As it will only be necessary to replace the cable in rare cases we recommend to have the cable replaced in a workshop, should it be necessary.

8.8. Rear Handbrake Cable - Replacement

The replacement of the rear handbrake cable is described below, but again we must point out that a special tool is required to remove a retaining ring. The operations are the same on both sides of the vehicle. Fig. 8.25 shows the parts to be removed for reference. Again petrol and diesel models are covered.

- Place the rear end of the vehicle on chassis stands after slackening the wheel bolts.

Fig. 8.25 – Details for the removal and installation of the rear handbrake cables.

1   Trailing arm
2   Front handbrake cable
3   R.H. rear handbrake cable
4   L.H. rear handbrake cable
5   Clip (fitted to Feb. 2001)
6   Pin (fitted to Feb. 2001)
7   Special tool to remove retaining tabs on frame floor.

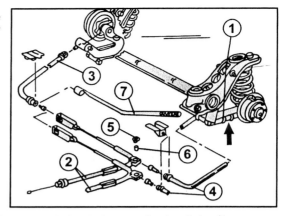

• In the case of a petrol models remove the lower engine compartment panelling, in the case of a diesel model remove the bottom section of the noise encapsulation. Refer to earlier description.

• Remove the wheel on the side in question (mark the wheel position on the hub before removal.

• In the case of drum brakes remove the brake shoes as already described. In the case of disc brakes remove the expander (spreader) locks of the brake shoes as described during the removal and installation of the parking brake shoes.

• Disconnect the handbrake cable from the adjuster.

• Remove the rear axle shaft flange (section "Rear Axle and Suspension"). The taper roller bearing must only be removed if required.

• Disconnect the L.H. brake cable from the front handbrake cable (2). On models produced before the 28.1.2001 the clip (5) must be fitted in the recess shown by the arrow in Fig. 8.25 during installation.

• Remove the L.H. and R.H. handbrake cables (3) and (4) from the retaining tabs on the frame floor: This requires the special tool mentioned above and shown with (7) in the illustration to free the tabs.

• Unclip the L.H. and R.H. handbrake cables (3) and (4) from the anchor bracket on the trailing arm (1) in the area shown by the arrow.

• In the case of fitted drum brakes disconnect the L.H. and R.H. cables from the handbrake levers on the brake shoes and push the cables out of the brake back plates with a screwdriver.

• In the case of disc brakes remove the bolts and remove the handbrake cables out of the back plates

The installation is a reversal of the removal procedure. The brake cables must be adjusted after installation. Also check the cable adjusters and adjust them if necessary. If new brake shoes have been fitted drive the vehicle on a clear road with about 50 mph and pull the handbrake lever to the first notch, but not longer than 10 seconds. After stopping, pull the lever by 2 to 3 notches (clicks) and check that the wheels are locked and rotate freely after the handbrake has been released. The rear of the vehicle must of course be jacked up for the check.

8.9.   Handbrake Cables – Adjustment (all models)

Fig. 8.26 shows the parts involved in the adjustment of the cables. The cables must be re-adjusted if the handbrake lever can be pulled by more than 3 notches without locking the rear wheels. Its is assumed that the brake shoes inside the brake discs

140

have been adjusted as described earlier on and that in the case of drum brakes the shoes have been correctly fitted and set to their basic position. Proceed as follows:
- Place the rear end of the vehicle on chassis stands.

Fig. 8.26 – Details for the adjustment of the handbrake.
1   Handbrake lever
2   Front handbrake cable
3   R.H. rear handbrake cable
4   L.H. rear handbrake cable
5   Cable adjuster
6   Locknut

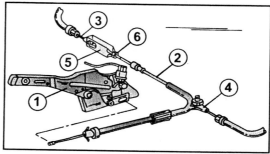

- In the case of a petrol models remove the lower section of the noise encapsulation, in the case of a diesel model remove the bottom parts of the noise encapsulation. Refer to earlier description.
- Pull the handbrake lever (1) to the first notch. When the lever is not pulled the cable must be under slight tension, but must not sag.
- Slacken the locknut (6) at the adjuster (5) and screw in the adjuster until the brake shoes contact the brake drums or brake discs/drums and it no longer possible to rotate the rear wheels.
- Slacken the adjuster (5) until both wheels can be rotated freely. Tighten the locknut (6) against the adjuster (5).
- Apply the handbrake and check that both rear wheels are locked (wheels off the ground, of course). Then release the lever and check that both wheels can be rotated completely freely.
- Refit the underbody panels and lower the vehicle to the ground.

8.10.   Brake Servo Unit

Brake servo units should not be dismantled, as special tools are required to dismantle, assemble and test the unit. Remember that a failure of the servo unit to act will not affect the efficiency of the braking system but, of course, additional effort will be required for the same braking distance to be maintained.

ATTENTION! If you coast downhill, for whatever reason, with a vehicle equipped with a brake servo unit, remember that the vacuum In the unit will be used up after a few applications of the brake pedal and the brake system will from then onwards operate without power-assistance. Be prepared for this.

The operation of the brake servo unit can be checked as follows:
- Operate the brake pedal several times to exhaust the vacuum in the system and then depress it towards the floor and keep it there. When the engine is started the pedal should go a little further direction floor.
- Allow the engine to idle and the switch off. Again depress the brake pedal several times. During the first application the pedal travel must be more then during subsequent applications.
- Faults in the brake servo unit can be attributed to leaking vacuum hose or a damaged non-return valve in the brake servo system.

8.10.0. BRAKE SERVO UNIT – REMOVAL AND INSTALLATION

The removal of the brake servo unit is in many aspects similar as the removal of the master brake cylinder as the latter must be removed to gain access to the servo. Fig. 8.17 can be referred to, but we advise you to read the instructions first, as some of the parts are not easily removed. After the cylinder (6) has been removed, proceed as follows:

• Operate the brake pedal a few times to exhaust any vacuum remaining in the system and disconnect the vacuum line (11) from the brake servo unit (7),

• In the case of vehicle built before the end of February 2001 disconnect the plug connector from the release switch and the solenoid valve (12). Also on these models remove the diaphragm travel sensor (14) after withdrawing the connector plug. The mentioned parts are not fitted to all models.

• In the case of a vehicle with traction system detach a brake pipe from the hydraulic unit. Protect the open pipe end in suitable manner. Tighten the union nut during installation to 1.4 kgm (10 ft.lb.).

• Pull the locking clip at the upper end of the brake pedal from the connecting bolt. During installation make sure that the clip enters the groove of the bolt properly.

• The brake servo unit (9) can now be unscrewed and removed from the pedal mounting bracket.

The installation is a reversal of the removal procedure. The sealing ring (8) must always be replaced. When fitting the servo unit take care not to trap the cable for the brake fluid level warning switch is not trapped. Experience has shown that the cable can slip into the gap. Tighten the collar nuts to 2.5 kgm (18 ft.lb.). Bleed the brake system as described below. After starting the engine check the correct functioning of the servo unit.

8.11. Bleeding the Brakes

Bleeding of the brake system should be carried out at any time that any part of the system has been disconnected, for whatever reason. Bleeding must take place in the order left-hand rear side, right-hand rear, left-hand front and right-hand front. If only one of the brake circuits has been opened, either bleed the front or the rear circuit. The workshop uses a bleeding device, but the following instructions should bleed the brake system successfully. The procedure given below should be followed and it should be noted that an assistant will be required, unless a so-called "one-man" bleeding kit is available.

Fig, 8.27 – Bleeding the brake system with disc brakes at the front and drum brakes at the rear.

Always use clean fresh brake fluid of the recommended specification and never re-use fluid bled from the system. Be ready to top up the reservoir with fluid (a brake bleeding kit will do this automatically) as the operations proceed. If the level is allowed to fall below the minimum the operations will have to be re-started.

142

Obtain a length of plastic tube, preferably clear, and a clean container (glass jar). Put in an inch or two of brake fluid into the container and then go to the first bleed point. Take off the dust cap and attach the tube to the screw, immersing the other end of the tube into the fluid in the container. Where the bleed screws are located is shown in Figs. 8.27 and 8.28 for disc/drum and for disc/disc models.

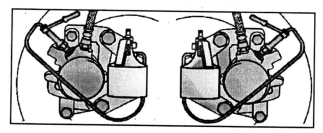

Fig, 8.28 – Bleeding the brake system with disc brakes at the front and at the rear.

Open the bleed screw about three quarters of a turn and have your assistant depress the brake pedal firmly to its full extent while you keep the end of the tube well below the fluid level in the container. Watch the bubbles emerging from the tube and repeat the operation until no more are seen. Depress the brake pedal once more, hold it down and tighten the bleed screw firmly (1.0 kgm).

Check the fluid level, go to the next point and repeat the operations in the same way. Install all dust caps, depress the brake pedal several times and finally top up the reservoirs.

8.12.   ABS System

Work should not be carried out on the ABS system, with the exception of the removal and installation of the speed sensors on front and rear wheels. The sensors are inserted into the steering knuckles, in the case of the front wheels and in the case of the rear wheels.

The following precautions must be taken after carrying out any work on a vehicle with ABS system:

- When carrying out electric welding work, withdraw the plug from the electronic control unit.
- If the vehicle is re-sprayed outside a Mercedes body shop, point out that the electronic control unit must not be subjected to temperatures of more than 95° C for a short while or more than 85° C for more than 2 hours.
- Tighten the battery terminal clamps well when re-connecting the battery.
- After work has been carried out on the brake system check the ABS system as follows:
- Start the engine and check if the warning light, marked "ABS" goes off immediately and does not come on after a speed of 3 to 7 mph is reached.

8.12.0.   WHEEL SPEED SENSORS

Front Wheel Speed Sensors
The wheel speed sensor is shown on one side in Fig. 8.29. It can be removed as follows:

Fig. 8.29 – Removal and installation of a front wheel speed sensor.
1   Bolts
2   Wheel speed sensor
3   Connector plug, sensor

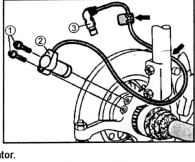

- Unclip the cable for the wheel speed sensor (3), shown with the arrow in the illustration from the spring strut and wheel housing in question (identical on both sides).
- Pull the plug connector (3) from the wheel speed sensor (2). On the R.H. side the connector must be separated from the plug of the brake pad wear indicator.
- Remove the two bolts (1) and pull out the sensor. Before installation check the rotor on the wheel hub for damage or dirt. The bolts (1) are tightened to 2.0 kgm (14.5 ft.lb.) during installation.

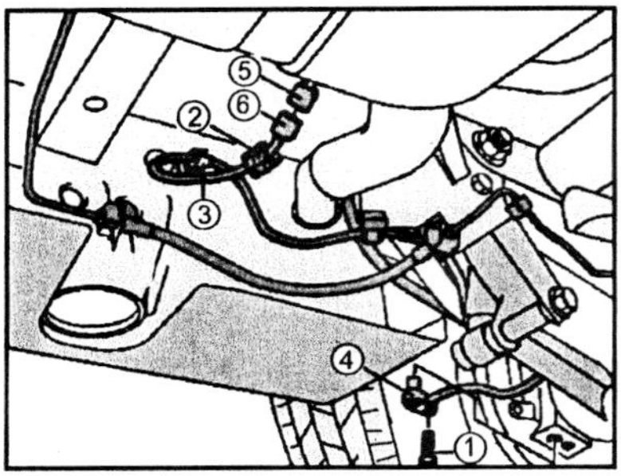

Fig. 8.30 – Removal and installation of a rear wheel speed sensor.
1   Hexagon socket bolt
2   Rubber grommet
3   Clip
4   Speed sensor
5   Plug connector, L.H. sensor
6   Plug connector, R.H. sensor

Rear Wheel Speed Sensors

The wheel speed sensor is shown on one side in Fig. 8.30. It can be removed as follows:

- If the L.H. sensor is removed, remove part of the wing liner by opening two clips at the bottom of the liner.
- Pull the rubber grommet (2) out of the frame floor. Make sure that the grommet is correctly seated during installation.
- Disconnect the plug connector from the left or the right speed sensor (4).
- Remove the bolt (1) and remove the sensor. Before installation check the rotor on the wheel hub for damage or dirt. The bolt (1) are tightened to 0.8 kgm during installation.

8.13.   Vacuum Pump (diesel models only)

The vacuum pump is attached at the position shown in Fig. 8.31 on the side of the cylinder head. Removal and installation takes place as follows:

- Remove the coolant expansion tank and place it to one side with the hoses connected.
- Detach a coolant hose on the R.H. side of the engine compartment from the body.
- Disconnect the vacuum hose (2) from the vacuum pump (1). The two detents of the quick-release fitting must be pressed together, as shown by the arrows as the vacuum hose is pulled off at the same time.
- Remove the bolts (3) from the pump (1) and remove the pump from the front cover. Take off the gasket (4) and immediately clean the timing housing cover face. If the same pump is refitted also clean the pump sealing face. The gasket must always be replaced.

144

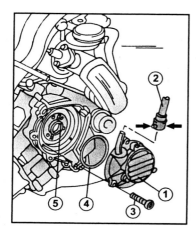

Fig. 8.31 – Details for the removal and installation of the vacuum pump as fitted to diesel engines.
1   Vacuum pump
2   Vacuum line
3   Torx-head bolt, 1.4 kgm
4   Sealing ring
5   Inlet camshaft

The installation is a reversal of the removal procedure. The driver for the pump at the inner face must engage with the drive slot in the inlet camshaft (5). Tighten the bolts (3) to 1.4 kgm (10 ft.lb.). The vacuum line (2) is pushed on until it snaps in position.

8.14.   Tightening Torques – Brakes

Brake caliper to knuckle, front: .... 11.5 kgm (83 ft.lb.)
Cylinder housing to brake caliper, front: .... 3.0 kgm (22 ft.lb.)
Brake pipe to brake hose, front: .... 1.4 kgm (10 ft.lb.)
Brake hose to caliper, front: .... 1.8 kgm (13 ft.lb.)
Bleeding valve to caliper, front, with "O" seal, front and rear: .... 1.0 kgm (7 ft.lb.)
Bleeding valve to caliper, front, without "O" seal, front and rear: .... 0.7 kgm (5 ft.lb.)
Brake caliper to brake carrier, rear: .... 5.5 kgm (40 ft.lb.)
Brake hose to caliper, rear: .... 1.8 kgm (13 ft.lb.)
Brake pipe to brake hose, rear: .... 1.4 kgm (10 ft.lb.)
Brake pipe to rear wheel cylinder, drums: .... 1.4 kgm (10 ft.lb.)
Wheel brake cylinder to back plate, drums: .... 1.5 kgm (11 ft.lb.)
Brake drum to wheel hub: .... 1.0 kgm (7 ft.lb.)
Brake disc to wheel hub, front and rear: .... 1.0 kgm (7 ft.lb.)
Master cylinder to brake servo unit: .... 2.0 kgm (14.5 ft.lb.)
Brake pipe union nuts to master cylinder: .... 1.6 kgm (11.5 ft.lb.)
Vacuum pump bolts: .... 1.4 kgm (10 ft.lb.)
Front wheel speed sensor: .... 2.0 kgm (14.5 ft.lb.)
Rear wheel speed sensor: .... 0.8 kgm (6 ft.lb.)
Brake servo unit: .... 2.5 kgm (18 ft.lb.)
Wheel bolts: .... 11.0 kgm (80 ft.lb.)

---

9   Electrical Equipment

9.0.   Battery

Voltage: .... 12 volts
Polarity: ....   Negative earth (ground)
Condition of Charge:
    Well charged: 1.28
    Half charged : 1.20
    Discharged: 1.12

9.1.0. CHECKING THE BATTERY

As you may know, the battery is not fitted in the engine compartment, but underneath a cover in the foot well of the passenger seat. The following precautions must be taken if any work is carried out on the battery:

- Keep the battery and all surrounding parts dry and clean.
- The battery electrolyte must always be to the correct level (see below). Only use distilled water to top up the battery.
- Never store a discharged battery for longer periods.

Fig. 9.1 – Removal and installation of the battery.
1   Securing bolts
2   Battery bracket
3   Earth (ground) cable
4   Positive (plus) cable
5   Gassing hose
6   Positive pole cover
7   Battery

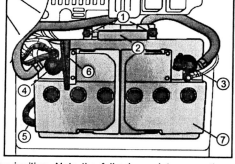

Removal and Installation of the Battery

As you know, the battery cannot be seen under normal circumstances as it is located in the foot well and is covered up. Before disconnecting the battery cables always switch off the ignition. Note the following points every time the battery cables are disconnected.

- All data in the electronic component parts of the vehicle will be lost as soon as one of the cables is disconnected from the battery.
- If a radio with anti-theft code is fitted, have the code handy before the battery is disconnected. Pre-set radio stations will also be lost, the clock must be reset. We would like to point out that from a certain model year it is only possible to have the radio reset in a workshop.
- If a new battery is fitted, take the old one to the supplier for disposal.

Remove the battery is follows:
- With the ignition key switched off, open the battery cover in the front passenger foot well. There you will see a handle, marked with "+" and "-". Fold the handle upwards and rotate it towards the left. Do not disconnect the earth cable from the battery cover. The battery will now be seen as shown in Fig. 9.1.
- Disconnect the battery cables. First disconnect the earth (ground) cable (3) from the battery (7). Slacken the clamp bolt from the positive cable (4) and pull off the terminal.
- Using a long extension with a suitable socket remove the two bolts (1) and take off the bracket (2).
- On one side of the battery disconnect the gassing line (5), The battery can now be lifted out of its compartment.

During installation take care that the gassing line (5) is not trapped. Position the battery securing bracket (2) into its correct position, fit the two bolts and tighten them. Re-connect the positive cable (4) and push the rubber cap over the terminal. Finally fit and tighten the negative cable.

Reset the radio code or have it reset in the workshop. Set the time clock.

The electric window operation must be adjusted. To do this, open and close the side windows. When the windows are closed, keep the switch pushed for a further second. The mechanism is no reset to the operation position.

Battery Electrolyte Level

The battery is in general maintenance-free, but here and then it is useful to check the electrolyte level in a conventional battery and correct it by filling in distilled water. To check the level unscrew the cell plugs. A torch will be necessary if the battery is fitted. The electrolyte should be approx. 5 mm above the battery cells.

Battery with "magic eye"

The "magic eye" is fitted to the upper surface of the battery and has different indicators which point to the charging condition of the battery:

- If the indicator shows green, the battery is in good condition.
- If the indicator shows black, the battery must be re-charged.
- If the indicator is colourless or yellow, the electrolyte level is low and the battery will have to be replaced very soon.

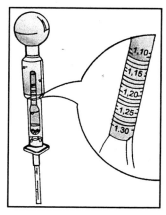

Fig. 9.2 – Hydrometer to check the spec. gravity of the electrolyte.

Checking the Battery Voltage

To check the battery voltage of a conventional battery, connect a voltmeter and apply between the two battery terminals. A voltage of 12.5 volts or more should be obtained. The strength of the electrolyte can be checked with a special hydrometer, for example of the type shown in Fig. 9.2. Squeeze the rubber ball to suck out some of the electrolyte. The float inside the tube will indicate the specific gravity of the electrolyte, which should be compared with the values given below.

A battery can be re-charged, but only a partial charge of not more than 5 hours should take place. Use of the vehicle will complete the charge and this will prevent overcharging with subsequent rise in temperature and drop in electrolyte level.

9.1.   Alternator

9.1.0.   ROUTINE PRECAUTIONS

The vehicle covered in this manual employs an alternator and control unit. This equipment contains polarity-sensitive components and the precautions below must be observed to avoid damage:

- Check the battery polarity before connecting the terminals. Immediate damage will result to the silicon diodes from a wrong connection—even if only momentarily.
- Never disconnect the battery or alternator terminals whilst the engine Is running.
- Never allow the alternator to be rotated by the engine unless ALL connections are made.
- Disconnect the alternator multi-pin connector before using electric welding equipment anywhere on the vehicle.

- Disconnect the battery leads if a rapid battery charger is to be used.
- If an auxiliary battery is used to start the engine. take care that the polarity is correct. Do not disconnect the cables from the vehicle battery.

9.1.1. REMOVAL AND INSTALLATION

The following information are valid for models with petrol and diesel engine. Certain differences must be noted during the removal, as the alternator with water cooling at the rear is connected completely different. It is impossible to list the various models, as on some models the connections have changed over from one type to the other. Figs. 9.3 and 9.4 show the connections of the alternator on the rear. We also would like to point out that the front axle carrier and the engine must lower to reach all attachments and connections if a water-cooled alternator is fitted. Remove the alternator is follows:

- Disconnect the battery earth cable as described above.

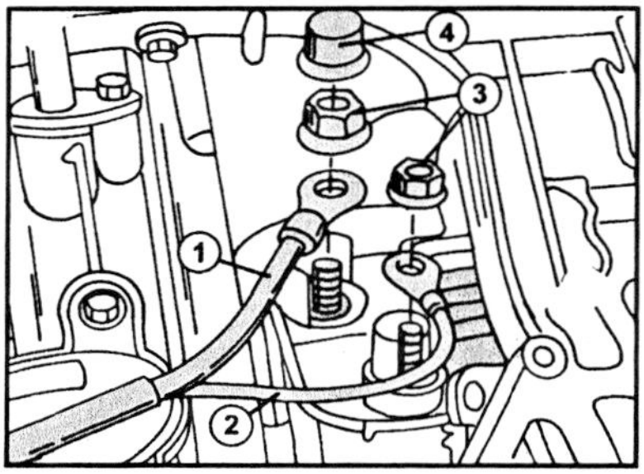

Fig. 9.3 – Connections on the rear of the alternator without alternator cooling.

1   Cable to terminal 30 (B+)
2   Cable to terminal 61 (D+)
3   Cable securing nuts
4   Protective rubber cap

- Remove the bottom section of the sound-proofing capsule.
- Slacken the Poly V- belt and lift it off the alternator pulley.
- In the case of a generator with water cooling (Fig. 9.4) lower the engine together with the front axle carrier as already described earlier on.
- In the case of a vehicle with A/C system remove the compressor. *Under no circumstances disconnect any refrigerant lines*. Use a piece of wire and tie the compressor to some part of the vehicle floor, with the lines attached.

If the parts shown in Fig. 9.3 are connected to the rear of the alternator:
- Remove the protective cap (4), unscrew the nuts (3) and remove the two cables (1) – terminal 30 (B+) and (2) – terminal 61 (D+) fro the rear of the alternator. During connection of the cable (2) tighten the nut to 0.6 kgm, the nut for the cable (1) to 1.8 kgm.
- Remove the two alternator mounting bolts from below (from the timing housing cover) and remove the alternator from underneath.

The installation is a reversal of the removal procedure. The alternator mounting bolts are tightened to 2.0 kgm (14.5 ft.lb.). Tighten the cable connections as specified above. Refit and tension the Poly V-belt. After installation reset the radio and set the clock. Operate the electric windows as described during the installation of the battery.

If the parts shown in Fig. 9.4 are connected to the rear of the alternator:
- Drain the cooling system.
- Remove the two alternator mounting bolts from the front of the timing housing cover.
- Withdraw the plug connector (1) from terminal "61".
- Slacken the hose clamps and detach the cooling hoses (2) and (3).

148

Fig. 9.4 – Connections on the rear of the alternator with alternator cooling.
1   Cable to terminal 61 (D+)
2   Coolant hose
3   Coolant hose
4   Cable to terminal 30 (B+)

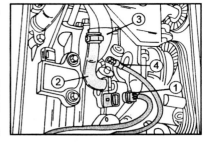

- Detach the electrical cable (4) from the alternator terminal "B+". The nut is tightened to 1.8 kgm during installation.
- Remove the alternator downwards from underneath the vehicle.

The installation is a reversal of the removal procedure. The alternator mounting bolts are tightened to 2.0 kgm (14.5 ft.lb.). Tighten the cable nuts as given above. Refit and tension the Poly V-belt. After installation reset the radio and the clock. Operate the electric windows as described during the installation of the battery.

Refill the cooling system, start the engine and check the hose connections for leaks.

9.1.2.   ALTERNATOR - SERVICING

We do not recommend that the alternator or control unit should be adjusted or serviced by the owner. Special equipment is required in the way of test instruments and the incorrect application of meters could result in damage to the circuits. Try to obtain an exchange unit if the fitted alternator shows signs of malfunction.

Fig. 9.5 – Replacing the carbon brushed and the voltage regulator of an alternator.
1   Collar nuts
2   Cover
3   Collar nut
4   Collar nut
5   Terminal stud bracket
6   Screws
7   Collar nuts
8   Regulator
9   Protective cap
10   Assembly cover
11   Carbon brushed
12   Alternator

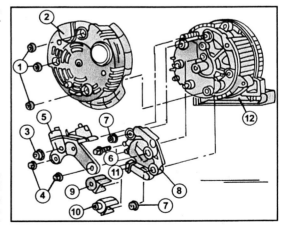

The alternator is fitted with sealed-for life bearings and no routine attention is required for lubrication. Keep the outside of the alternator clean and do not allow it to be sprayed with water or any solvent.

The alternator brush gear runs in plain slip rings and the brushes have a long life, requiring inspection only after a high mileage has been covered. To inspect the brushes, we recommend the removal of the alternator. Then proceed as follows with the help of Fig. 9.5.

- Remove the three collar nuts (1) and remove the cover (2) from the alternator (12).
- Remove the collar nuts (3) and (4) and remove the terminal stud bracket (5).
- Remove the bolts (6) and the collar nuts (7), take off the protective cap (8) and

remove the voltage regulator (8) which at the same time is the brush holder. Remove the regulator carefully as the brushes will be pushed out of their guides.

Fig. 9.6 – The protruding length of the brushes must be measured..

• Take out the two screws from the brush holder assembly and withdraw for inspection. Measure the length of the brushes, shown by "a" in Fig. 9.6. If the protruding length is less than 5.0 mm (0.2 in.) or approaching this length, replace the brushes. New brushes will have to be soldered in position. We would like to point out that it is not an easy operation to guide the brushes over the slip rings when the slip ring cover is being fitted.

During installation place the regulator (8) with the assembly cover (10) in position (supplied with repair kit) and tighten the collar nuts (7). Fit the bolts (6). If the regulator is being replaced you will find new bolts in the repair kit. The assembly cover (10) is now removed. This brings the carbon brushed (11) against the slip ring of the alternator..

Fit the protective cap (9).

Coat the heads of the bolts (6) with the protective paste included in the regulator repair kit.

Place the terminal stud bracket in position and attach it with the collar nuts (3) and (4). Finally fit the cover (2) with the collar nuts (1).

9.2. Starter Motor

9.2.0. REMOVAL AND I NSTALLATION

The connections at the rear of the starter motor are shown in Fig. 9.7. The engine together with the front axle carrier must be lowered to gain access to the starter motor.

If an air conditioning system is fitted remove the compressor and attach it with a piece of wire to the vehicle floor with the refrigerant lines connected. *Under not circumstances disconnect any of the pipes.*

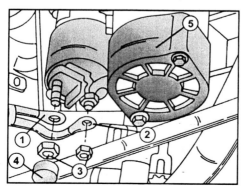

Fig. 9.7 – Connections at the rear end of the starter motor.
1   Cable to terminal 30
2   Cable to terminal 50
3   Securing nuts
4   Protective cap
5   Starter motor

• Disconnect the battery earth (ground) cable.

• Refer to the illustration and disconnect the electrical leads (1) and (2). Remove the protective cap before the nuts (3) are removed. The nut securing cable (1) must be tightened to 0.6 kgm, the nut securing the cable (2) to 0.9 kgm. In the case of a diesel engine tighten the nut (1), terminal 30, is tightened to 1.5 kgm.

- Remove the starter motor (5) from the transmission and remove it towards the bottom. The bolts are tightened to 2.0 kgm during installation. Take the opportunity to check the starter motor ring gear for wear or damage.
- The installation is a reversal of the removal procedure noting the torque values already specified.

9.2.1.   SERVICING

It may be of advantage to fit an exchange starter motor if the old one has shown fault. Exchange starter motors carry the same warranty as a new unit are therefore a better proposition.

9.3.   Headlamps
9.3.0.   BULB REPLACEMENT

The replacement of the headlight and other bulbs takes plate from the rear of the headlamp unit. The arrangement of the headlamp units has, however, been changed from March 2001 onwards. Figs. 9.8 and 9.9 show the two versions. Fig.9.8 shows the version as fitted to Vaneo models. There has been no change on these vehicles.

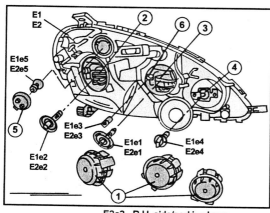

Fig. 9.8 – Removal and installation of the headlamp unit bulbs to the end of February 2001 and Vaneo models.
1 Housing cover
2 Dipped beam connection
3 High beam connection
4 Fog lamp connection
5 Flasher lamp connection
6 Parking light socket
E1   L.H. headlamp unit
E1e1 L.H. high beam
E1e2 L.H. dipped beam
E1e3 L.H. side/parking lamp
E1e4 L.H. fog lamp
E1E5 L.H. turn signal lamp
E2   R.H. headlamp unit
E2e1 R.H. high beam
E2e2 R.H. dipped beam

E2e3   R.H. side/parking lamp
E2e4   R.H. fog lamp
E2E5   R.H. turn signal lamp

On A-Class vehicles and Vaneo models before the 28th of February 2001 it is also possible to gain access to the individual bulbs via a cover in the L.H. wing liner. To open the cover turn two securing clips in the wing liner by a quarter of a turn and open the cover. In the following description we will refer to any differences as applicable between the two headlamp versions. The references made are the electrical identifications, as used in the wiring diagrams.

- Disconnect the battery. Open the engine bonnet to obtain access from the inside if the vehicle has been manufactured after 1st of March 2001.
- If the L.H. headlamp unit (E1) is removed unhook the windscreen washer reservoir from the body.

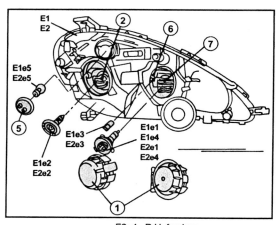

1 Housing cover
2 Dipped beam connection
5 Flasher lamp socket
6 Parking light socket
7 High beam and fog lamp
  connection
E1   L.H. headlamp unit
E1e1   L.H. high beam
E1e2   L.H. dipped beam
E1e3   L.H. side/parking lamp
E1e4   L.H. fog lamp
E1E5   L.H. turn signal lamp
E2   R.H. headlamp unit
E2e1   R.H. high beam
E2e2   R.H. dipped beam
E2e3   R.H. side/parking lamp
E2e4   R.H. fog lamp
E2E5   R.H. turn signal lamp

- If the R.H. headlamp unit (E2) is removed unhook the coolant expansion tank from the body (does not apply to petrol models without expansion tank).
- *Replacing the bulb for the L.H. main beam (E1e1) and the R.H. main beam (E2e1):* Detach the housing cover (1) in question and disconnect the main beam bulb (3) in the case of A-Class vehicles to the end of February 2001 and Vaneos or over the main beam bulbs and the fog lamp bulbs (7) in the case of A-Class vehicles after March 2001 and loosen the securing clips. Withdraw the bulb holder. The bulbs can also be held in position by means of a bayonet fitting. In this case rotate the fitting in anti-clockwise direction and pull out the bulb.
- *Replacing the bulb for the L.H. dipped dipped beam (E1e2) and the R.H. dipped beam (E2e2):* Detach the housing cover (1) and disconnect the dipped beam bulb connections (2) and remove the bulb in the manner described above for the main beam bulbs.
- *Replacing the bulb for the L.H. side and parking light (E1e3) and the R.H. side and parking light (E2e3):* Pull out the socket for the lamp in question (6) from the L.H. headlamp unit (E1) or the R.H. unit (E2).
- *Replacing the bulb for the L.H. fog lamp (E1e4) and the R.H. fog lam (E2e4):* Detach the housing cover (1) in question and disconnect the fog lamp connections (4) in the case of A-Class models produced before the end of February 2001 and Vaneo models or the connections for the high beam and fog lam (7) on A-Class models produced after March 2001 and loosen the fixing clips.
- *Replacing the bulb for the L.H. indicator lamp (E1e5) and the R.H. flasher lamp (E2e5):* Turn the socket of the bulb in question counter-clockwise and withdraw it.

The installation of the new bulb is carried out in reverse order. Do not touch the glass of the bulb with the fingers on. Use tissue paper. If a bulb of the main beam or the dipped beam has been replaced, have the headlamp adjusted checked at an early opportunity.

9.4.   Tail Light Unit Bulbs

The tail light units consist of bulb carrier, the reflector and the coloured cover fitted to the outside of the vehicle. The cover, also referred to as lens, is sealed off with the sealing ring and attached to the inside together with the reflector. The bulbs are inserted from top to bottom in the following order: Brake light bulb, reversing light bulb, flasher lamp bulb, tail light bulb and in the driver side tail light bulb and rear fog lamp bulb. The replacement of all bulbs is carried out in the same manner:

- Open the luggage compartment lid and open the cover in the luggage boot trim.
- On the side of the bulb holder press together the retaining lugs and withdraw the bulb holder. The bulb(s) can now be replaced by pushing them towards the inside and turning them towards the left.
- Fit the new bulbs in reverse order. Do not touch the glass with the fingers only. Use tissue paper.

Fig. 9.10 – The number plate lights. The bolts (1) secure each light to the body panel.

9.5. Number Plate Lights

The number plate lights are fitted at the positions shown in Fig. 9.10. To remove a light, unscrew the bolts (1) and take off the complete light (2). The electrical connector is automatically disconnected as the lamp is removed. Replace the bulb and refit the light. There is a seal under the lamp which must be checked for damage before the light is attached.

9.6. Windscreen Wipers

The wiper linkage must be removed before the wiper motor can be replaced. The removal is not straight forward and we suggest to read the instructions in full before you decide to remove the linkage or the wiper motor as several parts must be moved to gain access to the actual parts of the wiper system.

Removal and Installation of Wiper Arms

- Switch on the wipers (during dry condition operate the washer system) and wart until the wiper blades return to the park position. Mark the position of the two wiper blades on the windscreen. We suggest to attach a piece of sticky tape to the windscreen and mark the outline of both wiper blades on the tape, using a pencil.
- Switch off the ignition and open the engine bonnet.
- Pry off the cover with a suitable screwdriver and slacken the nut securing the wiper arm to the spindle without removing it.
- Move the wiper arm to and fro on the spindle until it is free. Take care that the wiper arm cannot snap back onto the glass as the removal takes place. Unscrew the nut fully and pull off the washer arm. A washer is fitted under the nut.

The installation is a reversal of the removal procedure. Fit the wiper arm over the spindle when the wipers are in the parked position (follow the marks on the sticky tape). Place the washer in position, fit the nut and tighten the nut to 2.0 kgm (14.5 ft.lb.). After installation check that the wipers function correctly.

Removal and Installation of Wiper Linkage

- Open the engine bonnet and remove the two wiper arms as described above.

153

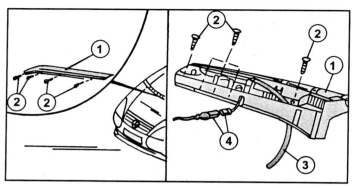

Fig. 9.11 – Removal of the air inlet (left) and the water collector (right).

- Remove the air inlet from the position shown in Fig. 9.11 on the L.H. side (shown with the bonnet closed). The removal takes placed when the bonnet is open. Remove the four bolts (2) and take off the air inlet (1). The bonnet must be partially closed to remove the inlet. During installation make sure that the inlet is seated correctly.

- Remove the water collector. This is item (1) in the R.H. view of Fig. 9.11 and is located below the air inlet. To remove it, disconnect the plug connector (4) for the heated windscreen washer supply, disconnect the supply hose to the washer jets (3) from the washer pump. The washer for the windscreen must be removed to disconnect the hose. Locate the 5 screws (2) and unscrew them. The bonnet must be partially closed to remove the waster collector (1). During installation ensure that the rubber seal is correctly seated on the windscreen.

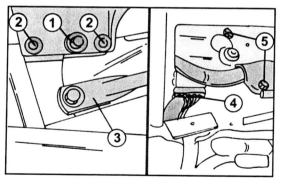

Fig. 9.12 – Removal and installation of the windscreen wiper linkage.
1   Wiper bearing mounting
2   Securing bolts
3   Long wiper linkage
4   Wiper motor plug
5   Securing bolts

- Refer to Fig. 9.12 and disconnect the plug connector (4). Remove the two bolts (2) and remove the wiper bearing (1) from its mount. Unclip the long wiper linkage from the transfer lever and pivot the linkage upwards until it free of the transfer lever. This is the lever shown in Fig. 9.13 with (3). During installation place the wiper linkage onto the transfer lever and press it in position.

- Undo the nut (4) in Fig. 9.13 and remove the wiper bearing from the mount. A washer and a rubber washer must be removed.

The installation is in general a reversal of the removal procedure, but the following points should be noted:

- Install the linkage system and secure it with the two screws (2) in Fig. 9.13.

154

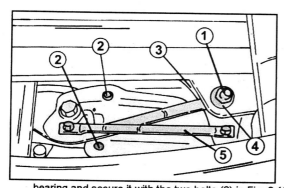

Fig. 9.13 – Removal and installation of the wiper linkage. The numbers are referred to in the text.

- Insert the wiper bearing (1) in Fig. 9.13 into the mount, fit the rubber washer and the flat washer and fit the nut (4). Tighten the nut to 1.2 kgm.
- Fit the long wiper linkage to the transfer lever and press in position.
- Fit the second wiper bearing and secure it with the two bolts (2) in Fig. 9.12.
- All other operations are now carried out in reverse.

Removal and Installation of Wiper Motor

After removal of the wiper linkages as described above pry off the wiper linkage (5) in Fig. 9.13 from the crank arm on the wiper motor. After removal of the three screws securing the wiper motor the motor can be lifted out. Tighten the bolts to 1.2 kgm during installation. Ensure that the crank arm is in alignment with the wiper linkage during installation. It is also important that the distance between the ball head of the transfer lever and the wiper linkage is exactly 10.2 mm. If this is not the case it is possible that the wiper may strike the right-hand A door pillar. If necessary correct the distance.

| 10 | Exhaust System |

10.1.   Removal and Installation of Exhaust System

Fig. 10.1 shows the exhaust system as it is fitted to A-Class models with diesel engine. There are some difference during the removal of the system fitted to Vaneo models. Note that the self-locking bolt (5) and the gasket (2) must be replaced during installation. Proceed as follows, but note the difference in the case of a Vaneo model:

- A split exhaust system is fitted, i.e. the front exhaust pipe can be detached at the end with the catalytic converter. A special retaining clamp is used to secure the parts together. A seal is fitted between the two pipe ends.
- The exhaust pipe with the catalytic converter can be detached from the silencer at the other end. An exhaust clamp with clamp bolts and nuts is used to clamp the two pipe ends together.

Remove the system as follows, noting the differences between A-Class and Vaneo models:

- Detach the exhaust pipe clamp (3) from the connection on the converter close to the engine. In the case of a Vanoe model remove the retaining clamp from the connection of the front exhaust pipe and the pipe of the catalytic converter.
- Unscrew the bolt (5) on the oil sump (all models). The front exhaust pipe on Vaneo models can now be removed. Also on these models release the exhaust pipe clamp at the connection between the rear end of the converter pipe to the silencer.

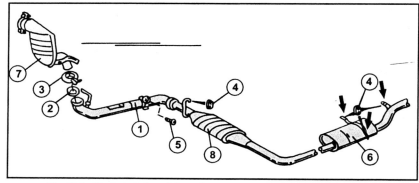

Fig. 10.1 – Exploded view of the exhaust system as fitted to passenger cars.

1 Exhaust system	4 Rubber hangers	7 Converter (engine side)
2 Sealing ring	5 Securing bolt	8 Converter (underfloor)
3 Exhaust pipe clamp	6 End silencer	

- Remove the rubber hangers (4) from the brackets at the rear silencer and at the underfloor catalytic converter. Remove the complete exhaust system (1) downwards (A-Class) or remove the underfloor converter and the rear silencer (Vaneo). The catalytic converter near the engine (8) can also be removed (all models).

The installation is a reversal of the removal procedure. Do not re-use any of the rubber hangers if they appear to be damaged or stretched. Replace them. The exhaust tail pipe trim (if fitted) must be re-used if the exhaust system has been replaced.

10.2.   Removal and Installation of primary Converter

Fig. 10.2 shows the parts to be removed. Various operations must be carried out before the converter can be removed. Some of them have already been described in other sections and should be referred to. The primary converter is flanged to the turbo charger and connected to the front exhaust pipe/converter assembly (A-Class) or to the turbo charger and the front exhaust pipe (Vaneo).

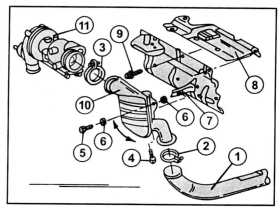

Fig. 10.2 – Removal and installation of the primary converter (engine side).

1	Exhaust system
2	Exhaust pipe clamp
3	Exhaust pipe clamp
4	Bolt for converter
5	Bolt for converter
6	Washer
7	Support strut
8	Heat shield
9	Torx-head bolt
10	Catalytic converter
11	Turbo charger

- .Remove the intake module from the cylinder head as described in section "Engine" in connection with the removal of the cylinder head cover and the cylinder head.

156

- Remove the heat shield (8) after removal of the screws (9).
- Remove the fan shroud as described in section "Cooling System".
- Detach the exhaust system (1) from the catalytic converter (10) as described above. Noting the differences between the passenger cars and the van models. Clean the sealing surfaces before installation. Check the pipe clamp (2) and replace if necessary.
- Unscrew the bolts (4) and (5) out of the converter and remove the converter. To do this, move the converter towards the windscreen washer fluid reservoir, turn it by about a quarter of a turn towards the right and lift it up and out. Take care not to damage the radiator during the removal.

The installation is a reversal of the removal procedure, noting the points already given during the removal.

10.3. Removal and Installation of Exhaust Manifold

Fig. 10.3 shows the parts to be removed. The removal and installation are fairly easy.

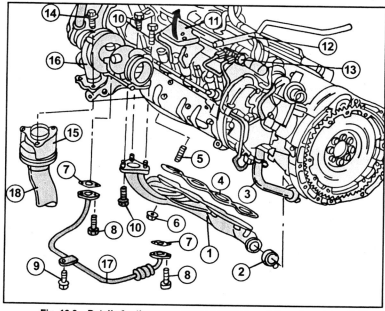

Fig. 10.3 – Details for the removal and installation of the exhaust manifold.

1 Exhaust manifold	7 Gasket	13 Bolt
2 Securing clamp	8 Allen-head bolt	14 Torx-head bolt
3 EGR pipe	9 Torx-head bolt	15 Noise insulation
4 Exhaust manifold gasket	10 Bolts	16 Turbo charger
5 Stud bolt	11 Heat shield	17 Oil return pipe
6 Nut	12 Support strut	18 Charge air hose

Remove the catalytic converter as already described.

- Unscrew the Torx-head bolts at the heat shield of the exhaust gas re-circulation pipe (3). There is not need to remove the heat shield.

- Detach the exhaust gas re-circulation pipe (3) from the exhaust manifold (1). Check the securing clamp (2) and replace if necessary.
- Remove the bolt (13) from the heat shield and the supporting strut (12). The heat shield must be carefully bend up in the direction of the arrow to gain access to the bolt (10).
- Detach the exhaust manifold (1) from the turbo charger (16).
- Detach the noise insulation (15) from the turbo charger (16) in order to permit access to the hexagon socket bolts (8). Remove the bolts.
- Unscrew the Torx-head bolt (9) from the bracket of the oil return pipe (17).
- Detach the oil return pipe (17) from the turbo charger and the crankcase and take it out. Watch out for draining oil. The gaskets (7) must be replaced during installation. The oil pipe is tightened to 0.9 kgm.
- Remove the nuts (6) from the exhaust manifold (1) and lift the manifold up and out. The self-locking nuts must be replaced. Clean the sealing faces and replace the gasket (4). Replace the studs (5) if the threads are damaged. The nuts are tightened to 2.1 kgm (15 ft.lb.). The studs, if removed, are tightened to 0.9 kgm.

The installation is a reversal of the removal procedure, noting the points already given during the removal.

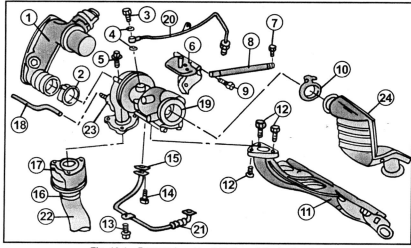

Fig. 10.4 – Removal and installation of the turbo charger.

1 Air intake manifold	9 Bolt	17 Noise insulation
2 Hose clamp	10 Pipe clamp	18 Vacuum hose
3 Banjo bolt	11 Exhaust manifold	19 Turbo charger
4 Sealing rings	12 Bolts	20 Oil feed pipe
5 Torx-head bolt	13 Torx-head bolt	21 Oil drain hose
6 Heat shield	14 Allen-head bolt	22 Charge air hose
7 Bolt	15 Gasket	23 Vacuum unit
8 Support strut	16 Hose clamp	24 Catalytic converter

10.4.　Removal and Installation of Turbo Charger

Fig. 10.4 shows the parts associated with the removal and installation of the turbo charger. Removal takes place as follows:

- Place the front end of the vehicle on secure chassis stands and remove the bottom part of the noise encapsulation as described earlier on in the manual.
- Detach the retaining clamp (2) and remove the air intake manifold (1) from the turbo charger (19). During installation arrange the clamp (2) so that the bolt head of the clamp is at the front and facing upwards. The clamp must be replaced if no longer in good condition.
- Remove the induction module as described in section "Engine" during the removal of the cylinder head.
- Remove the catalytic converter from the turbo charger but do not remove it completely, but lace it to one side. The pipe clamp (10) must be checked before it is re-used.
- Detach the vacuum hose (18) from the vacuum unit (23).
- Remove the charge air hose (22) with the noise insulation (17) from the turbo charger. The bolts (5) are removed. Tighten the bolts to 0.9 kgm during installation. Inspect the hose clamps (16) before re-using it. Also inspect the condition of the seal at the noise insulation. Again replace it if necessary.
- Detach the oil feed line (20) from the turbo charger. A banjo bolt (3) is used to connect it. The two sealing rings (4) must always be replaced, the bolt (3) is tightened to 3.0 kgm (22 ft.lb.).
- Detach the oil drain pipe (21) at the bottom of the turbo charger. Some oil will flow out and must be collected. Two Allen-head bolts (14) secure the pipe. The gasket (15) must be replaced.
- Detach the support (8) and the heat shield (6) from the turbo charger. Carefully bend the heat shield up in order to gain access to the bolts (12). Note that the bolt (7) must be slackened before installation of the support to ensure a stress-free installation. The bolt (9) is tightened to 3.0 kgm (22 ft.lb.).
- Detach the turbo charger (19) from the exhaust manifold (11). Remove the bolts (12). Tighten the bolts to 2.1 kgm (15 ft.lb.) during installation. Before fitting the parts together clean the sealing faces thoroughly.
- Lift the turbo charger upwards and lift it out.

The installation is a reversal of the removal procedure, noting the points already given during the removal.

11   Automatic Transmission

A four-speed automatic transmission is fitted to certain models, but not all models have the same transmission, as the gear ratios have been selected for the fitted engine.

The removal and installation of the transmission is a very comprehensive operation. Due to the electronic functions of some component parts, which can only be carried out by a dealer, we cannot recommend to remove the transmission yourself.

Fluid Level and Fluid Change.

The fluid level in the transmission changes with the temperature of the transmission fluid. The fluid dipstick is marked with two levels, one for a temperature of around 30° C (cold) and one for around 80° C (hot). These are shown in Fig. 11.1 with "A" and "B". On the other side of the dipstick you will find the temperatures in Fahrenheit (F). If the fluid level is correct you will find the fluid between the "Min" and "Max" marks. The transmission is filled with automatic transmission fluid (ATF). Dexron II fluid is recommended. The total capacity of the transmission is 6.3 litres, but only 3.3 litres will be used during a fluid change..

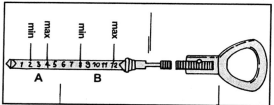

Fig. 11.1 – View of the fluid dipstick as fitted to an automatic trans-mission. The fluid must be within the area "A" when the fluid is cold or the area "B" when the fluid is hot.

Absolute cleanliness is to be observed during a fluid level check that even small particles entering the transmission can lead to malfunctions. Do not use fluffy cloth to wipe the dipstick. Tissue paper is best.

Fig.. 11.2 – Break off the lug on the plate (1) and pus the pin downwards in the direction of the arrow. The cap (2) can then be removed.

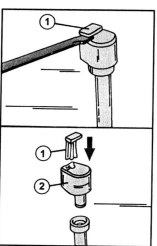

Filling in additional fluid is not straight forward. As you can see in Fig. 11.2, the upper end of the filler tube is fitted with a locking pin, which must be removed. To do this brake off the plate (1) of the pin with a screwdriver as shown and press out the remaining pin in the cap downwards. Remove the cap (2). The pin must, of course, be replaced.

The engine must be running at idle speed when fluid is filled in through the filler tube (a funnel is required). Apply the handbrake and depress the brake pedal and change through all gears. Finally leave the gear selector lever in position "P" and re-check the fluid level.

Finally refit the cap to the filler tube ands press in a new locking pin until it locks in position.

The fluid can only be changed at a dealer as a diagnostic system is used to carry out the operation.

12. SERVICING AND MAINTENANCE

Most of the maintenance operations can be carried out without much difficulties. In many cases it is, however, better to have certain maintenance operations carried out in a workshop as experience and special equipment, for example test instruments, are required to carry out a certain job. Most important are the regular inspections and checks which are described below. Operations to be carried out after a certain mileage are described later on in this section and the text will advise when specific jobs should be left to a Mercedes Dealer.

12.1. Regular Maintenance

Oil Level Check: Check the engine oil level every 500 miles. With the vehicle standing on level ground, remove the oil dipstick and wipe it clean with a clean rag or a piece of tissue paper. Re-insert the oil dipstick and remove once more. The oil level

160

must be visible between the upper and the lower mark on the dipstick. If the oil level is below the lower mark, top-up with engine oil of the correct viscosity. Never overfill the engine - the level must never be above the upper dipstick mark.

Checking the Brake Fluid Level: - The brake fluid reservoir is in the engine compartment on the drivers side. The reservoir is transparent and it is easy to check whether the fluid level is between the "Min" and "Max" mark. If necessary, top-up to the "Max" mark with the correct brake fluid.

Checking the Brake Lights: The operation of the brake lights can either be checked with the help of another person or you can check it by yourself by driving the vehicle backwards near the garage door. Operate the brake pedal and check if the reflection of the brake lights can be seen on the garage door by looking through the rear view mirror.

Checking the Vehicle Lights: In turn check every vehicle light, including the horn and the hazard warning light system. Rear lights and reversing lights can be checked in the dark in front of a garage door, without leaving the vehicle.

Checking the Tyre Pressures: Check the tyre pressures at a petrol station. Pressures are different for the various models. Either your Operators Manual or tyre charts will give you the correct pressures.

If continuous speeds of more than 100 mph are anticipated, increase the tyre pressure by 0.2 kg/sq.cm. (3 psi.).

Checking the Coolant Level: See Section "Cooling System". Never open the radiator filler cap or the cap of the expansion tank when the engine is hot.

Checking the Fluid Level in the Automatic Transmission: The fluid level should be checked at regular intervals to ensure the correct operation of the transmission. Check the level as described in Chapter 11.

12.2.   Service every 6000 Miles

Changing the Engine Oil and Oil Filter: Some petrol stations will carry out an oil change free of charge – You only pay for the oil. The same applies to the oil filter (there may be a small extra charge), but not every petrol station will be able to obtain a Mercedes filter. To change the filter yourself, refer to the relevant page.

Lubrication Jobs: Apart from the engine lubrication there are further lubrication points which should be attended to. These include the throttle linkage and shafts (only grease the swivel points), the engine bonnet catch and the hinges (use a drop of engine oil) and perhaps the door mechanism.

12.3.   Additional Service Every 12,000 Miles

Checking the Idle Speed: If the engine no longer idles as expected, have the idle speed checked and if necessary adjusted at your Dealer.

Air Filter Service: Remove the air filter element for cleaning.

Checking the Brake System: If no trouble has been experienced with the brake system, there is little need to carry out extensive checks. To safeguard for the next 6000 miles, however, follow the brake pipes underneath the vehicle. No rust or corrosion must be visible. Dark deposits near the pipe ends point to leaking joints. Brake hoses must show no signs of chafing or breaks. All rubber dust caps must be in position on the bleeder valves of the calipers. Insert a finger underneath the master cylinder, where it is fitted to the brake servo unit. Moisture indicates a slightly leaking cylinder.

The brake pads or the brake shoes linings must be checked for the remaining material thickness as has been described in Section "Brakes" for the front and rear brakes.

Adjusting the Parking Brake: Adjust the parking brake as described in Section "Brakes" under the relevant heading.

Brake Test: A brake test is recommended at this interval. Your will decide yourself if the brakes perform as you expect them to. Otherwise have the brakes tested on a dynamometer. The read-out of the meter will show you the efficiency of the brake system on all four wheels.

Checking the Wheel Suspension and Steering: In the case of the front suspension remove both wheels and check the shock absorbers for signs of moisture, indicating fluid leaks.

Check the free play of the steering wheel. If the steering wheel can be moved by more than 25 mm (1 in.) before the front wheels respond, have the steering checked professionally.

Check the rubber dust boots of the track rod and suspension ball joints. Although rubber boots can be replaced individually, dirt may have entered the joints already. In this case replace the ball joint end piece or the suspension ball joint.

Check the fluid level in the reservoir for the power-assisted steering. Refer to the "Steering" section for details. If steering fluid is always missing after the 12,000 miles check, suspect a leak somewhere in the system - See your dealer.

Tyre Check: Jack up the vehicle and check all tyres for uneven wear. Tyres should be evenly worn on the entire surface. Uneven wear at the inner or outer edge of front tyres points to misalignment of the front wheel geometry. Have the geometry measured at your dealer. Make sure that a tread depth of 1.6 mm is still visible to remain within the legal requirements. Make sure to fit tyres suitable for your model, mainly if you buy them from an independent tyre company.

Re-tighten Wheel Bolts:- Re-tighten the wheel bolts the value given in the tightening torque sections (front or rear suspension). Tighten every second bolt in turn until all bolts have been re-tightened.

Checking the Cooling System: Check all coolant hoses for cuts, chafing and other damage. Check the radiator for leaks, normally indicated by a deposit, left by the leaking anti-freeze. Slight radiator leaks can be stopped with one of the proprietary sealants available for this purpose.

Checking the Clutch: Check the clutch operation. The fluid reservoir should be full. If it is suspected that the clutch linings are worn near their limit, take the vehicle to a dealer. A gauge is used to check the protrusion of the slave cylinder push rod. It is a quick check and may prevent the clutch driven plate to wear down to the rivets.

Checking the Anti-freeze: The strength of the anti-freeze should be checked every 12,000 miles. Petrol stations normally have a hydrometer to carry out this check. Make sure that only anti-freeze suitable for Mercedes engines is used.

Checking the Manual Transmission Fluid Level: Refer to Chapter "Manual Transmission".

12.4. Additional Service every 36,000 Miles

Automatic Transmission Oil and Filter Change: See your dealer.

Air Cleaner Element Change: Refer to the relevant section.

Oil Filter Change: Replace the oil filter as described.

Clutch: The wear of the clutch driven plate should be checked by a dealer with the special gauge available.

12.5. Once every Year

Brake Fluid Change: We recommend to have the brake fluid changed at your dealer. Road safety is involved and the job should be carried out professionally. If you are experienced with brake systems, follow the instructions in the "Brakes" section to drain, fill and bleed the brake system.

FAULT FINDING SECTION

The following section lists some of the more common faults that can develop in a motor car with diesel engines. For the purpose of this manual, references to diesel engines are of course, first and foremost, as the detection faults in a petrol engine is a job for a special workshop, dealing with fuel injection system. The section is divided into various categories and it should be possible to locale faults or damage by referring to the assembly group of the vehicle in question.

The faults are listed In no particular order and their causes are given a number. By referring to this number it is possible to read off the possible cause and to carry out the necessary remedies, if this is within the scope of your facilities.

ENGINE FAULTS

Engine will not crank:	1, 2, 3, 4
Engine cranks, but will not start:	5, 6, 7, 8
Engine cranks very slowly:	1, 2, 3
Engine starts, but cuts out:	5, 6, 9, 10
Engine misfires in the lower speed ranges:	5, 6, 9, 11
Engine misfires in the higher speed ranges:	5, 6, 11, 12
Continuous misfiring:	5, 6, 7, 10 to I5, 21, 22
Max. revs not obtained:	5, 6, 12, 22
Faulty idling:	5, 6, 8 to 11, 13, 15, 16, 21 and 22
Lack of power:	3, 5 to 11, I3 to 15, 22
Lack of acceleration:	5 to 8, 12, 14 to 16
Lack of max. speed:	5 to 8, 10, 12, 13 to 15 ,22
Excessive fuel consumption:	3, 5, 6, 15 ,16
Excessive oil consumption:	16 to 19
Low compression:	7, 11 to 13, 16, 20 to 22

Causes and Remedies

1. Fault in the starter motor or its connection. Refer to "Electrical Faults".
2. Engine oil too thick. This can be caused by using the wrong oil, low temperatures or using oil not suitable for the prevailing climates. Depress the clutch whilst starting (models with manual transmission). Otherwise refill the engine with the correct oil grade, suitable for diesel engines.
3. Moveable parts of the engine not run-in. This fault may be noticed when the engine has been overhauled. It may be possible to free the engine by adding oil to the fuel for a while.
4. Mechanical fault. This may be due to seizure of the piston(s), broken crankshaft, connecting rods, clutch or other moveable parts of the engine. The engine must be stripped for inspection.
5. Faults in the glow plug system. Refer to "Glow Plug Faults" (diesel only).

6. Faults in the fuel system. Refer to "Fuel Faults".
7. Incorrect valve timing. This will only be noticed after the engine has been re-assembled after overhaul and the timing belt has been replaced incorrectly. Re-dismantle the engine and check the timing marks on the timing gear wheels.
8. Compression leak due to faulty closing of valves. See also under (7) or leakage past worn piston rings or pistons. cylinder head gasket blown.
9. Entry of air at inlet manifold, due to split manifold or damaged gasket.
10. Restriction in exhaust system, due to damaged exhaust pipes, dirt in end of exhaust pipe(s), kinked pipe(s), or collapsed silencer. Repair as necessary.
11. Worn valves or valve seats, no longer closing the valves properly. Top overhaul of engine is asked for.
12. Sticking valves due to excessive carbon deposits or weak valve springs. Top overhaul is asked for.
13. Cylinder head gasket blown. Replace gasket and check block and head surfaces for distortion.
14. Camshaft worn, not opening or closing one of the valves properly, preventing proper combustion. Check and if necessary fit new camshaft.
15. Incorrect valve (tappet) clearance. There could be a fault in the hydraulic tappets.
16. Cylinder bores, pistons or piston rings worn. Overhaul is the only cure. Fault may be corrected for a while by adding "Piston Seal Liquid" into the cylinders, but will re-develop.
17. Worn valve guides and/or valve stems. Top overhaul is asked for.
18. Damaged valve stem seals. Top overhaul is asked for.
19. Leaking crankshaft oil seal, worn piston rings or pistons, worn cylinders. Correct as necessary.
20. Loose glow plugs, gas escaping past thread or plug sealing washer damaged. Correct (diesel only).
21. Cracked cylinder or cylinder block. Dismantle, investigate and replace block, if necessary.
22. Broken, weak or collapsed valve spring(s). Top overhaul is asked for.

LUBRICATION SYSTEM FAULTS

The only problem the lubrication system should give is excessive oil consumption or low oil pressure, or the oil warning light not going off.

Excessive oil consumption can be caused by worn cylinder bores, pistons and/or piston rings, worn valve guides, worn valves stem seals or a damaged crankshaft oil seal or leaking gasket on any of the engine parts. In most cases the engine must be dismantled to locate the fault.

Low oil pressure can be caused by a faulty oil pressure gauge, sender unit or wiring, a defective relief valve, low oil level, blocked oil pick-up pipe for the oil pump, worn oil pump or damaged main or big end bearings, In most cases it is logical to check the oil level first. All other causes require the dismantling and repair of the engine. If the oil warning light stays on, switch off the engine IMMEDIATELY, as delay could cause complete seizure within minutes.

COOLING SYSTEM FAULTS

Common faults are: Overheating, loss of coolant and slow warming-up of the engine:

Overheating:

1. *Lack of coolant:* Open the radiator cap with care to avoid injuries. Never pour cold water in to an overheated engine. Wait until engine cools down and pour in coolant whilst engine is running.
2. *Radiator core obstructed by leaves, insects, etc.:* Blow with air line from the

back of the radiator or with a water hose to clean.

3. *Cooling fan not operating:* Check fan for proper cut-in and cut-out temperature. If necessary change the temperature switch or see your Dealer.
4. *Thermostat sticking:* If sticking in the closed position, coolant can only circulate within the cylinder head or block. Remove thermostat and check as described in section "Cooling".
5. *Water hose split:* Identified by rising steam from the engine compartment or the front of the vehicle. Slight splits can be repaired with insulation tape. Drive without expansion tank cap to keep the pressure in the system down, to the nearest service station.
6. *Water pump belt torn:* Replace and tension belt.
7. *Water pump inoperative:* Replace water pump.
8. *Cylinder head gasket blown:* Replace the cylinder head gasket.

Loss of Coolant:

1. *Radiator leaks:* Slight leaks may be stopped by using radiator sealing compound (follow the instructions of the manufacturer. In emergency a egg can be cracked open and poured into the radiator filler neck.
2. *Hose leaks:* See under 5, "Overheating".
3. *Water pump leaks:* Check the gasket for proper sealing or replace the pump.

Long Warming-up periods:

1. *Thermostat sticking in the open position:* Remove thermostat, check and if necessary replace.

DIESEL FUEL SYSTEM FAULTS

The information below are given for diesel engines in general, not specifically aimed at CDI engines.

Engine is difficult to start or does not start	1 to 13
Engine starts, but stop soon afterwards:	14 to 20
Engine misfires continuously:	1 to 13
Bad idling:	14 to 20
Black, white or blue exhaust smoke:	21 to 29
Lack of power:	30 to 39
Excessive fuel consumption:	40 to 47

Causes and Remedies

1. Fuel tank empty. Refuel.
2. Pre-glowing time too short. Operate until warning light goes "off".
3. Cold starting device not operated. Pull cable and push in after approx. 1 mm.
4. Glow plug system inoperative. Refer to "Glow Plug Faults".
5. Electro-magnetic cut-off device, loose or no current. Check cable to cut-off at top of injection pump. Ask a second person to operate ignition key and check if a "click" is heard. Either interrupted current supply or defective cut-off device.
6. Air in fuel system. Operate starter motor until fuel is delivered.
7. Fuel supply faulty. Slacken the injection pipes at injectors, and check if fuel is running out. Other faults: kinked, blocked or leaking injection pipes, blocked fuel filter, tank breathing system blocked. Wrong fuel for cold temperatures.
8. Injection pipes refitted in wrong order after repair.
9. Injection timing of pump out of phase: Have the adjustment checked and corrected.

10. One or more injectors faulty, dirty or incorrect injection pressure. Have injectors repaired or replace them.
11. Injection pump not operating properly. Fit an exchange pump or have it repaired.
12. Valves not opening properly.
13. Compression pressures too low. See item "8" under "Engine Faults[1]".
14. Idle speed not properly adjusted. Adjust.
15. Throttle cable not properly adjusted or sticking. Re- adjust or free-off.
16. Fuel hose between filter and pump not tightened properly. Tighten connections.
17. Rear mounting of injection pump loose or cracked. Tighten or replace.
18. See items 6, 7, 9, 11, 12 and 13
19. Engine mounting not tightened properly or worn. Tighten or replace.
20. Sticking accelerator pedal. Free-off pedal.
21. Engine not at operating temperature. Check exhaust smoke colour again when engine is warm.
22. Too much acceleration at low revs. Use individual gears in accordance with acceleration.
23. Air cleaner contaminated. Clean or replace.
24. Fuel filter contaminated. Replace.
25. Max. speed adjustment incorrect. Re-adjust.
26. Injectors are dripping. Have them checked or replace faulty ones.
27. Injector nozzles sticking or broken. Replace injector.
28. Injection pressure too low. Have injectors checked and adjusted.
29. See items 9, 11, 12 and 13
30. Throttle cable travel restricted. Re-adjust. Check that floor mats cannot obstruct pedal movement.
31. Throttle cable not correctly adjusted. Re-adjust.
32. Operating lever loose on pump. Re-tighten.
33. Max. speed not obtained. Re-adjust max. speed or have it adjusted.
34. Injector pipes restricted in diameter (near connections). Disconnect pipes and check that diameter is at least 2.0 mm (0.08 in.).
35. Heat protection sealing gaskets under injectors not sealing or damaged. Remove injectors and check. Replace if necessary. Fit the washers correctly.
36. Injection pressure of injectors wrong. Have them re-adjusted.
37. See items 6, 7, 9, 11 and 13
38. See item 20.
39. See items 23, 24, 26 and 27.
40. Road wheels dragging. Brakes seized or wheel bearings not running freely.
41. Engine not running "free". Refers to new or overhauled engine.
42. Fuel system leaking. Check hoses, pipes, filter, injection pump, etc. for leaks.
43. Fuel return line blocked. Clean with compressed air if possible.
44. Idle speed too high. Re-adjust.
45. Max. speed too high. Re-adjust.
46. See items 10, 11, 12 and 13.
47. See items 24, 26, 27 and 28.

CLUTCH FAULTS

Clutch slipping:	1, 2, 3, 4, 5
Clutch will not disengage fully:	4, 6 to 12, 14

Whining from clutch when pedal is depressed: 13
Clutch judder: 1, 2, 7, 10 to 13
Clutch noise when idling: 2, 3
Clutch noise during engagement: 2

Causes and Remedies

1. Insufficient clutch free play at pedal.
2. Clutch disc linings worn, hardened, oiled-up, loose or broken. Disc distorted or hub loose. Clutch disc must be replaced.
3. Pressure plate faulty. Replace clutch.
4. Air in hydraulic system. Low fluid level in clutch cylinder reservoir.
5. Insufficient play at clutch pedal and clutch release linkage. Rectify as described.
6. Excessive free play in release linkage (only for cable operated clutch, not applicable). Adjust or replace worn parts.
7. Misalignment of clutch housing. Very rare fault, but possible on transmissions with separate clutch housings. Re-align to correct.
8. Clutch disc hub binding on splines of main drive shaft (clutch shaft) due to dirt or burrs on splines. Remove clutch and clean and check splines.
9. Clutch disc linings loose or broken. Replace disc.
10. Pressure plate distorted. Replace clutch.
11. Clutch cover distorted. Replace clutch.
12. Fault in transmission or loose engine mountings.
13. Release bearing defective. Remove clutch and replace bearing.
14. A bent clutch release lever. Check lever and replace or straighten, if possible.
- The above faults and remedies are for hydraulic and mechanical clutch operation and should be read as applicable to the model in question, as the clutch fault finding section is written for all types of clutch operation.

STEERING FAULTS

Steering very heavy: 1 to 6
Steering very loose: 5, 7 to 9, 11 to 13
Steering wheel wobbles: 4, 5, 7 to 9, 11 to 16
Vehicle pulls to one side: 1, 4, 8, 10, 14 to 18
Steering wheel does not return to centre position: 1 to 6, 18
Abnormal tyre wear: 1, 4, 7 to 9, 14 to 19
Knocking noise in column: 6, 7, 11, 12

Causes and Remedies

1. Tyre pressures not correct or uneven. Correct.
2. Lack of lubricant in steering.
3. Stiff steering linkage ball joints. Replace ball joints in question.
4. Incorrect steering wheel alignment. Correct as necessary.
5 Steering needs adjustment. See your dealer for advice.
6. Steering column bearings too tight or seized or steering column bent. Correct as necessary.
7. Steering linkage joints loose or worn. Check and replace joints as necessary.
8. Front wheel bearings worn, damaged or loose. Replace bearing.
9. Front suspension parts loose. Check and correct.
10. Wheel nuts loose. Re-tighten.

11. Steering wheel loose. Re-tighten nut.
12. Steering gear mounting loose. Check and tighten.
13. Steering gear worn. Replace the steering gear.
14. Steering track rods defective or loose.
15. Wheels not properly balanced or tyre pressures uneven. Correct pressures or balance wheels.
16. Suspension springs weak or broken. Replace spring in question or both.
17. Brakes are pulling to one side. See under "Brake Faults".
18. Suspension out of alignment. Have the complete suspension checked by a dealer.
19. Improper driving. We don't intend to tell you how to drive and are quite sure that this is not the cause of the fault.

BRAKE FAULTS

Brake Failure: Brake shoe linings or pads excessively worn, incorrect brake fluid (after overhaul), insufficient brake fluid, fluid leak, master cylinder defective, wheel cylinder or caliper failure. Remedies are obvious in each instance.

Brakes Ineffective: Shoe linings or pads worn, incorrect lining material or brake fluid, linings contaminated, fluid level low, air in brake system (bleed brakes), leak in pipes or cylinders, master cylinder defective. Remedies are obvious in each instance.

Brakes pull to one side: Shoes or linings worn, incorrect linings or pads, contaminated linings, drums or discs scored, fluid pipe blocked, unequal tyre pressures, brake back plate or caliper mounting loose, wheel bearings not properly adjusted, wheel cylinder seized. Rectify as necessary.

Brake pedal spongy: Air in hydraulic system. System must be bled of air.

Pedal travel too far: Linings or pads worn, drums or discs scored, master cylinder or wheel cylinders defective, system needs bleeding. Rectify as necessary.

Loss of brake pressure: Fluid leak, air in system, leak in master or wheel cylinders, brake servo not operating (vacuum hose disconnected or exhauster pump not operating). Place vehicle on dry ground and depress brake pedal. Check where fluid runs out and rectify as necessary.

Brakes binding: Incorrect brake fluid (boiling), weak shoe return springs, basic brake adjustment incorrect (after fitting new rear shoes), piston in caliper of wheel cylinder seized, push rod play on master cylinder insufficient (compensation port obstructed), handbrake adjusted too tightly. Rectify as necessary. Swelling of cylinder cups through use of incorrect brake fluid could be another reason.

Handbrake ineffective: Brake shoe linings worn, linings contaminated, operating lever on brake shoe seized, brake shoes or handbrake need adjustment. Rectify as necessary.

Excessive pedal pressure required: Brake shoe linings or pads worn, linings or pads contaminated, brake servo vacuum hose (for brake servo) disconnected or wheel cylinders seized. Exhauster pump not operating (diesel). Rectify as necessary.

Brakes squealing: Brake shoe linings or pads worn so far that metal is grinding against drum or disc. Inside of drum is full of lining dust. Remove and replace, or clean out the drum(s). Do not inhale brake dust.

Note: Any operation on the steering and brake systems must be carried out with the necessary care and attention. Always think of your safety and the safety of other road users. Make sure to use the correct fluid for the power-assisted steering and the correct brake fluid.

Faults in an ABS system should be investigated by a dealer.

ELECTRICAL FAULTS

Starter motor failure:	2 to 5, 8, 9
No starter motor drive:	1 to 3, 5 to 7
Slow cranking speed:	1 to 3
Charge warning light remains on:	3, 10, 12
Charge warning light does not come on:	2, 3, 9. 11, 13
Headlamp failure:	2, 3, 11, 13, 14
Battery needs frequent topping-up:	11
Direction indicators not working properly:	2, 3, 9, 13, 14
Battery frequently discharged:	3, 10, 11, 12

Causes and Remedies

1. Tight engine. Check and rectify.
2. Battery discharged or defective. Re-charge battery or replace if older than approx. 2 years.
3. Interrupted connection in circuit. Trace and rectify.
4. Starter motor pinion jammed in flywheel. Release.
5. Also 6, 7 and 8. Starter motor defective, no engagement in flywheel, pinion or flywheel worn or solenoid switch defective. Correct as necessary.
9. Ignition/starter switch inoperative. Replace.
10. Drive belt loose or broken. Adjust or replace.
11. Regulator defective. Adjust or replace.
12. Generator inoperative. Overhaul or replace.
13. Bulb burnt out. Replace bulb.
14. Flasher unit defective. Replace unit.

WIRING DIAGRAMS
Wiring Diagram Index

Cable Colour Code

bl	=	blue		nf	=	natural colour
br	=	brown		rs	=	pink
ge	=	yellow		rt	=	red
gn	=	green		sw	=	black
gr	=	grey		vi	=	violet
				ws	=	white

Cable identification: a = size, square mm, b = basic colour, c = second colour

170

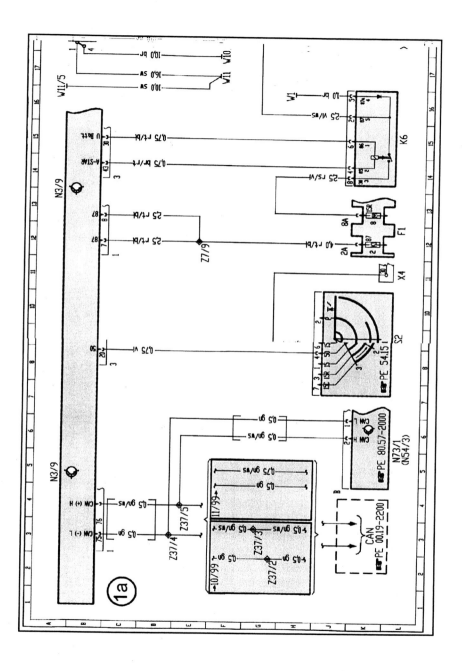

171

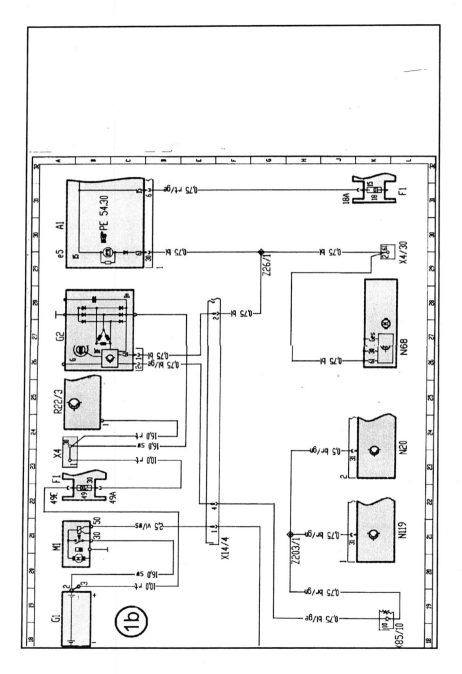

172

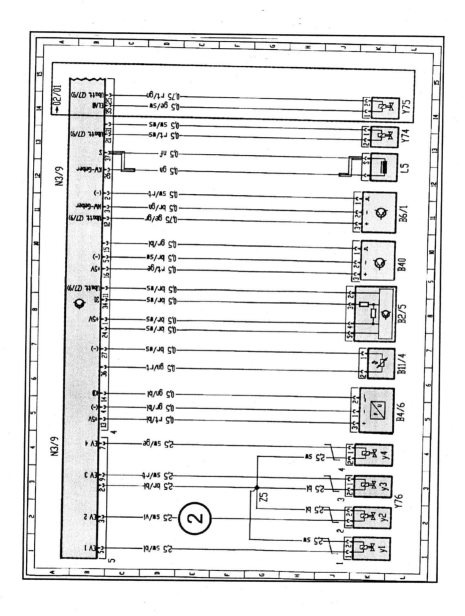

173

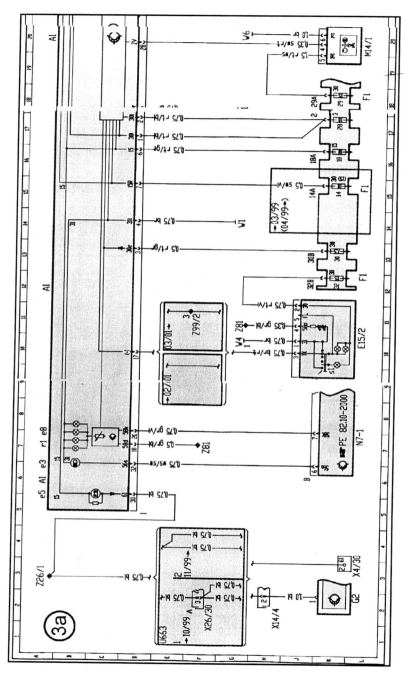

174

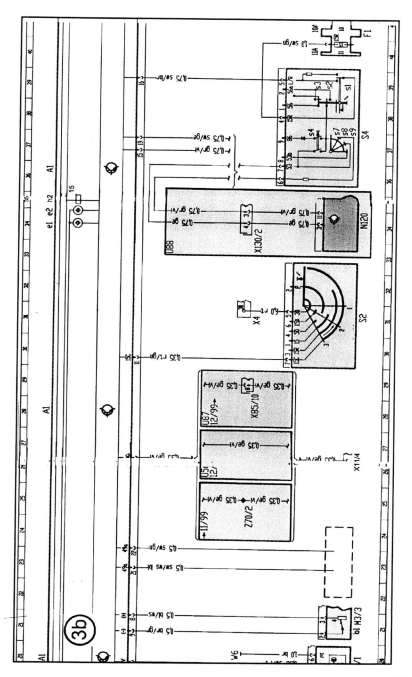

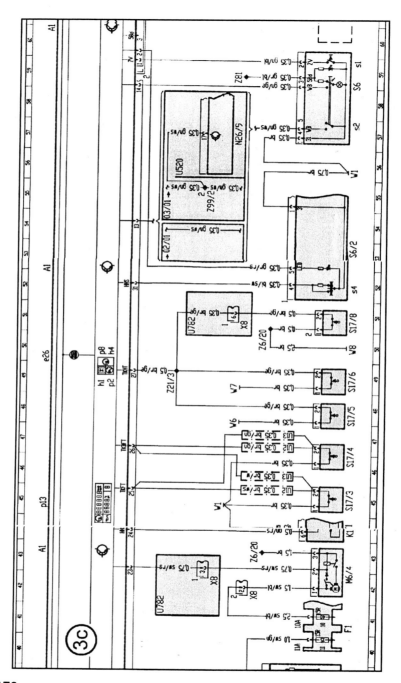

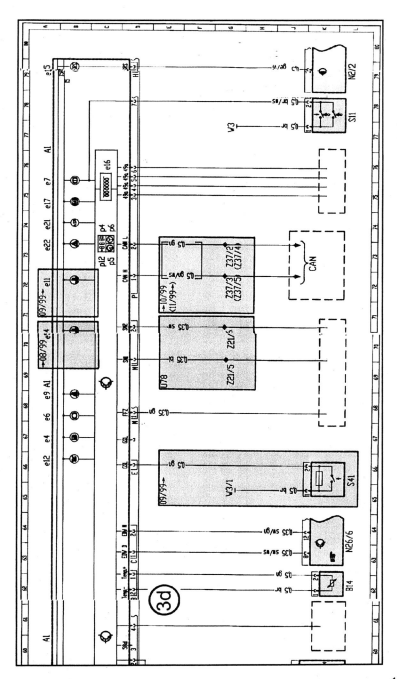

177

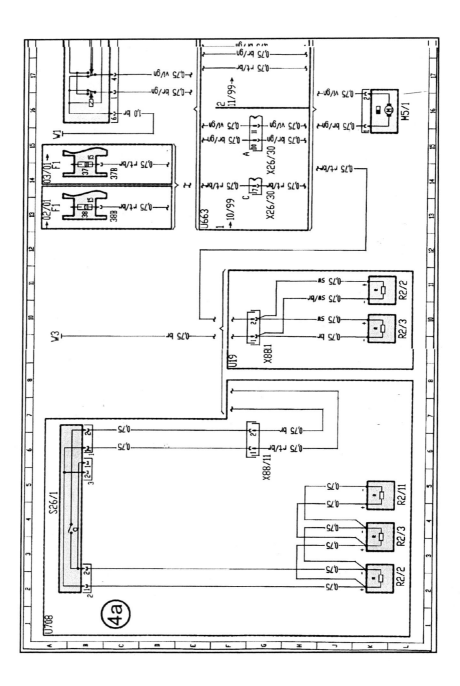

178

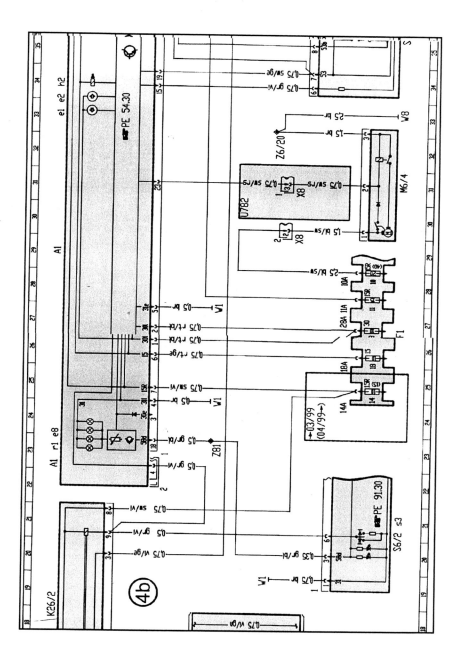

179

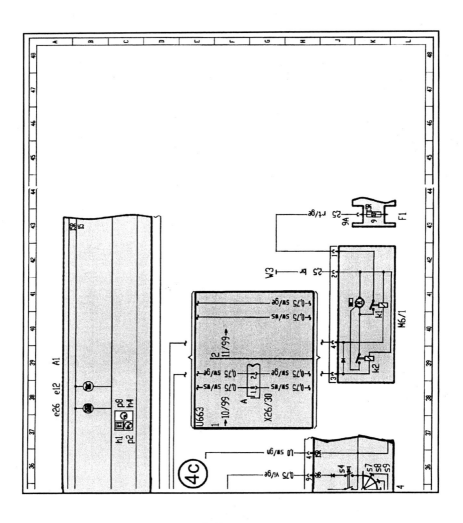

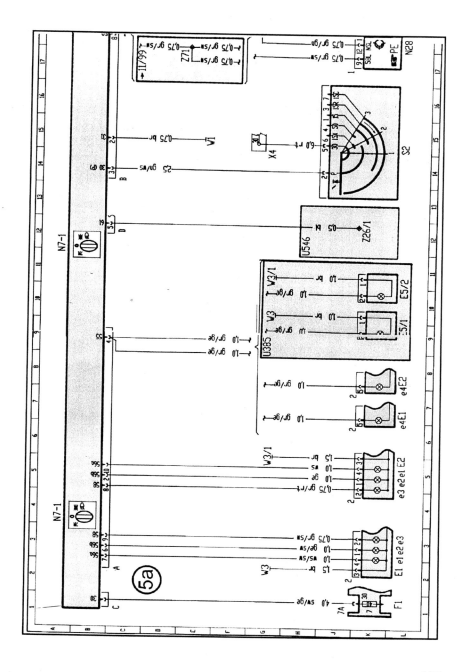

181

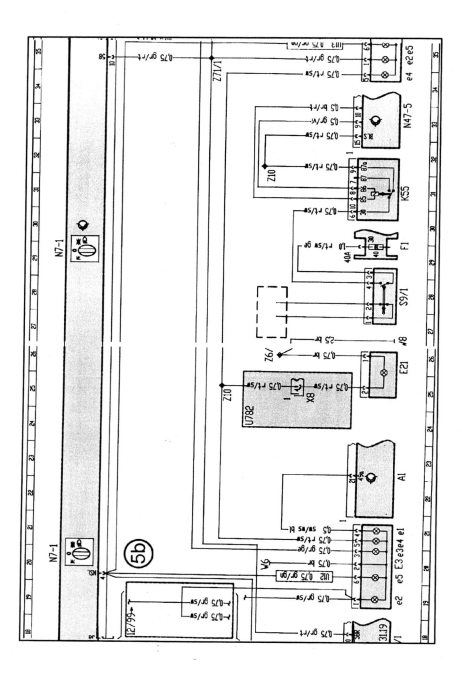

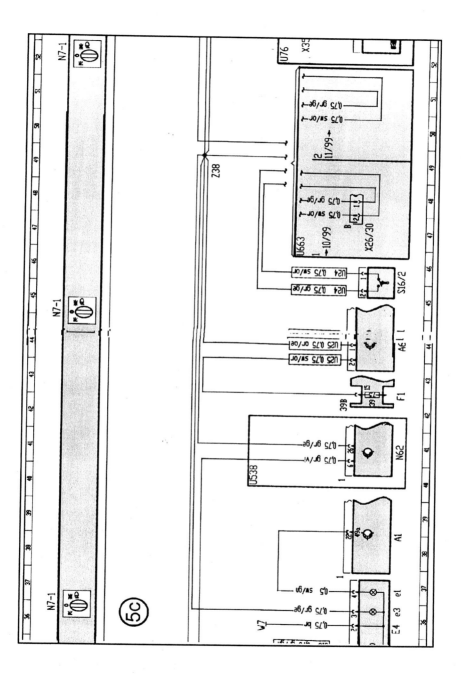

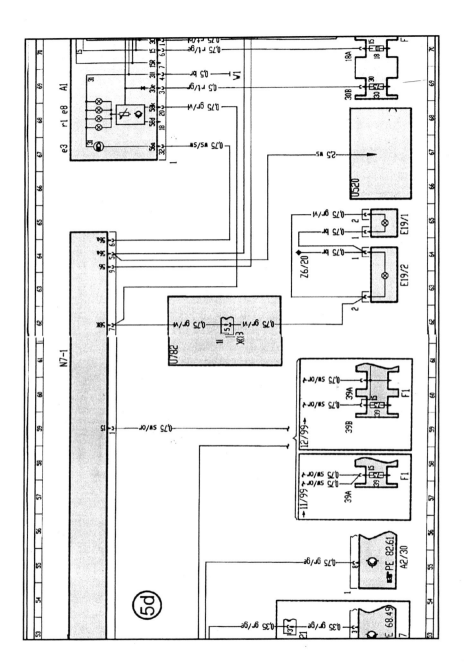

184

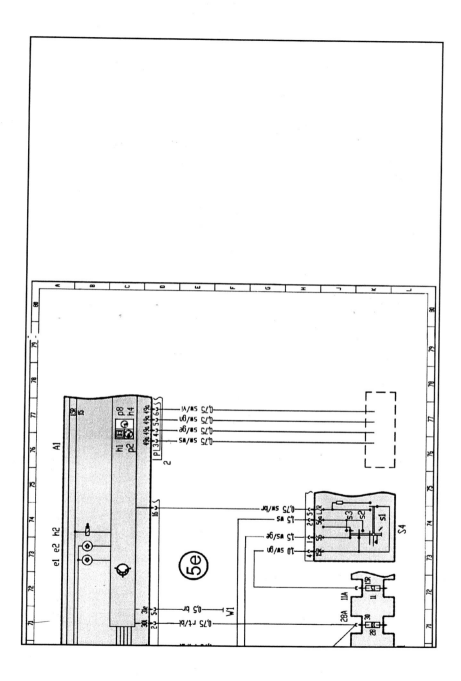

185

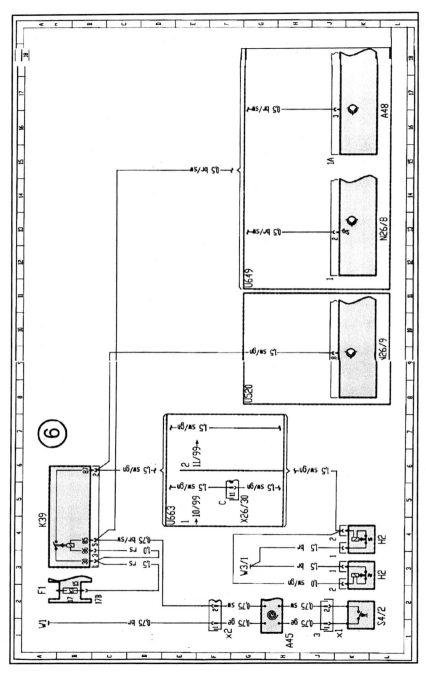

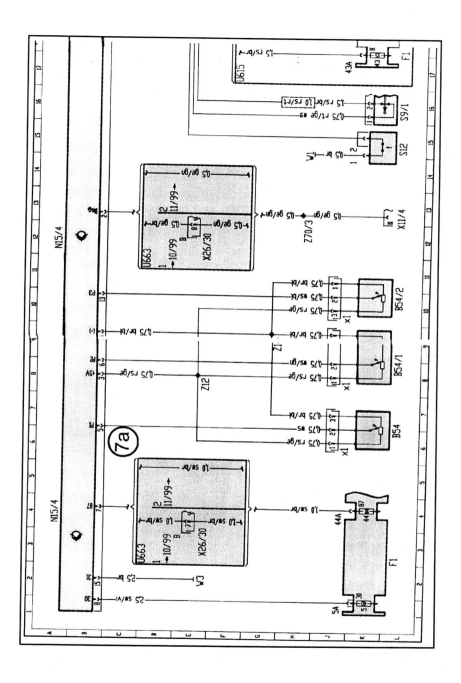

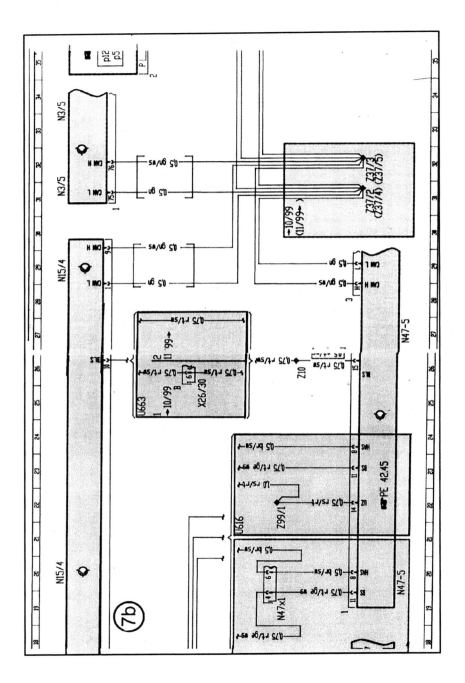

188

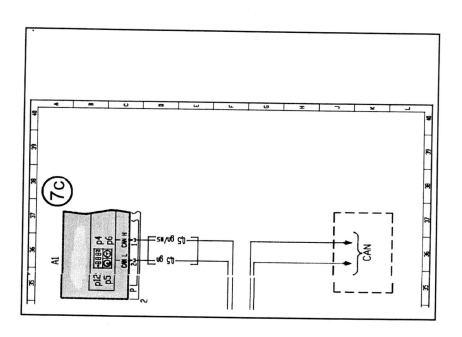

189

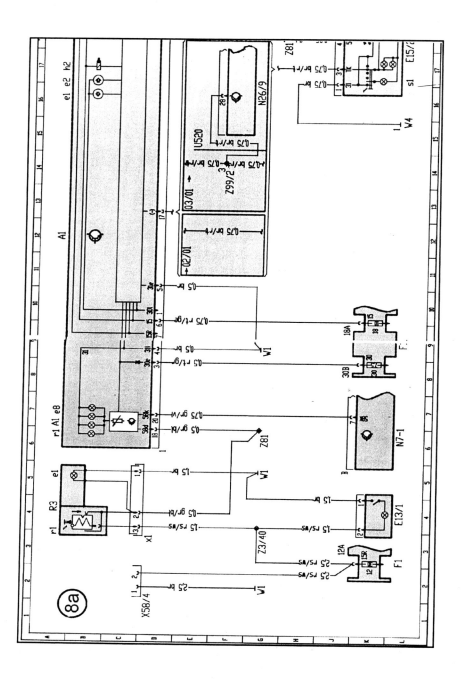

190

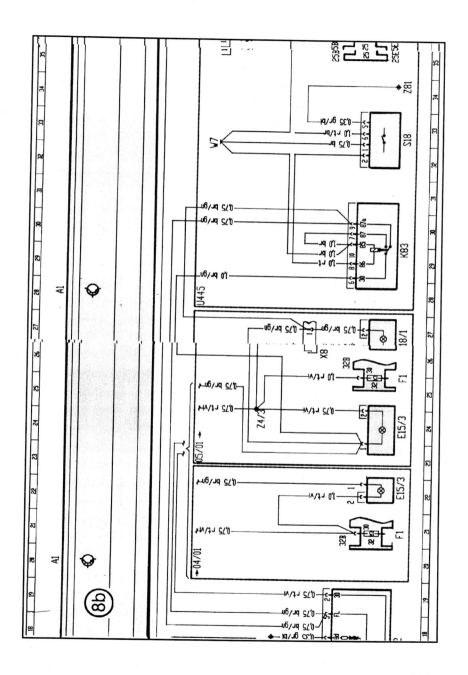

191

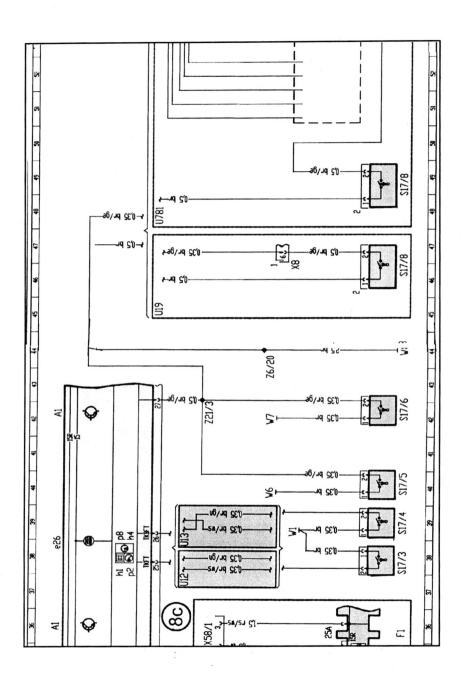

192

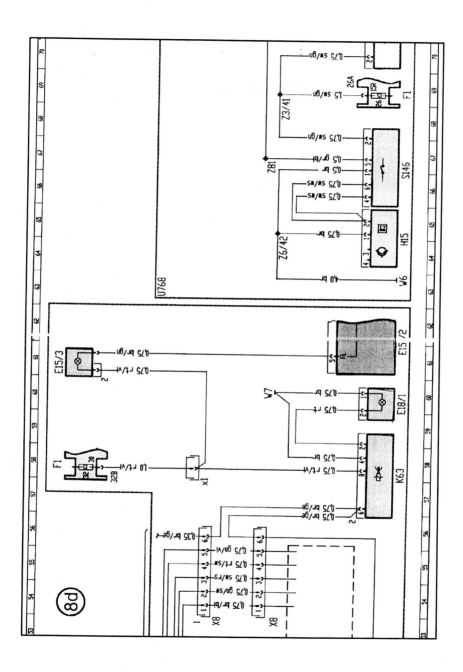

193

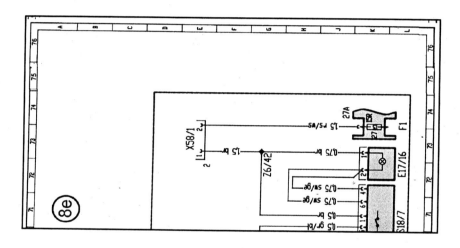

8e

X58/1

1,5 rs/ws

27A
27 | F1

1,5 br
X76/42
0,75 br
E17/16

0,75 sw/ge
0,75 sw/ge
0,5 br
0,5 gr/bl
S18/7

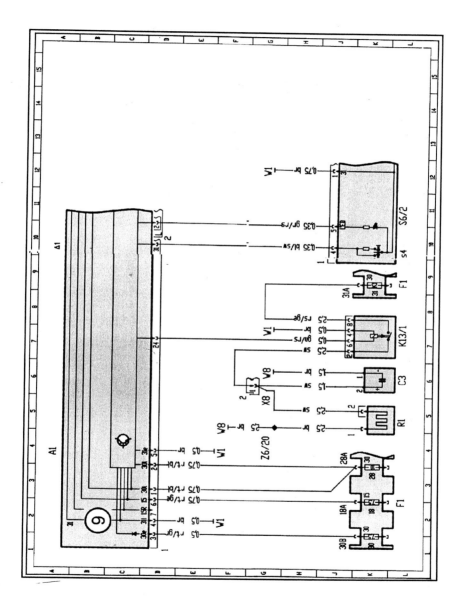

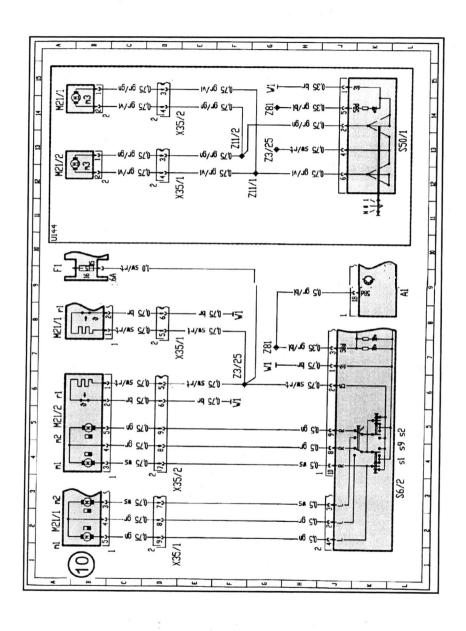

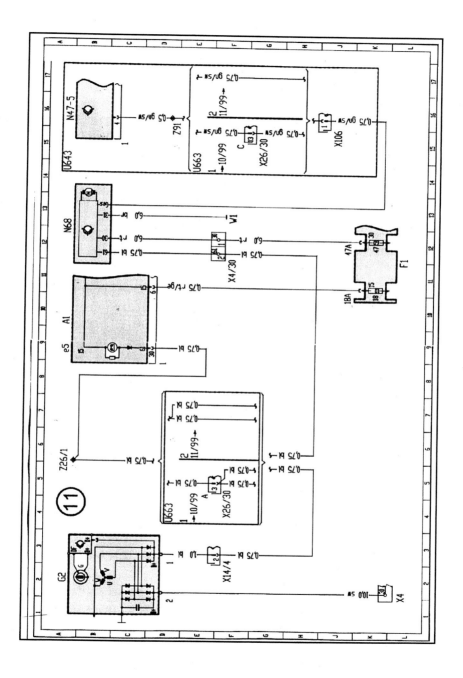

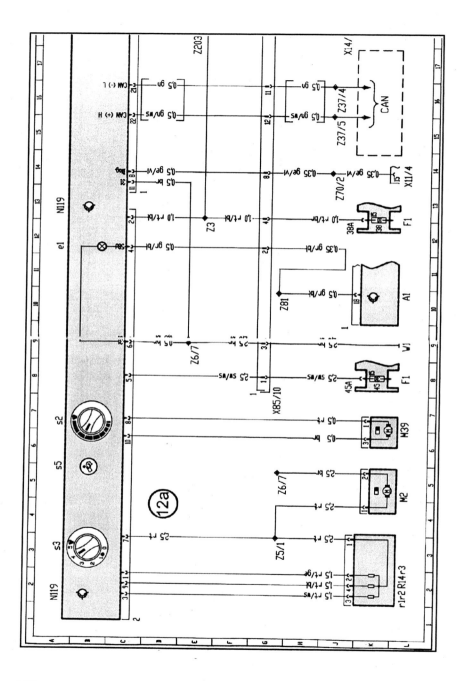

198

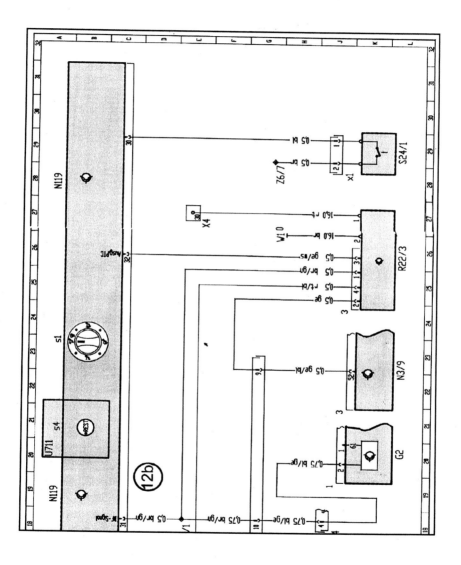

199

Legend for wiring diagrams 1a and 1b – Starter motor and alternator

ID.	Consumer	Coordinate
A1	Instrument cluster	30A
A1e5	Charge warning light	29A
F1	Fuse and relay box	12L, 23A 31L
F1f2	Fuse 2	12K
F1f8	Fuse 8	13K
F1f18	Fuse 18	31K
F1f49	Fuse 49	22B
G1	Battery	19A
G2	Generator (alternator)	27A
K6	Starter motor relay	15L
M1	Starter motor	21A
N3/5	CDI engine control unit	5A
N20	TAC control module	23L
N54/3	Radio frequency control module	5L
N68	Steering assist control module	27L
N73/1	DAS (FBS) control module	5L
N119	Heating pushbutton Control module	21L

R22/3	PTC heater booster	25A
S2	Starter motor switch	9L
W1	Main earth (under control module)	16H
W10	Earth (battery)	17F
W11	Earth (engine)	17F
W11/5	Earth strap (engine/body)	16A
X4	Terminal block (circuit 30, fuse and relay box, 2 pins	11L
X4/30	Circuit 30/61 connector	29L
X14/4	Circuit 50/61 connector	20F
X85/10	Connector, heating/A/C	18L
X26/1	Connector sleeve, 61	29G
Z37/2	CAN engine bus (low) connector sleeve, engine compartment	2G
Z37/3	CAN engine bus (high) connector sleeve, engine compartment	3G
Z37/4	CAN engine bus (low) connector sleeve - interior	2E
Z37/5	CAN engine bus (high) connector sleeve - interior	5E
Z203/1	Generator terminal DF	20H

Legend for wiring diagrams 2 – Common Rail (CDI) diesel injection

B2/5	Hot film MAF sensor	8L
B4/6	Rail pressure sensor	5L
B6/1	Camshaft Hall sensor	11L
B11/4	Coolant temperature sensor	6L
B40	Oil sensor (level, temperature)	9L
L5	Crankshaft position sensor	12L
N3/9	CDI control module	4A, 12A

Y74	Pressure regulator valve	13L
Y75	Electric shut-off valve	14L
Y76	Fuel injectors	2L
Y76/1	Fuel injector, cylinder 1	1K
Y76/2	Fuel injector, cylinder 2	2K
Y76/3	Fuel injector, cylinder 3	3K
Y76/4	Fuel injector, cylinder 4	4K
Z5	Connector sleeve (soldered connector in wiring harness)	3G

Legend for wiring diagrams 3a to 3d – Instrument cluster, display instruments, warning devices

A1	Instrument cluster	
A1e2	R.H. indicator warning light	31A
A1e2	L.H. indicator warning light	32A
A1e3	High beam warning light	6A
A1e4	Fuel reserve warning light	64A
A1e5	Charge warning light	5A
A1e6	Pad wear warning light	65A
A1e7	Brake fluid and handbrake warning light	73A
A1e8	Instrument illumination	7A
A1e9	Seat belt warning light	66A
A1e11	Coolant level light	70A
A1e12	Low engine oil warning light	64A
A1e15	Airbag warning lamp	77A
A1e16	Pre-glow warning light (diesel)	74C
A1e17	ABS warning light	72A
A1e21	ASR warning light	72A
A1e22	ASR indicator lamp	71A

A1e26	Check engine light	47A
A1e54	Coolant temperature warning lamp	68A
A1h1	Warning buzzer	46C
A1h2	Audible turn signal indicator	32A
A1h4	Main odometer	47C
A1p2	Fuel level gauge	46C
A1p4	Outside temperature indicator	72C
A1p5	Tachometer	70C
A1p6	Electric clock	72C
A1p8	Electronic speedometer	47C
A1p12	Gear indicator	70C
A1p13	Multifunction display	42A
A1r1	Instrument illumination variable resistor	7A
B14	Outside temperature temp. sensor	60L
E15/2	Front dome lamp	10L
E15/2s1	Dome lamp switch	9K
F1	Fuse and relay box	
F1f10	Fuse 10	38K

F1f11	Fuse 11	38K
F1f14	Fuse 14	15K
F1f18	Fuse 18	16K
F1f28	Fuse 28	17K
F1f29	Fuse 29	18K
F1f30	Fuse 30	13K
F1f32	Fuse 32	12K
G2	Generator	2L
K13/1	Rear window defroster relay	41L
M3/3	Fuel pump with level sensor	21L
M3/3b1	Fuel level sensor	21L
M6/4	Tailgate wiper motor	40L
M14/1	Central locking supply pump	20L
N2/2	Emergency retractor, airbag and side airbag control module	77L
N7-1	Light module	7L
N26/6	Towing control module	61L
N26/9	Multifunction control module (not all vehicles)	54G
S2	Starter motor switch	31L
S4	Combination switch	35L
S4s1	Turn signal switch	36K
S4s2	Flasher/main beam switch	37K
S4s3	Low (dipped) beam switch	37I
S4s4	Windscreen wiper switch	35I
S4s7	Intermittent wiper switch	35K
S4s8	Slow wiper switch	35K
S4s9	Fast wiper switch	35K
S6	Hazard warning and central locking switch group	56L
S6s1	Interior central locking switch	57L
S6s2	Hazard flasher switch	55L
S6/2	Cockpit switch group	51L
S6/2s4	Rear window defroster switch	49L
S11	Brake fluid level switch	75L
S17/3	L.H. front door contact switch	42L
S17/4	R.H. front door contact switch	44L
S17/5	L.H. rear door contact switch	45L
S17/6	R.H. rear door contact switch	46L
S17/8	Luggage boot lamp	48L
S41	Coolant level switch	61L
U12	Only for L.H.D. models	43I, 44I
U13	Only for R.H.D. models	44I, 45I
U78	Only for Japan	66E

U87	Only for A/C system	28F
U520	Only for Taxis	53E
U562	Valid for heater	26F
W1	Main earth (under control module box)	Various
W3	Earth (L.H. front wheel housing, at ignition coil)	75G
W3/1	Earth (R.H. front wheel housing, at ignition coil)	63G
W4	Earth (front dome lamp)	10G
W6	Earth (L.H. wheel housing in luggage boot)	20G, 45G
W7	Earth (R.H. wheel housing in luggage boot)	46G
W8	Earth (tailgate)	47L
X4	Terminal 30 terminal block	31G
X4/30	Terminal block 30/61	3L
X8	Terminal block, tailgate	39H, 40G
X11/4	Data link connector	26L
X14/4	Connector, terminal 50, 61	1H
X26/30	Engine wiring harness/cock-pit connector	1F
X85/10	Connector, heating/A/C	28H
Z6/20	Tailgate earth connector	40H
Z21/3	Feed for rear door switches	46E
Z21/5	Boot lid lock switch 1	66G
Z21/6	Boot lid lock switch 2	68G
Z26/1	Terminal 61 connector sleeve	3A
Z37/2	Engine CAN bus (low) connector sleeve-engine compartment	70G
Z37/3	Engine CAN bus (high) connector sleeve-engine compartment	69G
Z37/4	Engine CAN bus (low) connector sleeve-interior	70G
Z37/5	Engine CAN bus (high) connector sleeve-interior	69G
Z70/2	Diagnosis pin 15 sleeve	24G
Z81	Terminal 58d con. sleeve	7F
		11G
		58G
Z99/2	Terminal 87 con. sleeve	11F, 52F

Legend for wiring diagrams 4a to 4c – Windscreen wipers

A1	Instrument cluster	
A1e1	L.H. flasher warning lamp	33A
A1e2	R.H. flasher warning lamp	33A
A1e8	Instrument illumination	23A
A1e12	Low oil level warning lamp	38A
A1e28	Check engine light	38A
A1h1	Warning buzzer	37C
A1h2	Audible turn indicator	34A
A1h4	Main odometer	38C
A1p2	Fuel level gauge	37C
A1e8	Electronic speedometer	38C

A1r1	Instrument lighting rheostat	23A
F1	Fuse and relay box	
F1/9	Fuse 9	43K
F1f10	Fuse 10	28K
F1f11	Fuse 11	28K
F1f14	Fuse 14	25K
F1f18	Fuse 18	26K
F1f28	Fuse 28	27K
F1f37	Fuse 37	14B
F1f38	Fuse 38	13B
K26/2	Windscreen washer pump relay	18A

M5/1	Windscreen washer pump	16L
M6/1	Wiper motor	40L
M6/1k1	Stage 1 "wipe" relay	40K
M6/1k2	Stage 2 "wipe" relay	39K
M6/4	Tailgate wiper motor	31L
R2/2	L.H. heated windscreen washer nozzle	2L, 11L
R2/3	R.H. heated windscreen washer nozzle	3L, 9L
R2/11	Washer nozzle hose heater	4L
S4	Combination switch	35L
S4s4	Windscreen washer switch	36I
S4s7	Intermittent wiper switch	36K
S4e8	Slow wipe switch	36K
S4e9	Fast wipe switch	36K
S6/2	Cockpit switch group	20L
S6/2s3	Rear wiper switch	21L

S26/1	Heated windscreen wiper system thermo switch	4A
U19	Valid for standard equipment	8F
U708	Valid for washer nozzle hose heater	1A
W1	Earth (under control module)	15A
W3	Earth (left wheel housing at ignition coil)	9A, 42G
W6	Earth (tailgate)	33L
X8	terminal block (tailgate)	29H, 31H
X26/30	Engine wiring harness/cockpit connector	13G, 14G, 37G
X88/11	Water nozzle heater connector, 2 pins	5G, 9G
Z6/20	Tailgate earth connector	32G
Z81	Circuit 58d connector sleeve	23F

Legend for wiring diagrams 5a to 5e – Exterior lights

A1	Instrument cluster	
A1e1	L.H. flasher warning lamp	73A
A1e2	R.H. flasher warning lamp	73A
A1e3	Main beam warning light	67A
A1e8	Instrument illumination	68A
A1h1	Warning buzzer	76C
A1h2	Audible turn signal indicator	74A
A1h4	Main odometer	77C
A1p2	Fuel level gauge	76C
A1p8	Electronic speedometer	77C
A1r1	Instrument illumination rheostat	68A
A2/30	Navigation processor	55L
A61	Transmission range recognition module	44L
E1	L.H. headlamp unit	2L
E1e1	Main beam	2L
E1e2	Dipped beam	3L
E1e3	Side/parking light	3L
E1e4	Fog lamp	6L
E2	R.H. headlamp unit	5L
E2e1	Main beam	5L
E2e2	Dipped beam	5L
E3e3	Side/parking light	4L
E2e4	Fog lamp	7L
E3	L.H. tail lamp	20L
E3e1	Indicator lamp	21L
E3e2	Tail/parking lamp	19L
E3e4	Reversing light	20L
E3e4	Brake light	21L
E3e5	Rear fog lamp	20L
E4	L.H. tail lamp	36L
E4e1	Indicator lamp	37L
E4e2	Tail/parking lamp	35L
E4e4	Reversing light	36L
E4e4	Brake light	34L
E4e5	Rear fog lamp	35L
E5/1	L.H. fog lamp	9L

E5/2	R.H. fog lamp	10L
E19/1	L.H. number plate light	65L
E19/2	L.H. number plate light	63L
E21	High-mounted brake light	26L
F1	Fuse and relay box	
F1f7	Fuse 7	1K
F1f11	Fuse 11	72K
F1f18	Fuse 18	70K
F1f28	Fuse 28	71K
F1f30	Fuse 30	69K
F1f39	Fuse 39	42K, 58K, 60K
F1f40	Fuse 40	29K
H7	Automatic dimming rearview mirror	53L
K55	Brake light suppression relay	31L
N7-1	Light module	4A, 11A, 20A, 29A, 36A, 45A, 52A, 61A
N28/1	Trailer recognition module	17L
N47-5	ESP control module	33L
N62	PTS control module	41L
S2	Starter motor switch	15L
S4	Combination switch	74L
S4s1	Turn signal switch	74K
S4s2	Headlamp flasher/main beam switch	74K
S4e3	Dipped beam switch	74I
S9/1	Brake light switch	28L
S16/2	Reversing light switch	45L
U12	Valid for L.H.D. vehicles	29I
U13	Valid for R.H.D. vehicles	35I
U24	Valid for manual gearbox	46I
U25	Valid for auto transmission	44I
U76	Valid for entrance/exit lamps	52G
U385	Valid for code 990	8G
U520	Valid for Taxi	66I
U538	Valid for Parctronic system	40G
U546	Valid for Norway and Sweden	11H
W1	Main earth (under control	

	module)	15E, 69F, 72F
W3	Earth (left wheel housing at ignition coil)	2G, 9G
W3/1	Earth (right wheel housing at ignition coil)	5G, 11G
W6	Earth (tailgate)	27L
X4	Terminal block (circuit 30, fuse and relay box, 2 pins	14G
X8	Terminal block (tailgate)	25H
X26/30	Engine wiring harness/ cockpit connector	47K
	mirror	52H

Legend for wiring diagram 6 – Signal system

A45	Fanfare horns and airbag spring contact	1H
A45x2	Clock spring contact and fanfare horn relay plug	1F
A48	Special; signal operating unit	16L
F1	Fuse and relay box	2A
F1f17	Fuse 17	2B
H2	Fanfare horns	3L, 4L
K39	Fanfare horns relay	4A

Legend for wiring diagram 7a and 7b – Automatic clutch

A1	Instrument cluster	36A
A1p4	Outside temperature indicator	B36
A1p5	Tachometer	35B
A1p6	Electronic clock	36B
A1p12	Gear display	35B
B54	Shift direction turning angle sensor	6L
B54x1	Shift lever direction turning angle sensor connector	6I
B54/1	Selection direction turning angle sensor	8L
B54/1x1	Selector lever direction turning angle sensor connector	8I
F1	Fuse and relay box	3L, 18L
F1f5	Fuse 5	1K
F1f43	Fuse 43	17K
F1f44	Fuse 44	4K
N3/5	Engine control unit	31A, 33A
N15/4	Automatic clutch control module	4A, 12A, 20A, 29A
N47/1	Traction system control module intermediate connector	19G

Legend for wiring diagram 8a to 8e – Interior lights

A1	Instrument cluster	
A1e1	L.H. flasher warning lamp	16A

X35/21	Automatic dimming inside	
Z6/20	Tailgate earth connector	26G, 64H
Z10	Connector sleeve 2,	25F, 31G
Z26/1	Connector sleeve, 61	12K
Z38	Connector sleeve, reversing lamp	49F
Z71	Left tail lamp sleeve connector, circuit 58	17E
Z71/1	Right tail lamp sleeve connector, circuit 58	34E

N26/8	Steering control module	13L
N26/9	Special multifunction control module	9L
S4/2	Fanfare horns switch	1L
S4/2s1	Horns switch connector	1K
U520	Valid for Taxi	8G
W1	Earth (below control module)	1A
W3/1	Earth (right wheel housing at ignition coil)	3G
X26/30	Engine wiring harness/cockpit connector	4G

N47-5	ESP control module	19L, 27L
S9/1	Brake light switch	16L
S12	Parking brake indicator switch	16L
U615	Valid up to car No. 1J016125	17F
U616	Valid from car No. 1J016126	21F
W1	Main earth (under module)	14H
W3	Earth (left wheel housing at ignition coil)	2E
X11/4	Data link connector	12L
X26/30	Engine wiring harness/cockpit connector	3E, 11E, 25E
Z10	Connector sleeve 2	26H
Z12	Connector sleeve 4	8E
Z14	Connector sleeve 6	9G
Z37/2	Engine CAN bus (low) connector sleeve-engine compartment	31K
Z37/3	Engine CAN bus (high) connector sleeve-engine compartment	32K
Z37/4	Engine CAN bus (low) connector sleeve-interior	31K
Z37/5	Engine CAN bus (high) connector sleeve-interior	32K
Z70/4	Diagnostic socket pin 11	12H
Z99/1	Terminal 87 connector sleeve (traction system)	21G

A1e2	R.H. flasher warning lamp	16A
A1e8	Instrument illumination	7A

A1e26	Check engine lights	38A
A1h1	Warning buzzer	38C
A1h2	Audible turn signal indicator	17A
A1h4	Main odometer	39C
A1p2	Fuel level gauge	38C
A1p8	Electronic speedometer	39C
A1r1	Instrument illumination rheostat	6A
E13/1	Glove compartment lamp	4L
E15/2	Front dome lamp	17L, 61L
E15/2s1	Dome lamp switch	17L
E15/3	Rear interior lamp	22L, 24L, 61A
E15/3x1	Rear interior lamp connector	57E
E17/16	L.H. front foot well lamp	72L
E18/1	Luggage boot lamp	27L, 60L
F1	Fuse and relay box	
F1f12	Fuse 12	2K
F1f18	Fuse 18	9K
F1f25	Fuse 25	35K
F1f26	Fuse 26	69K
F1f27	Fuse 27	73K
F1f30	Fuse 30	8K
F1f32	Fuse 32	21K, 25K, 58B
K63	Boot lighting relay retrofit	58L
K83	Switchable rear lamp relay	29L
N7-1	Light module	6L
N26/9	Malfunction module	16G
R3	Front cigar lighter with ashtray illumination	4A
R3e1	Illumination	5A
R3r1	Heating element	3A
R3x1	Lighter connector	3D

S17/3	L.H. front door contact switch	38L
S17/4	R.H. front door contact switch	39L
S17/5	L.H. rear door contact switch	40L
S17/6	R.H. rear door contact switch	42L
S17/8	Boot lamp switch	46L, 49L
S18	Rear interior lamp switch	33L
U12	Valid for L.H.D. vehicles	37E
U13	Valid for R.H.D. vehicles	38E
U19	Valid for standard equipment	45D
U445	Family package, code U66	28E
U520	Valid for Taxi	15E
U768	Valid for driving school	63D
W1	Main earth (under control module)	2G, 5G, 9G, 39H
W4	Earth (front dome lamp)	15L
W6	Earth (left wheelhouse, boot)	40G
W7	Earth (right wheelhouse, boot)	33E
W8	Earth (tailgate)	44L
X8	Terminal block (tailgate)	26I, 46H, 53F, 53G
X58/1	Interior socket	38E, 73E
X58/4	Load compartment socket	1D
Z3/40	Circuit 15R connector sleeve, fused, F1f12)	3G
Z3/41	Driving school only	68G
Z4/3	Circuit 30 connector sleeve	24G
Z6/20	Tailgate earth connector sleeve	43G
Z6/42	Earth W6 connector sleeve	64G
Z21/3	Rear door connector sleeve	42E
Z81	Circuit 58d connector sleeve	6G
Z99/2	Circuit 87 connector sleeve	13G

Legend for wiring diagram 9 – Heated rear window

A1	Instrument cluster	4A, 10A
C3	Electronic capacitor (rear window noise suppressor)	6L
F1	Fuse and relay box	2L, 9L
F1f18	Fuse 18	2K
F1f28	Fuse 28	3K
F1f30	Fuse 30	1K
F1f31	Fuse 31	8K

K13/1	Rear window relay	7L
R1	Rear window defroster element	5L
S6/2	Cockpit switch group	11L
S6/2s4	Window defroster switch	10L
W1	Main earth (under module)	2F, 4F, 7G, 12G
W8	Earth (tailgate)	4F, 6G
X8	Tailgate connector	5G
Z6/20	Tailgate earth connector sleeve	4G

Legend for wiring diagram 10 – Outside rear view mirror

A1	Instrument cluster	9L
F1	Fuse and relay box	9A
F1f16	Fuse 16	9B
M21/1	L.H. electrically adjustable and heated outside mirror	2A, 8A, 14A
M21/1m1	Mirror up/down adjustment motor	A1
M21/1m2	Mirror in/out adjustment motor	A3
M21/1m3	Mirror fold-in motor	B14

M21/1r1	Mirror heater	8A
M21/2	R.H. electrically adjustable and heated outside mirror	5A, 12A
M21/2m1	Mirror up/down adjustment motor	4A
M21/2m2	Mirror in/out adjustment motor	4A
M21/2m3	Mirror fold-in motor	12B
M21/2r1	Mirror heater	6A
S6/2	Cockpit switch group	3L
S6/2s1	Vertical mirror adjustment switch	4L

S6/2s2	Horizontal mirror adjustment switch	5L
S6/2s9	Left/right outside mirror switch	4L
S50/1	Outside mirror switch with Mirror fold-in/fold-out switch facility	13L
U144	Valid for folding mirror	10A
W1	Main earth (under control module)	6F, 7G, 8F, 15G
X35/1	L.H. front door separation point	1E, 7E

Legend for wiring diagram 11 – Electric power steering pump

A1	Instrument cluster	10A
A1e5	Charge warning light	9A
F1	Fuse and relay box	11L
F1f18	Fuse 18	10K
F1f47	Fuse 47	12K
G2	Generator (alternator)	2A
N47-5	ESP control module	16A
N68	Steering assist control module	12A

Legend for wiring diagrams 12a and 12b – Heater

A1	Instrument cluster	10L
F1	Fuse and relay box	8L, 12L
F1f38	Fuse 38	12K
F1f45	Fuse 45	8K
G2	Generator (alternator)	20L
M2	Blower motor	5L
M39	Re-circulated air flap actuator motor	6L
N3/9	CDI control module (diesel)	22L
N119	Heating push button control module	2A, 13A, 19A, 25A
N119e1	Illumination	11A
N119s1	Air distribution switch	23A
N119s2	Temperature selector switch	6A
N119s3	Blower switch	3A
R14	Blower motor series resistor group	2L
R14r1	Resistance stage 1	1L
R14r2	Resistance stage 2	2L
R14r3	Resistance stage 3	3L
R22/3	PTC heater booster	26L

X35/2	R.H. front door separation point	3E, 13E
Z3/25	Circuit 15 connector sleeve (outside rearview mirror adjustment)	6F, 13G
Z11/1	Connector sleeve 1 (fold-in mirror)	12G
Z11/2	Connector sleeve 2 (fold-in mirror)	13F
Z81	Circuit 58d connector sleeve	7G, 14G

U643	Valid for model 168.032	14A
W1	Main earth (under control module)	13F
X4	Terminal block (circuit 30)	1L
X4/30	Circuit 30/61 connector	11F
X14/4	Circuit 50, 61 connector	2F
X26/30	Engine wiring harness/ cockpit connector	4F, 14G
X106	Steering pump connector	15J
Z26/1	Circuit 61 connector sleeve	5A
Z91	R.H. rear axle sensor connector sleeve	15D

S24/1	Temperature regulator micro switch	29L
S24/1x1	Connector for above	28I
U711	Valid for Taxi only	20A
W1	Main earth (under control module)	9L
W10	Earth (battery)	26G
X4	Terminal block (circuit 30)	27E
X11/4	Data link connector	14L
X14/4	Connector, circuits 50,61	17I
X85/10	Connector, heating or A/C	7G
Z3	Connector sleeve, term. 15	12E
Z5/1	Connector sleeve, blower	3G
Z6/7	Earth (W1) connector sleeve (feed from W1)	5G, 8E, 28G
Z37/4	Engine CAN bus (low) connector sleeve-interior	16I
Z37/5	Engine CAN bus (high) connector sleeve-interior	15I
Z70/2	Diagnostic socket pin 15 connector sleeve	13I
Z81	Circuit 58d connector sleeve	10G
Z20/3/1	Generator DF terminal post	17E

Other Mercedes-Benz Manuals available in the Pocket Mechanic Series

Mercedes-Benz 208D and all variants, 2.3, 2.4 and 2.9 Litre engines

Mercedes-Benz Sprinter, 208D and all variants, 2.3, and 2.9 Litre engines to 2000 (CDI not covered)

Mercedes-Benz Sprinter CDI, 2.2, and 2.7 Litre engines to 2006

Mercedes-Benz Vito and V-Class, 2.0 Litre 16V Petrol, and 2.3 Litre Diesel engines to 2000 (CDI not covered)

Mercedes-Benz E-Class, W124 and W210 Series, 4-cyl, and V6 Petrol Models, 1993 to 2000

Mercedes-Benz 124 Series, Petrol Models, 1985 to 1991

Mercedes-Benz 201 Series, Petrol Models, 1984 to 1991

Mercedes-Benz W123 Series, 102 Engine, 200 and 230. from 1980

Mercedes-Benz W124 Series, diesel models, from 1995

Available soon

Mercedes-Benz Vito and V-Class, CDI and petrol models From 2001 to 2003